Forensic Psycholog

Forensic Psychology in Practice

A Practitioner's Handbook

Edited by

Joanna Clarke
Pam Wilson

First published 2013 by
PALGRAVE MACMILLAN

Palgrave Macmillan in the UK is an imprint of Macmillan Publishers Limited,
registered in England, company number 785998, of Houndmills, Basingstoke,
Hampshire RG21 6XS.

Palgrave Macmillan in the US is a division of St Martin's Press LLC,
175 Fifth Avenue, New York, NY 10010.

Palgrave Macmillan is the global academic imprint of the above companies
and has companies and representatives throughout the world.

Palgrave® and Macmillan® are registered trademarks in the United States,
the United Kingdom, Europe and other countries.

ISBN 978–0–230–24777–2

This book is printed on paper suitable for recycling and made from fully
managed and sustained forest sources. Logging, pulping and manufacturing
processes are expected to conform to the environmental regulations of the
country of origin.

A catalogue record for this book is available from the British Library.

A catalog record for this book is available from the Library of Congress.

10   9   8   7   6   5   4   3   2   1
22 21 20 19 18 17 16 15 14 13

Printed and bound in Great Britain by
CPI Antony Rowe, Chippenham and Eastbourne

To all who practise forensic psychology

Contents

List of Figures and Tables

Figures

Tables

Foreword

Interest in forensic psychology continues to grow, and at what seems to be an ever-quickening pace. This shows in the numbers of students wishing to pursue it, the increasing practical value of it in several areas and the accelerating output of research. It shows, too, in the increasing number of texts being published in Europe as compared with the North American one, where the profession has been established for a longer period. Given the speed of these changes over recent years, it is easy to overlook the historic fact that the use of psychological evidence in courtrooms was one of the earliest forms of applied psychology. While this took a lengthy period to gain a foothold, it has become progressively more widespread to see forensic psychology being used in legal decisions at numerous points throughout the criminal justice and mental health systems.

The present text can make a fair claim to being unique. To resort to some familiar publishing jargon, the book you are holding can be described as filling what was a rather glaring gap in forensic psychology. This derives from its extensive, in-depth focus on the professional skills that are essential for the practice of forensic psychology. While many texts make reference to these areas, there is no methodical treatment available that covers interviewing, models of assessment, case formulation, report writing and communication in a well-connected way in a single volume. Here, readers will find wide-ranging treatment of the sometimes-challenging questions that arise when translating the ideas found in textbooks into real-life practice. They will then also be able to see how some of those skills can be applied with reference to an array of practical areas, some of which have been somewhat neglected and others that are relatively recent departures in the field.

To Kurt Lewin's famous and frequently quoted maxim, 'there is nothing so practical as a good theory', I have recently heard a fairly sceptical response, that theory and practice are the same thing in theory; just not in practice. Everywhere there is a need to bridge the perceived gap between the two. Without genuinely drawing on psychological theory and research, forensic psychology, apart from being detached from its 'parent discipline', would lose its scientific base and its direction of thought. But without some illustration of what psychological ideas mean when we use them to inform our work, our ability to do so appropriately and competently might not achieve its optimal effects.

Having been an external examiner of the forensic psychology programme at York, I am aware of the rich and varied experience of the staff team who are among the contributors to this book, and also of some of the innovative exercises they have developed for teaching and learning, and in assessment of students' work. The book is further strengthened by contributions from a number of highly experienced practitioners. It is firmly rooted in a thorough-going applied approach and is a very welcome addition to the sources we can all draw upon. I congratulate the editors and authors of *Forensic Psychology in Practice* in having achieved the goal they set in producing the book.

James McGuire
October 2012

Preface

From the perspective of most in the profession, forensic psychology is considered one of the most exciting and demanding domains of psychological practice. Working with clients who are by definition antisocial, in environments that are often anti-therapeutic, presents challenges and opportunities not often encountered in other branches of psychology. It is not a job for just anyone. However, whether in prison, hospital or the community, working with offenders presents a unique context in which to make a difference, at an individual, community and societal level.

The purpose of this book is to provide readers with a core understanding of the knowledge and skills required for effective practice as a forensic psychologist and the application of these skills to specific forensic populations. It is written as a practitioner's handbook, so that the reader may either read the whole, perhaps as a text underpinning an academic training programme, or focus on a particular chapter, particularly when faced with the challenges of working with a specific population.

Developing the requisite skills to work confidently and competently in this arena is really a lifelong process, but probably the steepest learning curve is at the start of one's career. Currently, there are 25 accredited postgraduate programmes designed to prepare people for this journey. Only two of these result in full Stage Two level qualification, enabling independent practice (Doctorate-level training). The remaining 23 (Masters-level training) qualify graduates to what is known as Stage One: the level at which an individual is considered to have the necessary skills and academic qualification to work psychologically with offenders, provided that practice is supervised. Supervision ensures that newly qualified (Stage One) practitioners are supported in the development of their theoretical knowledge and the application of that knowledge to practice.

The MSc in Applied Forensic Psychology at the University of York is the only Masters-level qualification to include the word 'Applied' in its title. It was developed in 2003 in partnership with HM Prison Service Directorate of High Security Prisons. At its heart is an emphasis on the application of psychological theory, principles and knowledge to the practice of forensic psychology. Consequently it has an equal balance of practice-based, methodological and theoretically driven modules designed to foster autonomy within the bounds of professional practice, independent learning and self-directed reflection.

Forensic psychology in practice, the module on which this book is based, is considered the core module. It provides theoretical and practical perspectives on key skills required by the effective practitioner, as they apply to a variety of forensic populations that are typically encountered in practice. The editors – as Course Director and one of the original instigators of the course – saw the clear benefit of developing this module and enhancing it into this book, in order to take what has been considered by students over the years to be a winning formula to a wider audience.

Acknowledgements

The editors would like to thank all the contributors to this book. Your expertise and experience brings both the book and the module on which it is based to life.

Thank you to all the graduates of the MSc in Applied Forensic Psychology, especially those who, in the early days, helped to source material for this book. Your passion for the subject, questions, challenges and contributions are a constant source of energy and renewal.

We would also like to thank Jenny and Paul at Palgrave Macmillan for their endless patience, invaluable advice and enthusiasm for this project.

Joanna Clarke would particularly like to acknowledge the inspiration, wisdom and support of Professor Michael Carroll. This book was really his idea.

Notes on Contributors

Joanna Clarke is the Director of the MSc in Applied Forensic Psychology at the University of York, a post she has held for the past four years. Prior to that, Jo spent over 20 years working with offenders and staff in both prison and community settings. Her main research and practice interests focus on individual and organizational factors that promote professional resilience in high-risk jobs. Within this arena she has written, presented and advised both nationally and internationally.

Jo is also fully committed to the professional development of forensic psychologists through her role at York, and is very proud to co-ordinate a programme that is recognized for the high calibre of trainees it produces. She is also hugely appreciative of the opportunities it provides to work with top professionals in the field.

Pam Wilson is Director of Pamela Wilson Associates Ltd, specializing in criminal justice psychology, through which she has recently delivered training both for academic course and for operational organizations in consultancy, crisis management and related topics. Previously, Pam spent 26 years with HM Prison Service, latterly as consultant psychologist for the Directorate of High Security, working with partner organizations on issues concerning the treatment and management of high-risk offenders. During this period, she took a keen interest in the training and development of forensic psychologists, and was instrumental in the initial concept for and development of the programme which gave rise to this book.

Kirstin Barnes is a Registered Forensic Psychologist with 13 years' experience of working at HMYOI Wetherby with juvenile offenders. Having started at Wetherby in 1999 as a psychological assistant, Kirstin then became a trainee forensic psychologist in 2000, going on to complete her MSc in Applied Forensic Psychology at the University of Leicester, and then achieving her chartership. After five years of managing the Psychology function, in 2010 she took on the role of Head of Reducing Reoffending which involves managing the Psychology department, the Offender Management team, public protection and substance misuse. Having spent all her career at Wetherby, Kirstin has a passion for working with young people and this is also her main area of expertise within forensic psychology. However, one of her other interests is in her role as a Negotiator Advisor for the area. Kirstin has attended a significant number of serious incidents at a number of different prisons over the last six years and is also involved in training negotiators.

Sarah Barnes is a PhD candidate at the University of York, UK, researching the potential pathway between being a survivor of childhood sexual abuse and later going on to offend sexually against children. After graduating in psychology at the University of Birmingham, UK, she successfully completed her MSc in Applied Forensic Psychology at the University of York before securing funding to complete her PhD. In her spare time, Sarah volunteers for Victim Support, a charity designed to provide support for victims and witnesses of crimes, and Circles of Support and Accountability, a charity that supports sexual offenders in the community.

Ruby Bell is a Consultant Clinical Forensic Psychologist, and Head of Forensic Psychology for Tees, Esk & Wear Valleys NHS Foundation Trust. She has over 20 years' experience of working with offenders in (high-secure) prison and (medium and low-secure) health settings. Her professional interests focus on the assessment of risk and the development and evaluation of interventions to reduce offending, with people who offend and have mental health problems.

Ruby is fully committed to the professional development of psychologists in forensic settings. Her team comprises equal numbers of chartered and trainee forensic and clinical psychologists and are involved in a diverse range of research initiatives within in-patient, prison and community-based practise. These include the development and evaluation of new, offending-focussed treatment programmes, and the design and implementation of a forensic service wide Cognitive Analytic Therapy skills and practice programme.

Tracy Brookes is a Chartered Psychologist, registered with the HPC as a Forensic Practitioner and is currently working at Stockton Hall psychiatric hospital, York. Prior to that, Tracy worked within a high-secure prison setting for over 14 years, during which she worked with both the offenders and prison service staff. More recently she was responsible for the production and supervision of a number of risk assessments and the subsequent reporting of the findings.

Phil Coombes is the Lead Psychologist and Deputy Clinical Director for Raphael healthcare a low-secure service provider specializing in the delivery of services to female population; he has held this for the past five years. Prior to this Phil worked for 10 years in a variety of forensic environments, working initially with delivery and management of offending programmes in prisons, then moving his practice to secure hospital settings. Phil's main interest has always been in the role trauma and attachment play and its impact upon the development and delivery of trauma-focussed interventions in forensic settings. He has a desire to continue to increase the profile and knowledge of forensic psychologists, both by lecturing on a number of forensic courses as well as supervising placement students.

Sue Evershed is a Consultant Forensic and Clinical Psychologist, currently the Lead Psychologist in the Men's Personality Disorder and National Women's Directorate at Rampton High Secure Hospital. Sue spent half of her 30-year career working in prisons with adult high-secure and adolescent offenders before moving to a health setting. During her career she has worked with many different offender populations including men and women, adults and adolescents and learning-disabled offenders, in high-, medium- and low-secure establishments within prison and hospital settings. Sue's main research and practice interests are focussed on improving the efficacy of managing and treating offenders and related practice and ethical issues. She is also keenly interested in the professional development of psychologists, contributing to both clinical and forensic courses including the York Forensic MSc, and regularly taking psychology students and trainees on placement.

Ruby Fitter is a Registered Forensic Psychologist with over 13 years' experience of working in adult prisons and more recently a Young Offender Institution (YOI) for juvenile offenders. Ruby is currently the Clinical Lead for individual assessments and interventions for young people at Wetherby YOI and takes a keen interest in developing the clinical skills of the staff that she supervises. As well as her current managerial and supervisory roles within Wetherby YOI, Ruby undertakes clinical assessments and interventions with young people who have been convicted of some high-risk offences, in particular those convicted of sexual offences. Besides her prison role, Ruby is an assessor for the BPS Qualification in Forensic Psychology.

Michelle Fletcher is a consultant forensic psychologist working for Forensic Psychology Practice (FPP), a forensic psychology consultancy company. Michelle has worked with FPP for approximately 15 months; prior to this she gained experience working in the private sector and secure psychiatric unit and spent several years working in the Scottish Prison Service. She has extensive experience of risk assessment and providing testimony in quasi-legal situations such as parole hearings and has trained other professionals in the use of various risk assessment approaches.

Rebecca Milner is a Lecturer in Applied Forensic Psychology at the University of York. Rebecca previously worked for the Prison Service and has 15 years' applied experience in the assessment and treatment of high-risk violent and sexual offenders. Rebecca has also been widely involved in the training and clinical/professional supervision of psychologists and other prison service staff. Her research interests include treatment and desistance in sexual offenders.

Matthew Shirley qualified as a Probation Officer in 2002 and has delivered accredited sex offender programmes for Hertfordshire Probation Trust since 2004. Additionally, he has concurrently held the post of Treatment Manager since 2007. He has been involved with the Internet Sexual Offences Treatment

Programme (i-SOTP) since it's initial pilot and has promoted the programme to probation colleagues in Northern Ireland and Latvia. In 2008 he co-presented a workshop on the i-SOTP with one of the programmes' authors (David Middleton) at the NOTA international conference. He qualified to train probation staff to deliver the i-SOTP in 2007 and has been active in delivering other accredited programmes training, as well as devising and presenting a range of sex offender-related training events to probation staff, other partner agencies (police, social services, LSCBs) and academic audiences.

Paul Summers has been a Teaching Fellow in the Department of Psychology at the University of York since 2007. Prior to this, Paul was employed by HM Prison Service and the drug agency Addaction. His ongoing doctoral research focuses on the impact of evidence on juror decision making. Paul is proud to be involved in preparing postgraduate students for applied practice and introducing undergraduate students to this relatively new, exciting and valued field of psychology.

Phil Willmot is a Consultant Forensic and Clinical Psychologist in the Men's Personality Disorder Service at Rampton Hospital. He has over 20 years' experience of working with sexual and violent offenders with personality disorders in both prison and hospital settings. Phil is also a Senior Fellow of the Institute of Mental Health, where his research interests include mechanisms of change in therapy for personality disorder and qualitative studies of forensic personality disorder.

1 Introduction

Pam Wilson

INTRODUCTION

Interest in the application of psychological knowledge and skills to criminal justice has seen unprecedented growth in recent years. This is reflected not just in
popular culture (a quick glance at the most popular TV programmes and books
will confirm this), but also in the massive growth in forensic psychology as a
profession. This in turn is demonstrated by the recruitment profiles of forensic
organizations, the development of academic training programmes and the huge
growth in academic writings on the subject. However, a scan of the academic
literature would suggest two separate emphases, theory and practice. For developing practitioners, this then requires a synthesis of different works to enable
the development of theory-driven practice. This book aims to address this by
providing, in one volume, both theoretical and practical considerations when
working with particular client groups.

This chapter sets the context for the book. A brief history of the profession
of forensic psychology is provided, including issues of definition and statutory
recognition. Attention then turns to the application of forensic psychology to
practice in key settings. Next, consideration of the skills specific to forensic psychologists is given; a taster for part one of the book. The challenges that forensic
clients present are then examined, followed by the challenges of forensic environments and issues for forensic psychologists working in a multidisciplinary
context. Finally, a chapter-by-chapter outline of the book is provided.

A BRIEF HISTORY OF FORENSIC PSYCHOLOGY AS A PROFESSION

Forensic psychology is hard to define and understand as a single, coherent discipline (Brown and Campbell, 2011). According to the British Psychological Society
(2012, p. 4), 'Forensic psychology is concerned with the psychological aspects of
legal processes in courts. The term is also often used to refer to investigative and

criminological psychology: applying psychological theory to criminal investigation, understanding psychological problems associated with criminal behaviour and the treatment of criminals'. This book will focus largely on the last of these concerns, which constitutes the practice area for the great majority of forensic psychologists, but also constitutes what Brown and Campbell describe as a narrowing of the term 'forensic' to mean 'criminological' – and perhaps also, more specifically, 'penal'.

Bartol and Bartol (2004) discuss the differentiation between broader and narrower definitions but also draw attention to the professional application of psychological knowledge, concepts and principles in practice, i.e., what psychologists working in the field actually do. This book builds on this concept, with the first part focussing on the theory underpinning forensic psychology and the skills needed to apply the theory to practice, and the second part building on these generic skills by considering their application to specific population groups.

In the United States, forensic psychology was only recognized as a specific specialist discipline as recently as 2001. In Britain, the British Psychological Society established the Division of Legal and Criminological Society in 1977, which effectively became the Division of Forensic Psychology in 1999, following much heated debate about the merits and implications of this title change. The introduction of Chartership in 1974 and, more recently, the incorporation of psychology within the remit of the Health Professions Council have both introduced considerable additional scrutiny of standards required by individuals in their practice. While there is some argument that forensic psychologists are using a narrower range of professional skills, especially if their practice mainly involves the delivery of manualized programmes, there is also a counter argument that the increased level of scrutiny of reports and professional opinion has led to a need for an enhanced professional knowledge and skill base. The associated rise in challenge and litigation has also required forensic psychologists to be in a position to routinely present their assessments and reports in court and to be subject to demanding cross examination.

FORENSIC PSYCHOLOGY IN THE PRISON SERVICE

A helpful brief history of psychology in UK prisons is provided by Robson (1999). Forensic psychology first emerged in the Prison Department in the mid-1920s, when the Prison Commission requested research into the vocational interests and aptitudes of borstal boys. Full-time psychologists were first appointed in the mid-1940s to provide assessments, and a decade later psychologists and psychological testers were employed to assist in the preparation of reports to court. At the same time, the first application of psychology to the selection and training of prison officers took place. The early 1960s saw an interest in improving the treatment of sentenced prisoners, and this led to the appointment of psychologists as advisors, with a broad remit concentrating the application of group methods to staff, managerial and organizational issues. This was then built on with key roles for psychologists in such matters as prisoner categorization and allocation procedures and the planning and evaluation of specialist prison regimes. A review of the strategy for prison psychological services in the early 1970s confirmed a focus on design, development and evaluation, rather than assessment of individual prisoners, and led to psychology becoming embedded in the prison service at all levels. The 1980s saw a further review, this time concentrating on resource pressures and the contribution of psychology to control and regime issues in establishments. The focus on organizational and system-centred tasks was reaffirmed, although work with individual prisoners and members of staff was also identified as important.

Since Robson's report, there has been a great expansion in the numbers of psychologists employed in prisons, and a refocussing of the work with prisoners, almost entirely due to the development and implementation of accredited programmes aimed at reducing re-offending. These have largely been based on cognitive behavioural principles, as a research-and-development-driven 'What Works' response to the nihilistic view prevalent in the 1970s that nothing worked to rehabilitate offenders. Psychologically informed practice has driven approaches that attempt to change offenders' future behaviour, and over time these have become more sophisticated, incorporating such issues as offence paralleling behaviour (see, for example, Jones, 2004) and the concept of 'Good Lives' – those factors which promote a positive lifestyle as well as addressing the offending itself (see, for example, Ward, 2010). Most recently, developments have been made to work with those offenders viewed as most difficult and entrenched, for example through initiatives aimed at those classified as psychopaths or with entrenched personality disorders, although funding issues are now calling some of this resource-intensive work into question.

The recent expansion in service delivery has been underpinned by a strong focus on professionalizing the work of psychologists and enhancing training, alongside an increasing emphasis on regulation and certification. It is argued by a number of authors, especially from an academic perspective (e.g., Brown and Campbell, 2010) that there has been an associated narrowing of the training base for forensic psychologists, which has largely been driven by the dual forces of the requirements of the Division of Forensic Psychology and the practicalities of the needs of employing organizations.

While forensic psychologists practicing in prison and other settings are involved in activities such as research and consultancy, the great majority of the work of most practitioner psychologists is directly with offenders, and this forms the focus of this book.

FORENSIC PSYCHOLOGY IN THE HEALTH SERVICE

The delivery of psychological services within National Health Service settings has traditionally been through clinical psychologists, who have as their aim 'reducing psychological distress and enhancing the promotion of psychological well-being' (British Psychological Society, 2012, p. 4). More recently, forensic psychologists have also been employed in health settings, with a somewhat different core focus on risk and offending behaviour. In many cases, individuals present with complex pathology, with linkages, if any, between mental health issues and offending being far from clear. As private provision has expanded in recent years, along with an increased focus on risk, more forensic psychologists have been employed alongside, and in some cases in place of, clinical colleagues. In the health context, psychologists are now being appointed as 'approved clinicians', as defined by the 2007 Mental Health Act, giving them lead responsibility for the care pathways of individuals for the first time.

FORENSIC PSYCHOLOGY IN THE PROBATION SERVICE

Forensic psychologists were rarely employed in the probation service until the focus came on offender risk assessment and management in the early 2000s, alongside a restructuring to bring prison and probation together under the umbrella of the National Offender Management Service. The role of forensic psychologists within the probation service essentially mirrors that in prisons: providing assessments and interventions using largely the same range of tools and accredited programmes. There is a particular emphasis on risk assessment and management, especially through the multi-agency public protection arrangements (MAPPA). There is an intention to develop a mixed economy of employed staff and private sector service provision, but resource pressures have seen far fewer forensic psychologists employed in the probation service than anticipated.

FORENSIC PSYCHOLOGY IN OTHER SETTINGS

Academia and research is the other main arena within which forensic psychologists work, which is crucial in order to drive forward the evidence base and to provide evaluations. As already mentioned, the remit of forensic psychology in the academic setting is wider than in the practitioner setting, and there are some apparent tensions about the definition and meaning of forensic psychology as a discipline. Perhaps the recognition of the need for broad-based training accompanied by practice components and the development of programmes attempting to marry these needs is assisting in the reduction of these tensions.

Private practice has grown considerably in recent years, particularly in response to a seemingly exponential increase in the requirement for assessment-based court reports. There has been a vast increase in the number of individuals in business providing such reports. The privatization of prisons and of health facilities has also contributed to an increase in the number of psychologists leaving the public sector to join private-sector organizations. The future is likely to see, as in other arenas which previously have been exclusively in the public sector, an expansion in areas of work where private practice is seen.

THE SKILLS SPECIFIC TO FORENSIC PSYCHOLOGISTS

Views differ about the extent to which forensic psychology, or any other specific discipline, has a large set of specific skills and competences associated with it, or whether all applied psychology is essentially using the same skill set, with some small nuances differing according to the area of work. It is the case that forensic psychologists adopt the stance of scientist practitioner. As explored above, forensic psychological practice has historically drawn from elements of both clinical and occupational psychology in work with individuals and organizations.

The Health Professions Council (2009) lay out required standards of proficiency for practitioner psychologists. There are a few standards of conduct, performance and ethics that are specific to forensic psychologists, and it can be argued that the application of these requires specific skills. However, close inspection of these shows that they do not really assist in differentiating a specific skill set. The specific skills are perhaps best considered in the context of the clients and the environment, as will be discussed next.

Approaches such as motivational interviewing and interventions which focus on positive attributes, not just offending behaviour – such as the 'Good Lives' model (Ward, 2010) are now key components of the toolbox of many practitioner forensic psychologists, but the essential skill is in bringing a coherent understanding and application of theory to the complex task of working with individuals, groups and organizations in order to reduce risk. The focus on risk of harm to others is perhaps the key differentiator when viewing the skill set needed in the forensic context. While all psychologists, as with other professional groups, need to operate defensible practice, this is rather more sharply brought to bear in the forensic context. Individuals who have been caught up in the criminal justice system are often quite litigious, and of course those serving long sentences or periods of detention in health settings have a great deal of time at their disposal to make challenges about their treatment. Psychologists, by nature of their work on risk assessment and interventions, are often at the 'sharp end' of this. This, and the requirement to produce and defend evidence in court, requires particular skills on the part of the forensic psychologist in honing their writing and presentation skills, as well as ensuring that the work undertaken is supported by a defensible evidential base.

The chapters in the first part of this book, covering theories and how they influence practice, interviewing forensic clients, forensic assessment, case formulation, report writing and motivational report disclosure, represent the backbone of the skills which each practitioner needs to flesh out in their own practice context.

THE CHALLENGES THAT FORENSIC CLIENTS PRESENT

Arguably the key challenge for the forensic psychologist in this arena, which defines the approach to all their work, is to identify who exactly is the client. There is very often a range of clients for any individual piece of work, and the individual offender is almost never the sole client. Indeed, there have been significant shifts over time, which have sometimes seen the offender almost being ignored in favour of the wider criminal justice system being viewed as the client, with reports being written, in the interests of public protection, using collateral and file information solely, with the offender not involved in the process at all. The present emphasis on motivational report writing and disclosure, covered in some detail in this book, represents the current view that involvement of the individual offender in decisions about their treatment and management is not only the most ethical but also the safest way to proceed.

Considering the offender as a key client, the lack of free volition when engaging in assessment or treatment, when compared to clients entering into any other relationship with a psychologist as therapist, presents a range of issues. One such ethical issue concerns the power held by the psychologist and the organization that they may be part of or represent. Another is ensuring that client engagement and motivation to change is genuine and not simply 'jumping through the hoops' inherent in the criminal justice system. This is touched on in Chapter 3 (Interviewing).

There are, of course, particular challenges presented by different client groups. The chapters that follow give valuable practical ideas and advice, grounded both in theory and in experience, about working specifically with juvenile, internet, female and sex offenders, as well as the emerging field of gang members and working with victims of crime. In each case, a theoretical overview relevant to the specific group is provided, followed by consideration of interviewing, assessment, case formulation and motivational report disclosure.

THE CHALLENGES OF FORENSIC ENVIRONMENTS

There is a range of challenges associated with working in any forensic environment. Perhaps the most obvious is that the key clients are by definition offenders, with psychologists frequently engaged in work with individuals and groups who have committed serious violent or sexual offences. All staff working within a closed environment, be it prison or hospital, need to have sufficient security awareness and training in order to protect themselves not only from the possibility of physical assault, but also, and far more commonly and much more insidiously, from the psychological techniques employed by offenders to gain favour with their therapists and gradually 'groom' them to behave in ways which may breach policy and rules. Boundary setting and supervision are essential components of safe practice. In an open environment, such as when working with clients on probation, the issues can be more complex, as inherent systems, structures and staff which promote safety and security in a closed environment are not in place.

The very same systems, structures and staff that create safety and security also present particular challenges for psychologists working in forensic environments. The emphasis is on reducing the risk of escape or of further offending by reducing opportunities for individuals to behave in ways which may be harmful to others, including physical boundaries such as walls, fences and locked doors and measures of social control such as limiting opportunities to mix with others and being supervised by staff. The policies and procedures in place to protect safety and security are often at odds with practices that might support a more therapeutic way of working with clients. The 'risk averse' culture that is often found makes it very difficult for clients to demonstrate change and hence to establish whether or not therapeutic input has been effective.

The impact of the media and the associated 'blame culture' can be very difficult and frustrating. The psychologist may be in a position to influence decisions, but is rarely the ultimate decision maker when it comes to such issues as moving an individual to a less secure environment or release. There may also be a lack of psychological mindedness or understanding among other staff groups, which can lead to therapeutic work being undermined, not necessarily deliberately, as behaviour is managed and controlled. Conversely, this can also lead to staff not seeing the risks that are being played out in behaviour, viewing serious offenders as 'just like the blokes down the pub'.

A further challenge for psychologists working in a forensic environment is that of budgetary and political control. It is rare indeed for a psychologist to have complete autonomy over their work. While it is, of course, important that the work of psychologists, as of other professional groups, is subject to scrutiny in respect of its costs and benefits, it is sometimes difficult to persuade 'the powers that be' to introduce evidence-based practice, particularly if this involves high costs, such as one-to-one work or intensive programmes. Some interventions may be highly politically driven, and this can be associated with a desire for rapid results, sometimes at the expense of more sustainable solutions.

There are also significant challenges in how forensic psychologists are viewed by other groups of staff. As a group, forensic psychologists working in penal and health settings tend to be young and predominantly female, with the majority still undergoing qualification training. This demographic provokes a number of differing responses among staff groups with whom psychologists work, including feeling a need to protect or parent, and scepticism that they can manage themselves within the environment. Psychologists need to work hard to establish professional credibility and to build a solid base of experience quite quickly, developing competence and confidence in their own work in order to demonstrate this to those around them. This may be at its most acute when considering young female psychologists working with male sex offenders. Clear boundary setting and effective use of supervision are paramount, as discussed in Phil Willmot's and Joanna Clarke's chapters in this book (Chapters 11 and 14 respectively).

One final, and rather different, challenge is that of who delivers psychologically based interventions in forensic environments. As the prominence of accredited, manualized programmes has spread, there has been a widespread shift towards utilizing staff from a range of backgrounds and disciplines to deliver the programmes, with the more costly and scarce forensic psychologists reserved for roles in the management of treatment, such as staff training and ensuring programme integrity.

AN INTRODUCTION TO THE BOOK CHAPTERS

The book is presented in two parts. The first starts with an overview of general theories of crime and how these relate to forensic practice, followed by chapters introducing specific skills required to work effectively with forensic clients, covering interviewing, assessment, case formulation and motivational disclosure of reports. The second part builds on these generic skills by considering their application to specific populations that most practitioners might expect to meet in the course of their work. Most of these chapters start with an overview of the theories relating to the particular client group, followed by special considerations regarding the application of the skills presented in Part I.

Part I: The Skills of Forensic Psychology

Chapter 2 introduces key theories of crime, predominantly exploring biological and sociological explanations before moving on to address psychological theories. In each case, the theory is briefly introduced, the evidence for it presented and its application explored. Thus this chapter sets the scene for the rest of the book, providing the reader with a grounding in the theory necessary to appreciate forensic psychology in practice.

Chapter 3 provides an analysis of the skills required for success in the complex task of interviewing forensic clients. An operational model of skilled performance is introduced to provide a framework, and various aspects of the interviewing process are explored, brought to life with illustrations and examples from the author's own practice.

Chapter 4 starts by exploring the various settings within which forensic assessment may be undertaken and the underpinning context and considerations. Key approaches to risk assessment – actuarial and structured professional judgement – are described, and their general limitations considered. Alternative assessments are then explored, with a final piece addressing ethical issues and dilemmas.

Chapter 5 makes a link between structured professional judgement (as described in Chapter 4) and creating a formulation of the presenting case. The literature is examined and then a basic model of case formulation is described, along with an exploration of the issues surrounding more complex models and their application.

Chapter 6 considers report writing from the perspective of the multiple roles and biases inherent in the task, including defining who the client is and recognizing who the readers are, as well as what questions need to be addressed. Specific ethical dilemmas when writing in a forensic environment are explored. A guide to the production of a balanced and comprehensive psychological report is provided.

Chapter 7 begins by arguing for the benefits of a collaborative approach to working with offenders, and specifically of motivational report disclosure, the aim being to help offenders to engage in therapeutic processes. Therapist characteristics and the challenges to collaborative working are explored, followed by theoretical concepts, incorporating a detailed overview of motivational interviewing. Finally, a case study is provided, to illustrate strategies that can be used to build a positive environment and collaborative relationship in order to facilitate motivational report disclosure.

Part II: Application of Skills to Forensic Populations

Chapter 8 commences with an overview of theories of juvenile offending. Special considerations relating to assessment, interventions and working with young people who have offended are explored, and a case example provided to illustrate the issues in a practice context.

Chapter 9 begins with a discussion of the term 'internet sex offender', exploring the range of behaviour that this can cover, before exploring the response of the criminal justice system to such offenders. Risk assessment, interviewing, treatment and interventions are addressed in turn. Finally, motivational report disclosure with this group is explored, making links to chapter 7.

Chapter 10 describes the female forensic population, highlighting the lack of research with this group and the need for specific services, rather than slight changes and adaptations to existing services. Theories relating to female offenders and pathways to offending are addressed and the role of trauma explored.

Assessment and treatment issues are examined, and consideration given to practical implications for working with women.

Chapter 11 starts with a theoretical overview relating to sex offenders. The importance of the psychologist-sex offender relationship is then explored, and special considerations for assessment, case formulation and report disclosure with this group are described.

Chapter 12 begins with a general overview of the phenomenon of gangs, followed by an exploration of relevant theory and definitional issues surrounding membership and identification. Responses in respect to addressing risk and practitioner involvement with gang members are explored, with notes of caution given to a lack of empirical evidence. Special considerations regarding therapeutic alliance, assessment, motivational report disclosure and enhancing staff knowledge are addressed.

Chapter 13 starts by explaining the reasons for the inclusion of a chapter about victims in this book, not least because a high proportion of offenders are also themselves victims. A theoretical overview is provided, incorporating a process model of victimization and recovery. Special considerations when working with victims, and issues concerning when professional involvement is most effective, are then explored. The chapter concludes with a case-study example.

Chapter 14 completes this part by moving the focus to the psychologist rather than the client group, addressing the importance of being a resilient practitioner when working in a forensic environment, with inherent high risk of exposure to traumatic events. It introduces and considers the application of a model to enhance individual and organizational resilience, then focuses on practical ways in which the individual practitioner can enhance their own resilience through energy management, supervision and mindfulness.

CONCLUSION

The aim of this handbook is to provide forensic psychologists and other forensic practitioners an easily accessible and practical guide to undertaking assessment and therapeutic work with offenders. That all the contributors have a wealth of experience in the field, and that the contents of the book are derived from a course of academic study, ensure that a comprehensive guide is provided to developing and enhancing a range of skills for application with a range of client groups.

REFERENCES

Bartol, C. R. and Bartol, A. M. (2004). *Introduction to Forensic Psychology*. (New Jersey: Sage Publications Inc.).

British Psychological Society (2012). *Member Networks* (Leicester: The British Psychological Society).

Brown, J. M. and Campbell, E. A. (2010). 'Forensic Psychology: A Case of Multiple Identities', in J. M. Brown and E. A. Campbell (Eds) *The Cambridge Handbook of Forensic Psychology* (Cambridge: Cambridge University Press).

Health Professions Council (2009). *Standards of Proficiency: Practitioner Psychologists* (London: Health Professions Council).

Jones, L. (2004). 'Offence Paralleling Behaviour (OPB) as a Framework for Assessment and Intervention with Offenders', in A. Needs and G. Towl (Eds) *Applying Psychology to Forensic Practice.* (Oxford: Blackwell), 34–63.

Robson, L. (1999). The history of the prison psychology service. Unpublished paper.

Ward, T. (2010). 'The Good Lives Model of Offender Rehabilitation: Basic Assumptions, Etiological Commitments and Practice Implications', in F. McNeil, P. Raynor and C. Trotter (Eds) *Offender Supervision: New Directions in Theory, Research and Practice* (Devon: Willan Publishing), 41–64.

Part I The Skills of Forensic Psychology

2 Theories of Crime

Rebecca Milner

INTRODUCTION

A forensic practitioner working with a client requires a set of specialist skills in order to assess, case formulate, treat and evaluate progress. In order to be able to use these skills effectively the practitioner will require a theoretical knowledge of the proposed explanations of how and why an individual engages in criminal behaviour. An awareness of the underlying possible explanations will add breadth and depth to assessment and case formulation and help to inform treatment considerations.

In the search for the explanation of crime many theories have been developed which attempt to explain the underlying mechanisms. The aim of this chapter is to explore three major strands, biological, sociological and psychological, and review the supporting evidence. Typically crime has been explained sociologically, while maintaining a focus on the behaviour of the individual; hence the inclusion of a number of different sociologically based theories within this chapter.

Following a review of the main theories of crime this chapter will present a case study with the aim of exploring how the different theories can be applied to practice.

BIOLOGICAL THEORIES

Early biological theories explaining crime stemmed from Darwinism and an evolutionary perspective, and focussed on the premise that crime was a result of inborn abnormalities. Early theorists believed that the criminal could be distinguished from the non-criminal by the identification of certain physical characteristics (Lombroso, 2006 [1911]). Harsh criticism of the methodology and lack of focus on environmental factors have given way to modern biological theories that focus on biochemistry, genetics and neurophysiology. These predisposing biological factors interact with the physical and social environment and can help to explain criminal behaviour (Rowe, 2002). These later theories are known as biosocial theories and look at how the learning of (antisocial) behaviour is different for individuals due to their underlying biology.

Mednick's biosocial approach postulates that genetic factors do not cause criminal behaviour, rather that an individual receives a susceptibility due to inheriting a slow autonomic nervous system (ANS). Individuals with a suboptimal ANS are slow to learn to control their impulsive behaviour and as such are more likely to commit crime (Mednick, 1977). As Rowe (2002) points out, this does not explain why individuals turn to crime rather than legitimate thrill-seeking behaviour.

Biosocial theories have also looked at brain dysfunction and how abnormalities in the frontal and temporal lobes may be linked to criminality. The frontal lobes are tasked with planning, inhibition and the ability to learn from experience (Comings, 2003). Damage to these areas would therefore result in behaviour that would be more likely to result in crime. Rosenbaum *et al.* (1994) found a significant number of violent men disclosed head injuries and made a link between head injury, which can reduce impulse control, and crime. One major limitation of head injury research is that it can be caused by childhood abuse and therefore the results that link it with crime are spurious (Cunningham *et al.* 1998).

Other biological factors that have been linked through the research to criminality include intelligence and low IQ (Crocker and Hodgins, 1997) hormones, e.g., testosterone (Dabbs *et al.*, 1995) and neurotransmitters and toxins (Curran and Renzitti, 2001).

Evidence

Mednick, Gabrielli and Hutchings (1984) studied adoptees in Denmark and found that the biological father and male adoptee conviction rates were considerably higher than the rates for the adoptive father. Their data suggests a genetic aetiology with some genetic component being inherited from the criminal biological parent increasing the risk of criminality in the biological child. Mednick *et al.* acknowledge the limitations of their study including lack of generalizability by using Denmark as the only research site and not being able to identify all of the subjects leading to bias in those being included. Gottfredson and Hirschi (1990) have been critical of this work, and in addition to pointing out flaws in the research, showed that in Swedish and American adoption research only a very small, non-significant relationship was found between biological parent and son's criminality.

Twin studies have been popular but have received much criticism due to the methodology and the difficulties in teasing out the biological and social factors. Akers and Sellers (2009) conclude that although twin studies of adult males have found evidence of a genetic influence, twin studies of delinquency in adolescence show little genetic effect. Rowe proposes that delinquency is a result of the combined processes of genetics and family environment (Rowe, 2002).

Raine (1993), in a series of biosocial studies, investigated biological risk factors for crime. He found that lower levels of physiological arousal at 15 years were related to criminality at age 24. Controlling for various social factors did not mediate the link between low arousal and criminality. Raine also investigated birth complications, hypothesizing that problems at birth would result in neurological and brain dysfunction deficits. He found that birth complications combined with maternal rejection at one-year predispose to violence. Raine argues that the combination of these factors launch a 'biosocial pathway' to violent crime. However many people may have low arousal and not turn to crime. It is not clear why some individuals seek out legitimate thrill-seeking such as travel or adventure sports and others become violent offenders.

Application

Early biological theories that proposed that crime was a result of innate biological make up did not offer much potential for rehabilitation. This view led to extreme medical measures such as prefrontal lobotomy, chemical castration and Electro-convulsive Therapy (ECT) during the 1950s to 1970s (Moyer, 1979). These measures, as well as being highly unethical, did not prove effective in reducing overall violence and were phased out. Biosocial theories have focussed instead on pharmacological treatments, dietary therapy, genetic counselling and the improvement of prenatal and perinatal care (Akers and Sellers, 2009). Additionally Raine (1993) suggests that biofeedback to regulate arousal could be used with antisocial individuals, and Fishbein (2001) suggests training to improve cognitive ability as a method of compensating for cognitive deficits as a result of brain dysfunction.

SOCIOLOGICAL THEORIES

Social Learning Theories

Sutherland's Differential Association Theory (1947)

Edwin H. Sutherland's theory is based on the premise that as human beings we learn how to behave as a result of our interactions with the social environment. Individuals who are immersed in and influenced by a culture whose rules or definitions are supportive of crime are more likely to engage in criminal acts.

Sutherland (1947) proposed 9 statements that are fundamental to his theory:

1. Criminal behaviour is learnt.
2. Criminal behaviour is learnt in interaction with other persons in a process of communication.

3. The principal part of the learning of criminal behaviour occurs within intimate personal groups.
4. When criminal behaviour is learnt, the learning includes (a) techniques of committing the crime, which are sometimes very complicated, sometimes are very simple, and (b) the specific direction of motives, drives, rationalizations and attitudes.
5. The specific direction of motives and drives is learnt from definitions of the legal codes as favourable or unfavourable.
6. A person becomes delinquent because of an excess of definitions favourable to violation of law over definitions unfavourable to violation of the law.
7. Differential associations may vary in frequency, duration, priority, and intensity.
8. The process of learning criminal behaviour by association with criminal and anti-criminal patterns involves all of the mechanisms that are involved in any other learning.
9. While criminal behaviour is an expression of general needs and values, it is not explained by those general needs and values, because non-criminal behaviour is an expression of the same needs and values.

Sutherland's theory does not allow for the influence of genetics or other organic factors. Also, while he goes some way to explain how 'white collar' workers from advantaged backgrounds are influenced by criminal thinking organizations, he does not explain how those from an advantaged background, and not exposed to criminal thinking, engage in crime.

Akers' Social Learning Theory (1977)

Ronald Akers extended the Differential Association Theory to look at the *process* of how people learn to be criminal. He based his theory on four major principles:

Differential association – which relates to the direct association with primary others such as family and friends, and indirect association with secondary groups such as teachers, neighbours and influence of the media.
Definitions – internally general beliefs and specific attitudes that a person holds about behaviour, and what is right and wrong. The more pro-criminal a person's definitions, the more likely they are to engage in criminal behaviour.
Differential reinforcement – based on operant conditioning and the anticipated rewards and punishment of behaviour. The more positive the outcome, the more likely the behaviour will occur. Punishment may also be positive. The more frequently an act is reinforced, the more likely it is to continue.
Imitation – which involves observing and then imitating the behaviour of others, including both primary and secondary groups.

Evidence

Akers's theory has been empirically tested and research has generally found a strong relationship between social learning variables and delinquency (e.g., Pratt *et al.*, 2006). Antisocial attitudes and criminal peers are strongly related to recidivism (Andrews and Bonta 1998). In comparison to other theories, when social learning measures are included in combined models including variables from other theories, social learning variables show the strongest effects (e.g., Thornberry *et al.*, 1994). As with other social theories, Akers does not give consideration to biological or organic influences. Also, social learning theories do not explain why transmission of crime through generations is not guaranteed; why do some criminals report no history of criminal modelling and some non-offending individuals come from several generations of criminals.

Application

The dilemma of applying social learning theories to treating offenders is that these theories postulate that the criminal behaviour of an individual is not due to his individuality but is related to the group in society to which he belongs. Therefore there are two possible options for treating crime according to this group of theories (Cressey, 1955). The first is to encourage the offender to associate with anti-criminal groups, such as through positive peer counselling or the use of mentors. The second is to change the attitudes of pro-criminal groups, for example through community out-reach and recreational programmes. Parent training, in order to allow carers to model prosocial behaviour, is part of this approach. In the UK, parent-training programmes have been introduced, for example, for parents of children who have high levels of unauthorized absences from school.

Another treatment approach is to aid the development of prosocial skills in those who have been exposed to pro-criminal behaviour through social skills training. There has been an explosion of cognitive-behavioural-based treatment programmes targeting social skills deficits such as thinking skills and relationship skills, particularly in the United States, Canada and the UK in the last thirty years. These programmes have received increasing empirical support (e.g., Landenberger and Lipsey, 2005), but are left with many outstanding issues, not least lack of follow-up studies and standardized evaluation procedures.

Strain Theory – Merton (1938)

Merton's theory attempts to explain why the majority of crime is committed in lower-class, minority and urban areas. He observed the cultural pressure to succeed in society, particularly financially and materialistically, and how education and the media uphold this. He proposed that this pressure creates a 'strain' as outstanding economic success is not necessarily always achievable by following legitimate channels such as education and conventional employment. The lower class and those living in disadvantaged areas are at an automatic disadvantage and in order to succeed individuals engage in illegitimate activities and crime. Merton identified five methods of individual response to strain that are very briefly summarized below.

1. Conformity – try to be successful within society's norms.
2. Innovation – use illegitimate methods to achieve success.
3. Rebellion – rebel against the standards and use own system.
4. Retreatism – do not attempt to achieve success.
5. Ritualization – ignore success and stick to the norms.

Evidence

Strain-type theories have been empirically tested, for example Agnew and White (1992) and Paternoster and Mazerolle (1994) conducted cross-sectional analyses and found that measures of strain were significantly related to delinquency. Although such studies have been criticized for not using an offending population (e.g., Hagan and McCarthy, 1997), Piquero and Sealock (2000) used a convicted sample and found that certain types of negative affect such as anger (hypothesized to have been caused by strain) predicted interpersonal aggression. They conclude that the relationship between strain and negative affect differs for different types of offences, but that general strain theory is supported. Studies in this field have been criticized for not assessing strain and it is a difficult and abstract concept to measure.

Strain theories have been criticized for their narrow scope in not explaining all types of crime, for example, crime committed by the more affluent or middle class, and why certain types of crime (e.g., gangs, white collar crime) are concentrated within certain bands of society (e.g., Clowhard and Ohlin (1960)).

Application

Agnew (1995) considered the application of his (later) strain theories to practice and suggested that treatment programmes which help reduce young peoples' exposure to the stimuli that promotes strain, and help develop coping strategies to cope with strain, may help to reduce offending. As Piquero and Sealock (2000) note it would be impossible to prevent strain influences in entirety but providing coping techniques in order to manage negative affect as a result of strain may be beneficial. Lilly, Cullen and Ball (2007) describe the types of intervention that may be provided to reduce exposure to strain. Essentially these provide opportunity to disadvantaged youth and those in prison in the form of increased educational, job and career training.

Labelling Theory

Labelling theory is based on the premise that crime is a consequence of labelling individuals as criminal. According to Akers and Sellers (2009), labels can act as cause and effect. When labels are an independent variable, they *cause* the continuation of criminal behaviour. When labels are a dependent variable (effect), certain individuals are selected for criminal labelling by society, and by making rules about which behaviour is deviant or not.

There are three main assumptions of labelling theory (from Scott, 2010, p. 31):

1. Crime is a label assigned to behaviour (by those in power) for social, economical and political reasons.
2. Reactions by the criminal justice system are governed by the characteristics of the person committing the crime (e.g., race, class) rather than the features of the crime itself.
3. Labelling a person as criminal leads to a self-fulfilling prophecy.

Evidence

Lilly, Cullen and Ball (2007) report that testing the causal effects of labelling has produced inconclusive results. They conclude that the impact of labelling remains unclear, as research has not yet addressed how susceptibility to criminal labels may be influenced by individual factors. One area that may be linked to labelling theory is the impact of imprisonment. Spohn and Holleran (2002) found that offenders were more likely to reoffend if they were sent to prison instead of placed on probation. Additionally, Gendreau, Goggin, Cullen and Andrews' (2000) meta-analysis found that being sent to prison, and longer the prison term, increased the risk of recidivism. However, being labelled as criminal may not be the mediating factor. It is possible that being sent to prison increases the risk of recidivism due to many other factors such as loss of employment, family, relationships (e.g., Sampson and Laub, 2003) or lengthy exposure to criminal peers and attitudes.

Application

It could be argued that the criminal justice system has worked to provide criminals with the labels needed to satisfy self-fulfilling prophecies. For example, in the UK the introduction of Anti Social Behaviour Orders for Juveniles and the National Sex Offender Register both apply labels to individuals. It is not clear whether these strategies have reduced or increased crime overall due to the difficulties with measuring the specific impact of such policies against the backdrop of many confounding factors.

Multi systemic therapy (MST) integrates labelling, strain, control and social learning theory and is a method of treating offenders and their families in an attempt to address more than one factor contributing towards crime (Henggeler *et al.*, 2009). It consists of family- and home-based treatment that targets parental discipline, relationships, peer associations and school performance. Several outcome studies have demonstrated effectiveness (e.g., Henggeler, Pickrel and

Brondino, 1999; Letourneau *et al.*, 2009). In a long-term follow-up to a randomized clinical trial of MST, Schaeffer and Borduin (2005) found that MST participants had significantly lower recidivism rates than controls and argued that the critical aspects of MST are the comprehensive nature and its provision to youths in their natural ecology. MST has been criticized for its poor cost effectiveness and, although the Schaeffer and Borduin study found MST to be cost effective, this needs further investigation, as does the treatment change process.

Self-Control Theory (Gottfredson and Hirschi, 1990)

The fundamental underlying principle is that individuals with a higher level of 'self control' will be able to resist the (short-term) gratification of crime. Those with a lower level of self-control are unable to restrain themselves, and when the opportunity arises (they do not necessarily plan or seek it), they are able to violate society's norms. Gottfredson and Hirschi contend that low self-control is a result of poor socialization and ineffective parenting; parents who do not impose appropriate sanctions or supervise their children. These children grow into adults who are drawn to excitement and short-term gratification such as substance abuse, reckless and irresponsible behaviours and essentially crime. They argue that the level of self-control, developed in the formative years, is stable across the lifespan, explaining career and persistent criminals and why the minority of people commit the majority of crime.

Evidence

There has been significant empirical support for the model and Pratt and Cullen's (2000) meta-analysis indicated that low self-control is a strong predictor of crime and other behaviours analogous to crime (e.g., speeding, excessive drinking). However, the effect of self-control was weaker across longitudinal studies and the hypothesis that self-control is stable across a lifespan was not supported.

Application

Managing self-control/impulsivity has been a focus in modern treatment programmes. For example Reasoning and Rehabilitation (Ross and Ross, 1995) along with programmes designed to treat violence and sexual offending all have modules which attempt to teach the offender skills to regulate his or her emotions and behaviour. These programmes have showed some success (Tong and Farrington, 2006). Impulsivity has typically been addressed via a cognitive behavioural approach, not one outlined by the developmental model. Self-control theory directs that poor parenting should be addressed in order to reduce crime and this raises the question about whether it is the product or source of self-control that is being treated.

PSYCHOLOGICAL THEORIES

Eysenck's Personality Theory

Various theories have been put forward which hypothesize that there are certain types of (stable) personality traits that are linked with criminal behaviour. For example, Yochelson and Samenow's (1976) criminal personality theory proposes that offenders develop a set of 'faulty' thinking patterns that lead them towards irresponsible behaviour and crime. However the pioneer of personality theory and the focus for this chapter is the work of Hans Eysenck.

Eysenck (1967) argued that genetic factors and environmental factors are key and that these are mediated by personality and contribute to criminal behaviour. Eysenck presented three dimensions of personality based on numerous cross-cultural studies, namely,

1. Extraversion-introversion (deals with social interactions)
2. Neuroticism (emotional reactions)
3. Psychoticism (aggressive/egocentric impulses)

Eysenck theorizes that the response to antisocial behaviour is usually punishment, and that it is the ability to learn this conditioned response that enables the individual to stop committing antisocial behaviour. Eysenck presented evidence (1967, 1980) that indicates that extraverted personality types do not form conditioned responses as well as introverts, and as such are more likely to commit anti social-acts. In addition, he proposed that extraverts have lower cortical arousal than introverts and so are more likely to seek stimulating, reckless behaviour. Those high on the Neuroticism scale have a higher level of resting anxiety, which impacts positively on their conditioning for socially acceptable behaviour. Finally he predicted that individuals high on the Psychoticism dimension would be more likely to commit criminal acts as aggressive and egocentric impulses combined with emotional coldness would make it difficult for them to control their antisocial behaviour.

Evidence

One of the strengths of Eysenck's theory is that he presents a series of cross-cultural studies to support his theory (e.g., Eysenck and Eysenck, 1971, 1974, 1977). Research on male prisoners typically found that prisoners have higher psychoticism, higher neuroticism and higher extroversion scores compared to non-offending controls, although the strength of these findings varied across studies. Other researchers have found similar trends, for example high neuroticism and high extroversion linked to offending (Steller and Hunze, 1984), although it should be noted that opposing theories and evidence has been presented (e.g., Gray, 1972).

Raine (1993), as discussed earlier, found that low levels of arousal predict later criminal behaviour, and antisocial juveniles who later desist from crime show very high levels of arousal, showing support for Eysenck's stimulation seeking theory.

However, Farrington (2002) administered the Eysenck Personality Inventory (EPI) to offenders and found that levels of impulsivity mediated the relationship between crime and extraversion. He proposed that it is impulsivity that is related to offending (a well-established finding) and not certain personality dimensions/traits.

Eysenck's work has also been criticized for not explaining individual differences between offenders and types of crime. Additionally, it is not clear how individuals can (and do) desist from offending if their propensity to crime lays with stable personality traits, supported by physiological predispositions.

Psychopathic Personality Theory

Initially coined by Cleckley (1941), Robert Hare believes that the psychopathic personality is characterized by a number of measurable and stable personality traits. These are developed as a result of the interaction of biological and social factors, and he proposes that the presence of these traits is strongly linked to criminal behaviour. Hare (1993) initially proposed 20 items which fell into two factors, affective and behavioural, and developed the Psychopathy Checklist – Revised (PCL-R, Hare (2003)) which is the most widely used tool for measuring the concept and used in over 20 countries. Hare (2005) reconceptualized psychopathy and presented four correlated facets falling within two factors; interpersonal, affective, lifestyle and antisocial. Psychopaths have been shown to have deficits in the following areas: failure to show a quicker response to emotionally laden words (Blair *et al.*, 2006), impaired recognition of fearful and distressed facial expressions (Marsh and Blair, 2008) and failure to show increased skin conductance to fear/distress stimuli (Veit *et al.*, 2002). The research suggests that psychopaths are fundamentally different on psychobiological measures from non-psychopaths.

Various aetiological theories have been presented to try and understand the development of psychopathy including genetics (twin studies, Viding *et al.*, 2005), environmental (e.g., role of poor parenting, Farrington, (1995)) and neurological, particularly the role of the amygdala (Tiihonen *et al.*, 2000) and orbito-frontal cortex (Morgan & Lilienfeld, 2000). Support has been found for all strands and Hare would argue that it is a combination of the three that lead to the development of psychopathy.

Evidence

Hare's conceptualization of psychopathy has had its critics, namely Cooke and Michie (1991) who proposes a three-factor model that does not include the antisocial facet. Cooke argues that antisocial behaviour is a consequence of psychopathy and should be kept distinct when trying to measure it. There is a fundamental flaw in the argument that psychopathy is a cause of criminal behaviour, if criminal behaviour is used to measure it (Akers & Sellers, 2009).

Much research has been carried out looking at the relationship between psychopathy and crime. For example men who have high scores on the PCL-R commit more violent and/or serious offences compared to low PCL-R scorers (Harris, Skilling and Rice, 2001; Pham, Philippot and Rime, 2000) and are more likely to recidivate, and commit community violence and violence while incarcerated (Edens, Skeem and Douglas, 2006).

Hare (1999) proposed that as psychopathy is so strongly linked to criminal behaviour, 20 per cent of the prison population would be high-scoring psychopaths. Additionally, psychopaths would commit over 50 per cent of serious crime. The presence of psychopathy in the prison population has been examined and Coid *et al.* (2009) report that 7.7 per cent of the male prison population in England and Wales are high-scoring psychopaths. As such it is clear that not every offender is a psychopath, and not every type of crime can be explained by the presence of psychopathy, a fact acknowledged by Hare.

Application

There is a long-running debate concerning whether antisocial personality, or psychopathy (as measured by the PCL-R) is treatable. Many interventions, including in the UK, exclude individuals who score highly (above 30), although more recent policy is not on the basis of the PCL-R alone (Offending Behaviour Programmes Unit, 2005). Diagnosing an individual as 'not treatable' raises important ethical and social issues; what does society do with people that cannot be treated?

Some international programmes have included high-scoring psychopaths on treatment programmes, with varying degrees of success (see Thornton and Blud, 2007 for a review). In the UK, forensic practitioners have developed an Accredited Violence Reduction Intervention (HM Prison Service, 2005) specifically for those with psychopathic personality disorder. No published evaluation is yet available, however initial reports indicate high levels of engagement in the programme and low attrition rates, alongside staff noting prosocial behavioural change and positive changes as measured by psychometrics (Atkinson and Tew, 2011).

There are several further key psychological theories which the forensic practitioner should be familiar with including the role of attachment/maternal deprivation theory (Bowlby, 1969) the Life Course perspective (Moffit, 1993) and Sampson & Laub (2003) and moral development (Kohlberg, 1981).

THIS CASE STUDY BASED ON REAL LIFE OFFENDER: MR A

Mr A is 40 years old and of Black-British ethnic origin. He is serving a life sentence for the murder of a man who he and two co-defendants believed to be a police informer. They went to his house, forced entry, assaulted him and interrogated him for an hour and then Mr A shot him in the back. Mr A denies premeditation for the murder and states that he shot the victim by mistake – he was so angry with him for not telling the truth that he momentarily 'lost control of his senses'.

A family in the inner city of London, UK, adopted Mr A when he was three weeks old. His biological father was in prison serving a sentence for Armed Robbery and Grievous Bodily Harm and his mother could not cope on her own. From an early age Mr A had temper tantrums and was quick to use aggression with his siblings. Despite this, he had a close relationship with his adoptive siblings and mother, who is described in probation reports as 'mild mannered and calm'. However the relationship with his adoptive father was strained, as his father had high expectations of him. He was known as the 'black sheep' of the family, being the only one with criminal convictions. His siblings became high achievers. No history of psychiatric illness is recorded, although on his medical file he was noted to have suffered a head injury at the age of six resulting in loss of consciousness. Mr A left school at the age of 16 having obtained no qualifications. He was considered a 'trouble maker' at school and hung around with older peers who were involved in criminal activity. He was suspended on several occasions for fighting and damaging property. He has a trade as a carpenter, although he has rarely worked for long periods due to becoming bored/under performing at work and on one occasion assaulting his boss. He has a number of previous convictions including theft, burglary, criminal damage, assault on a policeman, assault, drug possession and attempted robbery. His previous offences were mostly committed with others. He has a domineering, but charming, personality and presents as outgoing and a risk taker. Assessment in prison highlighted presence of psychopathic traits. Mr A exhibits high levels of frustration that can result in violence and has adjudications for fighting in prison.

The opposite table (Table 2.1) demonstrates the range of theories and how they contribute individually to explaining the case study. Certain elements are explained by the biological theories, for example the genetic influence of a criminal father and the early head injury. However these theories do not explain why most offending was committed in a specific social context, i.e., when in association with criminal others. The umbrella of sociological theories

Table 2.1 *Theory summary*

Theory	Main features	How theory explains case study	What is left unexplained by the theory	Treatment approach
Biological				
Genetic and biosocial	Individuals are 'born criminal'. Genetic link, with criminal parents increasing risk of criminality in child. Inherit slow autonomic nervous system. Prefrontal dysfunction linked to violence and impulsivity.	Mr A is an adoptee and his natural father has a criminal conviction. His criminality is due to his genetic inheritance. Head injury as a child may contribute to impulsive and aggressive behaviour.	Role of social environment. Crimes committed in specific social context, i.e., with criminal peers.	No treatment for having a criminal parent. Biosocial approach has suggested use of biofeedback to regulate under arousal combined with cognitive 'remediation' to compensate for deficits/ prefrontal dysfunction, e.g., increase verbal and social skills and impulse control. Medication for impulsivity.
Sociological				
Social learning theory	Criminal behaviour is learnt. Individuals influenced by a culture and rules/definitions supportive of crime are more likely to become criminal	Mr A associated with criminal peers at school and was likely influenced by their attitudes and criminal culture. Current offence committed with 2 co-defendants suggesting continued association with criminal others	Adoptive parents are 'mild mannered and law abiding' and siblings are pro-social, so does not explain disruptive/ explosive behaviour from an early age.	Learning prosocial skills through social skills training. Also relationship and thinking skills training. Encourage the individual to associate with prosocial groups. Pro-criminal groups are

(continued)

Table 2.1 Continued

Theory	Main features	How theory explains case study	What is left unexplained by the theory	Treatment approach
				targeted with a view to change their criminal attitudes through community programmes. Therapeutic communities
Self-control	Individuals with low levels of self-control are unable to resist crime when the opportunity arises, and are able to contravene society's set norms. Result of poor parenting and trait are stable across lifespan	Mr A appears to have low levels of self-control evidenced by behaviour at school (fighting, damaging property), at work (assaulting his boss) and during previous offending (assault, assaulting a police officer, speeding offences). In the current offence of murder, Mr A states he 'lost control of his senses'. Adjudications for fighting in prison. Trait seems stable across lifespan and different contexts.	No evidence of poor parenting. No offending in the home.	Treatment programmes designed to regulate emotions/self-control. Cognitive behavioural basis. Parent training.
Strain/Anomie	Immense cultural pressure to achieve economic success creates a strain on those who	Adopted into inner-city family (likely to be of low socio-economic status) and put	Not clear how offence of murder (or previous non instrumental violence)	Reduce youth's exposure to strain. Work at a community/

	are disadvantaged through poverty/class. Success can only be gained by illegitimate means.	under pressure to achieve by his father. Left school with no qualifications and unable to achieve success through legitimate means.	is related to strain to achieve economic success.	society level rather than individual, e.g., grants systems/projects for disadvantaged youth Teach coping skills to help individuals deal with negative effect caused by strain.
Labelling	Crime is a consequence of labelling individuals as criminal. Crime is a label assigned by those in power to those who are not in power. Labelling a person as criminal is a self-fulfilling prophecy.	Mr A was known as the 'black sheep' of the family. He was a also known/labelled as a trouble maker at school and his crimes are a result of this. Being labelled in this way by parents and education (those in power) would act as a self-fulfilling prophecy. Will now be labelled as criminal as a result of imprisonment.	Does not explain at an individual level why offence occurred. No account for the behaviour that comes before the label (i.e., 'black sheep').	No individual-specific treatment/intervention associated with labelling theory although arguments that intervention is needed at macro, societal level. Inclusion rather than exclusion. Multi systemic therapy incorporates strain, labelling, control and social theory, targeting individual needs at home and incorporating family and peers.

(continued)

Table 2.1 Continued

Theory	Main features	How theory explains case study	What is left unexplained by the theory	Treatment approach
Psychological Personality	There are certain personality traits that are linked to criminal behaviour.	He has a domineering and charming personality. Outgoing and a risk taker. Presence of psychopathic traits. These personality traits could be linked to high extraversion and psychopathy.	Does not explain why he committed offence-presence of these traits are found in non offending population. No explanation for offending in certain social contexts.	Various psychological treatments aim to treat underlying traits/cognitions and associated dysfunctional/offending behaviour. Dialectic Behavioural Therapy, Cognitive Analytical Therapy, Schema Focussed Therapy are all different strands of cognitive-behavioural therapy. The underlying premise is that if thinking is changed then behaviour will change.

give some explanation to this via learning from criminal others, being labelled by family and school and the strain placed on him to achieve by his father. The theory of self-control seems to account for much of his criminal and violent behaviour across several different contexts although is limited in explaining how he developed a lack of self-control, as aetiologically he appeared to have good parenting. Psychological personality theories would recognize the traits he displays and link them to his criminal behaviour, but would not explain why he turned to crime as opposed to other risk-taking behaviour or again the influence of criminal others.

Interestingly, when these theories are viewed in unison, they do cover many of the factors presented by the case study. As such, a theory knitting or integrative approach may be beneficial in order to understand the mechanisms underlying crime in this case, and others. Theory knitting works to combine the best aspects of a set of competing theories with the researchers/clinicians own ideas in order to solve a problem (Kalmar & Sternberg, 1988). An example of this can be seen in the sexual offender literature where Ward and Siegert (2002) combine the best elements of three existing theories to develop a new etiological theory of child sexual abuse.

Similarly, theory integration, where individual and often-competing theories are combined, has received attention from researchers as singular theories fail to explain criminal behaviour in isolation. Several years ago Hirschi (1979) suggested ways in which theories of crime could be assimilated and Liska, Krohn and Messner (1989) provided further directions for integration. More recently McQuire (2004) outlined the characteristics necessary for integrated theories to be effective. Several integrated theories do exist, for example Cohen and Machalet (1989) took an evolutionary ecological approach and combined individual causes of crime with social factors. Thornberry's (1987) interactional model was influenced by control, learning, strain and culture-conflict theories and focussed on how the individual reacts with the environment. Elliott, Huizinga and Ageton (1985) combined strain, control and social learning theory, focussing on the process of individual development and societal influence. Farrington (1994) draws on social learning, sub-cultural theory, control, differential association, rational choice and labelling theories and combines these into a four-stage model covering motivations for and engagement in criminal behaviour. The challenge faced by such approaches is to prove effectiveness while indicating how they merge and resolve the contrary underlying assumptions of the theory (Blackburn, 1993).

Referring back to the case study, a forensic clinician may well consider a range of perspectives when trying to build a case formulation. For example considering a biological influence (head injury) in addition to a lack of self-control and the influence of criminal others. This would lead to the formulation of a more holistic treatment plan, perhaps the inclusion of a neuropsychological assessment as well as addressing impulsivity and teaching social skills.

CONCLUSION

It is apparent that no theory can explain crime on its own or has enough empirical backing to convince the academic audience that it can claim sole influence. There are many factors at work to mould a criminal, for example being born with a genetic predisposition, being exposed to criminal influences, poor parenting, lack of self-control and underlying personality traits related to criminality. The approach with the most power of explanation may well be to integrate theories, taking the most useful features and building a new framework to address the problem. This may be usefully applied by forensic clinicians when trying to form a case conceptualization or formulation (see Chapter 5). The debate over which theory best explains crime becomes more interesting when applied to treatment, as the political, legal and ethical obligations have to be considered, in addition to trying to facilitate people from re offending. It could be postulated that as individualized intervention strategies have focussed on one approach they are not broad enough to cover all the contributory factors involved, and therefore are not wholly successful in treating people. Bowker (1998) suggests that efforts to influence male violence must occur at five levels; social, cultural, personality, biological and economic. This may well apply to crime as a whole and while not a panacea, those attempting to explain the development of crime, and those working to reduce crime, would do well to consider a spectrum of key approaches and utilize the best aspects from each.

RECOMMENDED FURTHER READING

Akers, R. L. and Sellers, C. S. (2009). *Criminological Theories: Introduction, Evaluation & Application,* 5th edn (New York: Oxford University Press). This is a comprehensive and easily accessible text that is current, and has an applied aspect.

Lilly, J. R., Cullen, F. T. and Ball, R. A. (2007). *Criminological Theory: Context & Consequences,* 4th edn (Sage Publications. London). This has a strong and in-depth focus on sociological perspectives that have dominated the theory base for many years and therefore should be understood.

REFERENCES

Agnew, R. and White, H. R. (1992). 'An Empirical Test of General Strain Theory', *Criminology,* 30(4), 475–500.

Agnew, R. (1995). 'Testing the Leading Crime Theories: An Alternative Strategy Focusing on Motivational Processes', *Journal of Research in Crime and Delinquency*, 32, 363–98.

Akers, R. L. (1977). *Deviant Behaviour – A Social Learning Approach*, 2nd edn (Belmont, CA: Wadsworth Publishing Co).

Akers, R. L. and Sellers, C. S. (2009). *Criminological Theories: Introduction, Evaluation & Application*, 5th edn (New York: Oxford University Press).

Andrews, D. A. and Bonta, J. (1998). *The Psychology of Criminal Conduct*, 2nd edn (Cincinnati, OH: Anderson Publishing Co).

Atkinson, R. and Tew, J. (2011). Chromis: From Conception to Evaluation. Paper presented at British and Irish Group for the Study of Personality Disorder conference. Oxford.

Blackburn, R. (1993). *The Psychology of Criminal Conduct. Theory Research and Practice* (Chichester, England: Wiley).

Blair, K. S., Richell, R. A., Mitchell, D. G. V., Leonard, A., Morton, J. and Blair, R. J. R. (2006). 'They Know the Words, But Not the Music: Affective and Semantic Priming in Individuals with Psychopathy', *Biological Psychology*, 73(2), 114–23.

Bowker, L. H. (eds) (1998). *Masculinities and Violence* (Thousand Oaks, CA, US: Sage Publications).

Bowlby, J. (1969). *Attachment and Loss, Vol. 1: Attachment* (NY: Basic Books).

Cleckley, H. (1941). *The Mask of Sanity; An Attempt to Reinterpret the So-Called Psychopathic Personality* (Oxford, England: Mosby).

Clowhard, R. A. and Ohlin, L. E. (1960). 'Delinquency & Opportunity', in F.P. Williams III, and M. D. McShane, *Criminology Theory: Selected Classic Readings*, 2nd edn (Cincinnati, OH, US: Anderson Publishing Co.), 149–62.

Coid, J., Yang, M., Ullrich, S., Roberts, A., Moran, P., Bebbington, P., Brugha, T., Jenkins, R., Farrell, M., Lewis, G., Singleton, N. and Hare, R. (2009). 'Psychopathy among Prisoners in England & Wales', *International Journal of Law & Psychiatry*, 32(3), 134–41.

Cohen, L. E. and Machalet, R. (1989). 'A General Theory of Expropriative Crime: An Evolutionary Ecological Approach', *American Journal of Sociology*, 94, 465–501.

Comings, D. E. (2003). 'Conduct Disorder: A Genetic, Orbitofrontal Lobe Disorder that is the Major Predictor of Adult Antisocial Behaviour', in A. Walsh and L. Ellis (eds) *Biosocial Criminology: Challenging Environmentalism's Supremacy* (New York: Nova Science), 145–64.

Cooke, D. J. and Michie, C. (2001). 'Refining the Construct of Psychopathy: Towards a Hierarchical Model', *Psychological Assessment*, 13(2), 171–88.

Cressey, D. R. (1955). 'Changing Criminals: The Application of the Theory of Differential Association', *American Journal of Sociology*, 61(2), 116–20.

Crocker A. G. and Hodgins, S. (1997). 'The Criminality of Non Institutionalized Mentally retarded Persons. Evidence from a Birth Cohort Followed to Age 30', *Criminal Justice and Behaviour*, 24, 432–54.

Cunningham, A., Jaffe, P. G., Baker, L., Dick, T., Malla, S., Mazahari, N. and Poisson, S. (1998). 'Theory Derived Explanations of Male Violence against Female Partners: Literature Update and Related Implications for Treatment and Evaluation'. *Focus*. London Family Court Clinic, 1–69. Retrieved from http://www.lfcc.on.ca/maleviolence.pdf, Accessed 12/2011.

Curran, D. J. and Renzetti, C. M. (2001). *Theories of Crime*, 2nd edn (London: Allyn & Bacon).

Dabbs, J. M., Carr, T. S., Frady, R. L., Riad, J. K. (1995). 'Testosterone, Crime and Misbehaviour among 692 Male Prison Inmates', *Personality and Individual Differences*, 18(5), 627–33.

Edens, J. F., Skeem, J. L. and Douglas, K. S. (2006). 'Incremental Validity Analyses of the Violence Risk Appraisal Guide and the Psychopathy Checklist: Screening Version in a Civil Psychiatric Sample', *Assessment*, 13(3), 368–74.

Elliott, D. S., Huizinga, D. and Ageton, S. S. (1985). *Explaining Delinquency and Drug Use* (Beverley Hills, CA: Sage).

Eysenck, H. J. (1967). *The Biological Basis of Personality* (Springfield, III: CC.Thomas).

Eysenck, H. J. (1980). *A Model for Personality* (New York: Springer).

Eysenck, S. B. G. and Eysenck, H. J. (1971). 'A Comparative Study of Criminals & Matched Controls on 3 Dimensions of Personality', *British Journal of Social & Clinical Psychology*, 10, 362–6.

Eysenck, S. B. G. and Eysenck, H. J. (1974). 'Personality & Recidivism in Borstal Boys', *British Journal of Criminology*, 14, 285–7.

Eysenck, S. B. G. and Eysenck, H. J. (1977). 'Personality Differences between Prisoners & Controls', *Psychological Reports*, 40, 1023–8.

Farrington, D. P. (1994). 'Introduction', in D. P. Farrington (ed.) *Psychological Explanations of Crime* (Aldershot: Dartmouth Publishing Company Limited).

Farrington, D. P. (1995). 'Development of Offending and Antisocial Behaviour from Childhood: Key Findings from the Cambridge Study in Delinquent Development', *Journal of Child Psychology*, 360(6), 929–64.

Farrington, D. P. (2002). 'Developmental Criminology and Risk-Focused Prevention', in M. Maguire, R. Morgan and R. Reiner (eds) *The Oxford Handbook of Criminology*, 3rd edn (Oxford: Oxford University Press).

Fishbein, D. H. E. (2001). *Biobehavioural Perspectice in Criminology: The Wadsworth Series in Criminological Theory* (Belmont, CA: Wadsworth/Thomson Learning).

Gendreau, P., Goggin, C., Cullen, F. T. and Andrews, D. A. (2000). 'Effects of Community Sanctions & Incarceration on Recidivism', *Forum on Corrections Research*, 12(2), 10–13.

Gottfredson, M. R. and Hirschi, T. (1990). *A General Theory of Crime* (Stanford: Stanford University Press).

Gray, J. A. (1972). 'The Psychophysiological Basis of Introversion-Extra-Version: A Modification of Eysenck's Theory', in V. Nebylitsyn and J. A. Gray (eds) *Biological Basis of Individual Behavior* (New York: Academic Press, Graziano, WG), 182–205.

Hagan, J. and McCarthy, B. (1997) 'Anomie, Social Capital and Street Criminology', in N. Passas and R. Agnew (eds) *The Future of Anomie Theory* (Boston MA: NorthEastern University Press), 124–41.

Hare, R. D. (1993). *Without Conscience: The Disturbing World of the Psychopaths Among Us* (New York: Pocket Books).

Hare, R. D. (1999). *Without Conscience: The Disturbing World of the Psychopaths Among Us*, 2nd edn (New York: Guilford Press).

Hare, R. D. (2003). *Manual for the Revised Psychopathy Checklist,* 2nd edn (Toronto, ON, Canada: Multi Health Systems).

Harris, G. T., Skilling, T. A. and Rice, M. E. (2001). 'The Construct of Psychopathy', *Crime & Justice*, 28, 197–264.

Henggeler, S. W., Pickrel, S. G. and Brandino, M. J. (1999). 'Multisystemic Treatment of Substance Abusing and Dependent Delinquents: Outcomes, Treatment Fidelity and Transportability', *Mental Health Services Research,* 1, 171–84.

Henggeler, S. W., Schoenwald, S. K., Borduin, C. M., Rowland, M. D. and Cunningham, P. B. (2009). *Multisystemic Therapy for Antisocial Behaviour in Children & Adolescents,* 2nd edn (New York: Guilford Press).

Hirschi, T. (1979). 'Separate and Unequal is Better', *Journal of Research in Crime and Delinquency,* 16(1), 34–8.

HM Prison Service (2005). *Chromis Manuals.* Offending Behaviour Programme Unit, London, UK.

Kalmar, D. A. and Sternberg R. J. (1988). 'Theory Knitting: An Integrative Approach to Theory Development', *Philosophical Psychology,* 1(2), 153–70.

Kohlberg, L. (1981). *Essays on Moral Development: Volume 1. The Philosopy of Moral Development* (Cambridge: Harper & Row).

Landenberger N. A. and Lipsey M. W. (2005). 'The Positive Effects of Cognitive-Behavioral Programs for Offenders: A Meta-Analysis of Factors Associated with Effective Treatment', *Journal of Experimental Criminology*, 1: 451–76.

Letourneau, E. J., Henggeler, S. W., Borduin, C. M., Schewe, P. A., McCart, M. R., Chapman, J. E. and Saldana, L. (2009). 'Multisystemic Therapy for Juvenile Sexual Offenders: 1 Year Results from a Randomised Effectiveness Trial', *Journal of Family Psychology,* 23(1), 89–102.

Lilly, J. R., Cullen, F. T. and Ball, R. A. (2007). *Criminological Theory: Context & Consequences,* 4th edn (London: Sage Publications).

Liska, A. E., Krohn, M. D. and Messner, S. F. (1989). 'Strategies and Requisites for Theoretical Integration in the Study of Crime and Deviance', in S. F. Messner,

M. D. Krohn and A. E. Liska (eds) *Theoretical Integration in the Study of Deviance and Crime. Problems and Prospects* (Albany: State University of New York).

Lombroso, C. (2006 [1911]). *Criminal Man* (M. Gibson and N. H. Rafter, trans) (London: Duke University Press). Original work published in 1911.

Marsh, A. A. and Blair, R. J. R. (2008). 'Deficits in Facial Affect Recognition among Antisocial Populations: A Meta-Analysis', *Neuroscience & Biobehavioural Reviews*, 32(3), 454–65.

McQuire, J. (2004). *Understanding Psychology and Crime: Perspectives on Theory and Action* (Maidenhead: Open University Press).

Mednick, S. A. (1977). 'A Bio-Social Theory of the Learning of Law Abiding Behaviour', in S. A Mednick and K. O. Christiansen (eds) *Biosocial Bases of Criminal Behaviour* (New York: Gardner Press).

Mednick, S. A., Gabrielli, W. F. and Hutchings, B. (1984). 'Genetic Influences in Criminal Convictions: Evidence from an Adoption Cohort', *Science*, 224, 891–4.

Merton, R. (1938). 'Social Structure & Anomie', *American Sociological Review*, 3, 672–82.

Moffitt, T. E. (1993). 'Adolescence-Limited and Life-Course-Persistent Antisocial Behaviour: A Developmental Taxonomy', *Psychological Review*, 100(4), 674–701.

Morgan, A. B. and Lilienfeld, S. O. (2000). 'A Meta Analytic Review of the Relation between Antisocial Behaviour and Neuropsychological Measures of Executive Function', *Clinical Psychology Review*, 20(1), 113–36.

Moyer, K. (1979). 'What is the Potential for Biological Violence Control?', in C. R. Jeffrey (ed.) *Biology and Crime* (Newbury Park, CA: Sage), 19–46.

Offending Behaviour Programmes Unit (June 2005). *Considering the Suitability of Programmes for Individuals with High Level of Psychopathic Traits: Notes to Aid Decision Making* (London, UK).

Paternoster, R. and Mazerolle, P. (1994). 'General Strain Theory & Delinquency: A Replication & Extension', *Journal of Research in Crime & Delinquency*, 31(3), 235–63.

Pham, T. H., Philippot, P. and Rime, B. (2000). 'Subjective and Autonomic Responses to Emotion Induction in Psychopaths', *L'Encephale: Revue de psychiatrie clinique biologique et therapeutique*, 26(1), 45–51.

Piquero, N. Z. and Sealock, M. D. (2000). 'Generalising General Strain Theory: An Examination of an Offending Population', *Justice Quarterly*, 17(3), 449–84.

Pratt, T. C. and Cullen, F. T (2000). 'The Empirical Status of Gottfredson & Hirschi's General Theory of Crime: A Meta-Analysis, *Criminology*, 38(3), 931–64.

Pratt, C. T., Sellers, C. S., Cullen, F. T., Winfree, L. T., Jr. and Madensen, T. (2006). The Empirical Status of Social Learning Theory: A Meta-Analysis. Unpublished manuscript, Washington State University, Vancouver, WA.

Raine, A. (1993). *The Psychopathology of Crime: Criminal Behaviour as a Clinical Disorder* (London: Academic Press).

Raine, A. and Liu, J. H. (1998). 'Biological Predispositions to Violence and Their Implications for Biosocial Treatment and Prevention, *Psychology, Crime & Law,* 4(2), 107–125.

Rosenbaum, A., Hoge, S. K., Adelman, S. A. Warnken, W. J., Fletcher, K. E., Kane, R. L. (1994). 'Head Injury in Partner-Abusive Men', *Journal of Consulting and Clinical Psychology,* 62(6), 1187–93.

Ross, R. R and Ross, R. D. (eds) (1995). *Thinking Straight: The Reasoning and Rehabilitation Programme for Delinquency Prevention and Offender Rehabilitation* (Ottawa: AIR Training and Publications).

Rowe, D. C. (2002). *Biology and Crime* (Los Angeles: Roxbury Publishing Co.).

Sampson, R. J. and Laub, J. H. (2003). 'Life Course Desisters? Trajectories of Crime among Delinquent Boys Followed to Age 70', *Criminology,* 41(3), 555–92.

Schaeffer, C. M. and Borduin, C. M. (2005). 'Long-Term Follow-Up to a Randomised Clinical Trial of Multisystemic Therapy with Serious & Violent Juvenile Offenders', *Journal of Consulting & Clinical Psychology,* 73(3), 445–53.

Scott, A. J. (2010). *Forensic Psychology. Palgrave Insights in Psychology* (Hampshire, England: Palgrave Macmillan).

Spohn, C. and Holleran, D. (2002). 'The Effect of Imprisonment on Recidivism Rates of Felony Offenders: A Focus on Drug Offenders', *Criminology,* 40(2), 329–58.

Sutherland, E. H. (1947). *Principles of Criminology,* 4th edn (Philadelphia: Lippincott).

Steller, M. and Hunze, D. (1984). 'Self Description of Delinquents with the Freiburg Personality Inventory: A Secondary Analysis of Empirical Studies', *Zeitschrift für Differentielle und Diagnostische Psychologie,* 5(2), 87–109.

Thornberry, T. P. (1987). 'Towards and Interactional Theory of Delinquency', *Criminology,* 25(4), 863.

Thornberry, T. P., Lizotte, A. J., Krohn, M. D., Farnworth, M. and Jang, S. J. (1994). 'Delinquent Peers, Beliefs & Delinquent Behaviour: A Longitudinal Test of Interactional Theory', *Criminology,* 32(1), 47–83.

Thornton, D. and Blud, L. (2007). 'The Influence of Psychopathic Traits on Response to Treatment', in H. Hervé and J. C. Yuille (eds) *The Psychopath: Theory, Research and Practice* (New Jersey: Lawrence Erlbaum Associates Inc), 141–70.

Tiihonen, J., Hodgins, S., Vaurio, O., Laakso, M., Repo, E., Soininen, H., Aronen, H. J., Nieminen, P. and Savolainen, L. (2000). 'Amygdaloid Volume Loss in Psychopathy', *Society for Neuroscience Abstracts,* 15, 2017.

Tong, L. S. and Farrington, D. P. (2006). 'How Effective is the "Reasoning and Rehabilitation" Programme in Reducing Reoffending? A Meta-Analysis of Evaluations in Four Countries', *Psychology, Crime and Law,* 12, 1.

Veit, R., Flor, H., Erb, M., Hermann, C., Lotze, M., Grodd, W. and Birbaumer, N. (2002). 'Brain Circuits Involved in Emotional Learning in Antisocial Behavior and Social Phobia in Humans', *Neuroscience Letters*, 328, 233–6.

Viding, E. R., Blair, J. R., Moffitt, T. E. and Plomin, R. (2005). 'Evidence for Substantial Genetic Risk for Psychopathy in 7 Year Olds', *Journal of Child Psychology & Psychiatry*, 46(6), 592–7.

Ward, T. and Siegert, R. S. (2002). 'Toward a Comprehensive Theory of Child Sexual Abuse: A Theory Knitting Perspective', *Psychology, Crime and Law*, 8(4), 319.

Yochelson, S. and Samenow, S. E. (1976). *The Criminal Personality* (New York: Jason Aronson).

3 Interviewing Forensic Clients

Joanna Clarke

INTRODUCTION

Interviewing is arguably the most important skill for any forensic practitioner. It is the foundation on which all other processes depend, from developing therapeutic rapport, eliciting meaningful information, formulating a balanced case and reporting in an informative and motivational way. But rarely does anyone receive formal training in anything other than the basic skills required to undertake such a task successfully. There seems to be a general acceptance that if someone is a reasonable communicator, they will be able to conduct a reasonable interview. However, as many will know through trial, error and, sometimes, bitter experience, this is not necessarily the case, especially with forensic clients.

It is not the aim of the chapter to provide a step-by-step guide to conducting an interview, from setting up your room to writing up your notes. There are some very useful texts covering these areas in-depth (see Recommended Further Reading). Nor is it intended to discuss specific therapeutic or analytic interviewing techniques, such as motivational interviewing (e.g., Miller and Rollnick, 2002), or cognitive interviewing (e.g., Gieselman *et al.*, 1985; Memon, 2000), although the former is touched upon in Chapter 7. Such advanced skills require specific training.

What this chapter does set out to do is provide practitioners with an operational model, developed by Hargie and Tourish (2000; Hargie, 2011), for managing and enhancing the interview process. Although not derived from the forensic field (it is based in the field of communication skills), it presents as one of the most applicable and useful models for understanding the mechanics and complexities of interviewing forensic clients, whatever the purpose. It is proposed that by having an infrastructure by which to manage the process of the interview, many of the other elements will fall naturally into place.

To enliven the theory, this chapter is punctuated with a number of examples, some personal to the author and others drawn from the experiences of colleagues, for either illustration or emphasis. Additionally at the end of relevant sections, tips are offered aimed at developing and/or enhancing the associated skills.

SOME SPECIFICS ABOUT INTERVIEWING FORENSIC CLIENTS

Before describing and illustrating the interview process, it is worth spending a few moments considering the experience of the interview from the perspectives of both practitioners and offenders.

The interview is arguably the foremost tool for gathering information (Memon, 2000), and as such is at the heart of forensic practice. Unlike other methods of data collection, such as observation, file review or administration of psychometrics, it is a unique type of interactive event (Hargie and Tourish, 2000) that enables the skilled practitioner to make educated meaning of a myriad of verbal and non-verbal information that cannot be gleaned by any other method. Consequently, interviews are the bedrock of investigations, sentencing recommendations, case formulation, risk assessments, selection for treatment and parole decisions to name just a few. Given this, it is highly likely that the average offender will have been interviewed many more times (and by many different people) than the average practitioner has conducted an interview. It is also quite probable that the average offender is far more accomplished than the newly qualified practitioner, at least in an intuitive way, at managing the interview process. This can present a rather daunting prospect to the inexperienced interviewer. It becomes even more important then that those developing their skills in this area have access to both theoretical and practical information in support of their learning.

Interviewing in a forensic setting adds a range of factors and dynamics that other interviewers would not have to consider. For example, the power imbalance between the participating parties is usually more in evidence in a forensic context than in any other. Generally, when applying for a job, undertaking a career interview or even opting into therapy, there is an element of choice. This exists even when there is much resting on the outcome, such as successfully getting the job. For the forensic client, a decision not to participate in interviews with forensic professionals can have far-reaching, and in some cases lifelong, consequences. While it may reasonably be argued that choice still exists, for many it feels like no choice at all.

Another dynamic that is very rarely mentioned, let alone written about, is that of gender and sexual chemistry. The reality of forensic practice is that the majority of trainee psychologists are females (predominantly relatively young) practicing in male institutions. For many heterosexual incarcerated men, female staff represent their only possibility to engage with women and this will, without doubt, impact on behaviour, especially in a one-to-one interviewing context. The same is true for men working in female institutions (see Chapter 10) and to a lesser degree, homosexual staff working in same-sex institutions. These issues are likely to be less prevalent in community settings, but nonetheless will still require attention. They will be returned to later in the chapter.

Also bear in mind that for both the psychologist and the offender the environment in which the interview takes place will influence behaviour. For example, in prisons or hospitals, offenders will need to return to wings or wards. This can often inhibit the process, as interviewees are understandably reluctant to discuss issues that leave them feeling vulnerable. Institutional offices are also notorious for interruptions, ranging from an apologetic knock to remove something from a shared office to a full-scale incident. Clearly this is a threat to the flow of an interview. Interviews in court settings have their own challenges, not least the possibility of acute emotion associated with court appearances as well as a host of other distractions. The point is that forensic settings are not always the most conducive to establishing the optimum conditions for successful interviewing. It is an aspect returned to later in the chapter.

There is no substitute for observing experienced practitioners demonstrate their skills and managing these challenges, and then practicing them oneself. However, it is not unusual to hear disheartened trainees wax lyrical about how smooth and easy their supervisor made it look, only to find themselves completely tied up in knots by a canny offender who does not appear to play by the rules. This may have something to do with experienced practitioners attending almost on autopilot to many cues in the interaction, but even veterans of the interviewing process can find themselves perplexed and thwarted if they fail to attend to all aspects of the process. The obvious analogy to apply to learning the skills of effective interviewing is that of learning to ride a bike or drive a car. There is little doubt that practice and experience are required to develop, enhance and maintain the necessary skills that may at first seem impossible to master, and even then accidents can and do happen. But the motor skills analogy is very useful and one from which Hargie and Tourish drew significantly in the development of their Operational Model of Skilled Performance.

INTERVIEWING AS A MOTOR SKILL

Hargie and Tourish (2000) argue that perceiving communication as a form of skilled behaviour provides a 'robust template for charting the nature and process of interpersonal interaction' (p. 72). They describe five key features of both motor skills and communication skills.

- Fluency – the apparent seamlessness of the process hinted at above (the equivalent of changing gear, looking in the mirror, turning the wheel and talking, all without stalling or going into the back of the car in front of you);

- Rapidity – the fast and usually correct decisions the individual makes to further the process, for example knowing how to manage silence or resistance;
- Automaticity – the ability to do all the required tasks without obvious conscious effort;
- Simultaneity – when a number of tasks are being attended to at once, such as responding to verbal and non-verbal cues while taking notes;
- Knowledge – implementing a range of skills from a wide repertoire at the most appropriate times.

Of course, in terms of motor performance, the application of these skills will almost certainly result in an anticipated response – if you put your foot on the brake, the car will stop (usually). Within the interview context however, the process is rarely as predictable, and the forensic element can add yet another dimension. The main issue is that the interaction is taking place between two unpredictable entities, one of whom by definition is antisocial and may not be motivated to abide by the 'rules' of social interaction, or have all the necessary skills to do so. Add to that an interviewer who has limited experience, and it is easy to see how the knots referred to previously get tied. Having a framework to which to refer can be highly reassuring to the new practitioner and provide a very helpful tool for reflection for the more experienced one.

The basis for the operational model of interviewing (see Figure 3.1) is recognition that individuals engage in a process that is driven by the pursuit of goals, attained through adopting appropriate behaviours, monitoring the responses of others and adjusting future behaviour accordingly (Hargie and Tourish, 2000). Contextually it is important to acknowledge that the psychological and physical characteristics of both interviewee and interviewer will influence the outcome,

Figure 3.1 *Model of skilled performance*

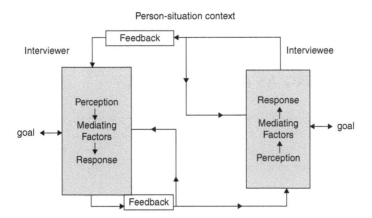

Source: Reproduced with permission from John Wiley & Sons.

as will the environment in which the interview takes place, all of which will be discussed in more detail in the following sections.

TIP

▨ As with driving, it is hard to master all the skills at once. Try recording yourself interviewing someone (audio visual is preferable given the power of body language) and review it with your supervisor. It might be less threatening to start with an interview of a colleague or friend, who can also provide you with honest feedback on your performance. It may cause you to feel self-conscious, but this is far preferable with supportive colleagues than with hostile offenders.

CASE STUDY

During a therapeutic group session, my task was to elicit an offence account from a particularly resistant and angry middle-aged man who had sexually abused his niece. It did not go well. After an hour and a half of what felt liked immense effort (and patience), we had achieved nothing. Even the other group members were clearly frustrated and angry with 'John'.

However, on reviewing the recording of the session, a significant contributor to John's resistance became crystal clear. Although I had been sitting next to him, in an attempt to support him, I had in fact been turned away from him for a majority of the session. Being asked questions as I looked over my shoulder – essentially having to respond to my back – was clearly not conducive to his disclosure. The shocking thing was, I had no idea I had been doing it. Although this occurred in a group, it is a lesson not only in how not to interview a client, but also the importance of self-monitoring and value of audio-visual recording.

GOALS

The goal of the interview is the starting point of the Skills Model. Clearly, both interviewer and interviewee will have goals, although the extent to which they concur will need establishing. Much will depend on the purpose of the interview, and for the forensic practitioner there can be a multitude. An interview to assess for sentencing will have different goals from one designed to assess for suitability for parole, for example. With this in mind, it is easy to see how the goal may have a significant impact on an offender's motivation to engage. Wicks (1982) contends that the absence of common goals is one of the most common problems impacting on the interview process; in the context of forensic clients it is likely to be one of the most common occurrences too.

An obvious solution as an interviewer is to clearly state the purpose of the interview at the outset, but given the power imbalance referred to previously, the impact that may have on the dynamic may still be negligible. It is also possible that such an overt statement of goals may well deprive the interviewer of observation of the client in a less-guarded state. Consider your own behaviour in a job interview. How likely is the interviewer to see a "natural" you? But assuming you are right for the job, how much better that could be. This emphasizes the importance of establishing rapport as quickly and as effectively as possible, an essential but sometimes elusive skill, especially with clients who are often suspicious and mistrustful of professionals. Defining rapport is in itself a challenge, but is essentially behaving in a way that enables the client to engage safely and comfortably with the interview (or therapeutic) process. Interviewer behaviours that can help include:

- Skilled listening (summarizing, reflecting, paraphrasing)
- Skilled questioning (knowing when to use open, closed, leading, assumptive questions)
- A collaborative approach (whereby the interviewer and interviewee sit together to address the main issues, as opposed to the interviewer sitting separately from the interviewee and the issues)
- A non-defensive, open and clear explanation of the goals, assessments, long-term implications and so on
- Working at the interviewee's pace
- Use of conversation and small talk (rather than launching straight into the purpose of the interview)

How effective strategies such as these will be depends to some extent on the dynamics between the two key players, and what works in establishing rapport with one client, might not with another. But a skilled interviewer will make the necessary adjustment fluently and probably automatically, simply by observing the interviewee's response and understanding the interviewee's goals.

In practice, then, it is clearly important to try to establish common goals as quickly as possible, and if necessary to find a way to work with differing goals. Sometimes the interviewer's goal may simply be to encourage an offender to engage in a process that he or she finds threatening or uncomfortable. On other occasions, the goals may be considerably more substantial, such as establishing levels of risk. Whatever the goals, it is important to ask the client directly what they want from the interview process and to explain your own goals clearly and simply. It is important to recognize that goals cannot or will not always be verbalized; sometimes an educated guess is in order. Allowing time for the client to ask questions and not getting defensive should, in most circumstances, assist in establishing collaborative goals.

TIPS

- Ask you client directly about their goals for the interview.
- State your goals clearly and ensure the client has understood.
- Record your agreed goals.
- Record any discrepancies.
- Understand that it is not always possible to get complete agreement and that it is does not have to be a barrier to successful interviewing.

PERCEPTION

The extent to which rapport can be established and goals agreed will be influenced hugely by both players' perceptions of each other. Dougherty, Turban and Callender (1994) found that positive first impressions led to an increase in rapport-building behaviours and a decrease in information gathering on behalf of the interviewer (at least in the context of semi-structured work-related interviews). Such adjustments based on initial perception can have significant consequences for both practitioner and client in a forensic context.

Whether we intend it or not, our initial perception of a client will be set in our own frame of reference, meaning it will be influenced by our personal prejudices, biases and stereotypes. When working with the extremes of antisocial and damaging human behaviour, managing these factors can present a substantial challenge. All too often in interviewing training, we are instructed to be non-judgemental. Paradoxically, the entire purpose of a forensic interview might be to make a professional judgement or series of judgements about the person being interviewed. Initial perceptions may be very telling, and, whatever they are based on should not be ignored. However, the skill is to be able to *suspend* those judgements made on initial perceptions until there is firm evidence to back them up. Hargie and Tourish state, 'skilled interviewers will be perceptive individuals' (2000, p. 80). They should also be skilled at managing their judgements.

Obviously, account also has to be taken of the client's perception of the interviewer, and similarly this will be processed through their existing perceptual framework. Their previous experience of forensic professionals and your own personal qualities such as gender, age, appearance and accent will all impact on the impression you make. Clearly, many of these things will be beyond your control, making it even more important that you manage those factors that you can. These will be discussed in more detail under the heading Person/Situation context.

CASE STUDY

A few years ago I was asked to undertake an assessment of an incarcerated offender who had previously refused to engage with psychologists. He was unable to progress without a full psychological assessment and very reluctantly agreed to see me on the basis that I was 'independent'. Establishing rapport took several sessions and involved many strategies to calm his paranoia. It transpired however that his paranoia had some basis, at least according to his perceptual framework. Early in his sentence he had been the subject of considerable (unwanted) attention from female members of the public. He described being horrified when, at around the same time, a trainee psychologist came to see him to do an assessment. He perceived this young, attractive female psychologist as flirtatious and making overt sexual advances to him. He had very clear and defined internal schema about the way professionals should behave, and whatever the ultimate truth of the situation, his perception was that she breached them. Bearing in mind he was already highly sensitized to unsolicited advances, this prevented him from engaging with female professionals for many years.

Whether or not this psychologist behaved inappropriately will not be established, but I do remember once, in my efforts to be friendly to a prisoner working in the staff canteen (by smiling and saying 'hello' each time I saw him), I was accused of being intimidating. His direct feedback was a rather salutary lesson in taking nothing for granted with regards to how others might see you. Indeed it may even have helped with the situation described above.

In addition to perception of each other, self-perception is also important. For the interviewer, Hargie and Tourish argue, this is largely about the capacity for self-monitoring, both within and outside the interview context. Sommers-Flannagan and Sommers-Flannagan (2003) go further, referring to developmental self-awareness, or consciousness of one's own personal history. Particularly, they contend that one's history of interpersonal relationships will impact on interviewing style and therefore outcome. In forensic settings this may have particular pertinence for practitioners who have, directly or indirectly, been victims of crime. It is vitally important not to underestimate the impact of one's interpersonal history and this will be returned to in Chapter 14.

Meta perception is described by Hargie and Tourish (2000) as 'the aptitude for perceiving the perception process' (p. 81). In other words, understanding how others perceive you, how they might think you perceive them and adjusting your behaviour accordingly. Here is where the skill of simultaneity comes into its own. Attending effectively to your own and others perceptions will shape not only how, when and why particular questions are asked, but also how you and your client respond to each other.

TIPS

- Think about how you come across to others. Ask a friend or trusted colleague to help you appraise your presentation.
- Know yourself. Identify your prejudices and biases and what is likely to trigger them. Supervision is the right forum for this.
- Understand the difference between <u>content</u> and <u>process.</u> Content refers to what is being said, the script of the interview. Process refers to how the interview happens, the mood of the interview (see Mediating Factors below for a more detailed description).
- If, during the interview process, you perceive a problem with the process, perhaps the offender becoming particularly hostile whenever you ask about family relationships, it might well be appropriate to make it explicit. For example, 'It seems to me Sarah, that whenever I ask about your family you get hostile and angry [you could give behavioural examples here]. What can I do differently to help us talk about what I see as a very difficult area for you?' Not only does this demonstrate your empathy, it also shows you are paying attention to the wider context of the interview. Additionally, it can help to unblock or at least loosen up a blockage (see *Recommended Further Reading* for a reference to motivational interviewing techniques that can be extremely effective in addressing challenges related to both content and process).

MEDIATING FACTORS

Hargie and Tourish refer to two main mediating factors: emotion and cognition, both of which mediate between the goal being pursued, the feedback received and the responses made. In practice, cognitive and emotional processes of both the interviewer and interviewee mediate the whole experience of the interview. In normal interviewing circumstances it is not unusual for emotion to be heightened and to impact on performance (usually on behalf of the interviewee, but not always). In the forensic context there is often an added dimension – that of pre-existing emotional and cognitive dysfunction. The significance of emotional and cognitive deficits in the offending population is well documented (see, for example, Ward, Hudson and Marshall, 1995; Hoaken, Allaby and Earle, 2007), although research is usually directed at the role of such dysfunction in the aetiology or maintenance of offending. In an interviewing context, the existence of cognitive and/or affective disorders can, and most likely will, impact on the process. It is therefore essential that the interviewer not only understands the ways in which their own cognitive and emotional functioning might mediate their experience, but also how that of the client can influence the process. Here, the knowledge component of the motor skills analogy comes into its own. For example, the use of conversation and small talk to develop rapport may backfire unexpectedly if the clients experience is mediated through paranoid, suspicious and mistrustful cognitions.

To moderate any potential negative impact of emotional and cognitive dysfunction on behalf of the offender, there are a number of steps an interviewer can take. First, ensure that you are as familiar as possible with the client's case and personal details. There is some argument for making your own assessment in the first instance by knowing only the bare minimum to keep you safe, however this is a weak argument in the face of the damage that can be caused by ignorance of factors that might otherwise have enhanced rapport development. Second, close attention and appropriate responses to non-verbal cues can help both interviewer and interviewee work with cognitive and emotional issues. This highlights the importance of simultaneity and knowledge skills, as well as attending to both content and process issues in the interviewing context. Where content refers to the 'what' of the interview (what is being said, the detail, information imparted and so on), process refers to the 'how'. How is the information imparted? How is the client responding? How does the client look when talking about particular themes? It is the process of the interview that is likely to yield to greatest information about emotional and cognitive states (see Feedback below).

For the interviewer, attention to their own emotion and cognition is equally important, and again, the forensic setting adds a dimension not present in day-to-day interviewing situations. For example, eliciting an offence account can require the interviewer to listen to and process sometimes graphic details of abuse perpetrated against another person. It is rare that such information does not trigger a strong emotional response in the receiver, and yet that response needs to be managed if the interview is to flow. Added to this, an offender might be particularly blasé, or defensive, or minimizing of the impact on the victim, triggering an additional range of responses to be managed. It is important not to underestimate the potential for emotional and cognitive impact that working with offenders can have. At both an acute level (managing in the moment) and a chronic level (managing the build-up over months and years of forensic work), recognizing personal emotional and cognitive reactivity is at the heart of effective practice. We have a duty of care, to our clients and ourselves, to ensure that we attend to it in order to prevent professional or personal impairment (see Chapter 14 – Resilience), as well as a professional obligation to ensure that we are fit to practice (see Section 2.4 of the British Psychological Society Code of Ethics and Conduct).

CASE STUDY

On one occasion, as a result of an 'emergency' call to the office to come and see a prisoner who was behaving in a somewhat bizarre and irrational way, I skipped the part where I should have read the file. Other than a distant recollection of the prisoner's name, I knew nothing about him. A staff member introduced me to 'Bobby', who was in his early 20's, approximately 6'4" and roughly 20 stone in weight. We were shown into the 6' by 6' office, where the desk and two chairs took up most of the room, and a result of his size, Bobby and I had to sit rather uncomfortably close together.

He immediately launched into an account of how he had predicted a recent plane crash and that he could easily run a mile in minute; it was very clear very quickly why staff were concerned. Both his emotional and cognitive presentation were impaired to a degree where rational conversation did not seem possible. As Bobby continued to describe the most unlikely of occurrences, it suddenly dawned on me why his name was familiar; in big red letters on the office notice board it clearly stated: BOBBY on B WING – Not to be seen alone by female staff. I should have read the file! The immediate perception of possible threat resulted in a massive adrenalin surge and I'm convinced that a more sensitive onlooker would have noticed my heart trying to escape from my chest. It was only by focusing on the immediate moment, recognizing that Bobby was not actually demonstrating any inclination to do me any harm, that I managed to regain my composure – at the point where he was telling me he would never offend again (phew!) because he would lose his family and that was a really big detergent [sic]. Suffice to say I managed to extricate myself unharmed, but it was a salutary lesson.

TIPS

- Spend some time at the start of an interview gauging an offender's cognitive and emotional state. If it's the first time you have met, is there anything in the file you should pay particular attention to, such as mental health diagnosis, drug/alcohol use, recent challenging events, that may impact on immediate presentation. If it is a familiar client, are things as they usually are.
- If you are uncertain, ask.
- Monitor and acknowledge your emotions. It is almost certain that you will come across things that shock, frighten or repulse you, as well as a myriad of other feelings. It is essential that you remember that in a

vast majority of cases, these are normal reactions to very often abnormal, situations, circumstances or account of human behaviour.

- DO NOT deny how you feel. To yourself or anyone else. If a sex offender asks what you think of their offence, it would be very odd for your response to be totally neutral. Practice a human response: 'Your behaviour towards your victim shocks and saddens me, and actually makes me quite angry' is a much more credible and honest response than 'we're not here to discuss what I think'. Some professionals may disagree with me, but this approach has never yet resulted anything other than the development of a positive client relationship.

RESPONSES

Hargie and Tourish (2000) argue that the response element of the model is the point at which skill becomes manifest. The responses of both parties in the process are important and will shape behaviour, because no matter what internal processing or emotion management is going on internally, it is ultimately what is done and observed that is most influential. The purpose and goals of the interview may well dictate the type of skill that is required. For example, for an initial assessment, where information gathering is perhaps a priority over rapport building, the key skill determinants are likely to be around questioning style. A therapeutic interview on the other hand will demand different responses in terms of empathic listening, reflection, summarizing and so on. This highlights the importance of responses being situation-specific and emphasizes the skills aspect of the model further. For example, responding to someone who discloses thoughts of self-injury will require a very different skill set from responding to someone who is having homicidal fantasies.

FEEDBACK

Feedback is the final link in the model. It is what enables the practitioner to act in a skilled manner. At a micro level, once a response has occurred, the resultant feedback enables the practitioner to modify or adjust subsequent responses accordingly. For example, a hostile and resistant response from an offender to the possibility of undertaking group intervention to reduce risk will provide ample information to the practitioner, who may then chose a number of alternative responses. Depending on the details of the client's response, the interviewer may chose to explore the resistance to group work or the client's understanding of the concept of risk or perceptions of offending behaviour programmes (as examples). Future feedback in response to these investigations will indicate whether or not the practitioner is on the right lines.

Feedback may come in the form of verbal or non-verbal cues, and from external or internal sources. As the model indicates, it is crucial for both interviewer and interviewee and essential to the interpersonal process – an interaction with no feedback is by far the hardest to manage. The following example aims to encapsulate these key components and illustrate not only the complexity of the feedback loop, but also the impact on other features of the model.

An offender smiles in response to a question about his abuse of a victim. This tiny muscular movement is likely to evoke a chain reaction so complex that it actually defies explication, but let us make a hypothetical attempt within the framework of the model. The smile may evoke a strong emotional reaction in the interviewer (**mediating factor**), who then needs to manage their own reactivity while making sense of the client's response and formulating their own appropriate (professional) **response** in turn. The smile might be interpreted as evidence of lack of remorse, or sadism. An experienced interviewer might also attend to the environment, consider the social skills of the offender, evidence of anxiety, learning disability or any other such indication that may help make sense of the behaviour. The interviewer might attend to process issues and ask why the client is smiling, recognizing that their initial **perception** of the client has been altered, while at the same time attending to the personal issues perhaps triggered by the smile or the change in **perception.** They will know that whatever **response** is made to the smile provides **feedback** to the offender, will effect the process and may well change the **goal** of the interview (now the goal is to understand this piece of feedback), while at the same time knowing that their own body language is likely to give away much more than anything they actually say. Meanwhile the offender has sat back and appears to be waiting for a **response** and so the cycle continues. When an interaction is broken down into small component parts in this way (however roughly), the motor skill analogy comes into its own and the fluency, rapidity, automaticity, simultaneity and knowledge components can be appreciated more readily.

THE PERSON/SITUATION CONTEXT

The context in which all communication takes places is of core importance, in that it can only be construed within that framework (Hargie and Tourish, 2000). Interviews conducted in prison will be different from those conducted in the community, for example. Total institutions such as prisons and hospitals will have their own cultures which impose a whole set of expectations on the behaviour of forensic practitioners and offenders in all circumstances, including interviews. How these expectations play out in the actual interview will depend on those features explained by the model as well as the host of features discussed below.

Often when working in forensic settings there is little option about where an interview takes places. Practitioners working in courts, prisons, hospitals and so on will usually have designated interview rooms, the set up of which is beyond the control of the interviewer as they are common-purpose rooms used by everyone. This does not mean, however, that account should not be taken of the environment and the impact it can have on the interview process. Prisons, for example, are often noisy places where interruptions are commonplace, alarm bells not infrequent and security objectives are often counter to therapeutic ones. The interviewer will need to accommodate these, perhaps by structuring the expectations of the client and preparing for interruptions. This is much easier in an environment that is familiar, but harder when visiting an institution. There are no hard and fast rules but the old adage 'prepare for the worst and hope for the best' applies well in such circumstances.

Perhaps more influential than the environment are features of the interviewer. Gender, culture, age, appearance and personality will all influence the process. These factors have all been widely discussed (and researched) in the general interviewing literature, but as has been highlighted several times already, they take on a different significance in forensic practice.

The issue of gender was raised at the start of this chapter, with reference to sexual chemistry and the importance of acknowledging and dealing with its presence. Gender is known to influence interviewing interactions in many other ways, for example in terms of levels and types of disclosure (Lamb and Garretson, 2003; Pollner, 1998). In a mental health setting, Pollner found respondents interviewed by women reported more symptoms of depression, substance abuse and conduct disorders. He suggests that this might be because women are more likely to create conditions for disclosure. This is borne out in part by Lamb and Garretson's research with children, who found that when interviewing child witnesses, women fostered greater compliance among both male and female children. Importantly though, they also found that the gender difference was minimized when interviewers adhered to best practice guidelines for the types of interview being conducted. Although there is a dearth of such guidelines in general forensic interviewing, ensuring consistency of approach, engaging in regular supervision and remaining mindful of the impact of gender can all help in ensuring good practice.

CASE STUDY

I, and a number of my female colleagues, have experienced the romantic attentions of incarcerated men, and it can be extremely potent. Indeed it is not unknown for staff members to jeopardize security, personal safety and professional credibility for the apparent love of an offender. Perhaps this was particularly significant twenty odd years ago, when it was still unusual to find women working in male institutions, but even recently I have heard of cases of resignation, dismissal and even marriage resulting from illicit relationships between forensic practitioners and clients, both in secure settings and in the community.

Thinking realistically about this issue, it should not provoke any surprise, given that the survival of the species is based on sexual chemistry that can be stronger than any physical barrier or professional code of practice. Perhaps what is more surprising is that volumes have not already been written about it, either from the perspective of academic interest, but perhaps more importantly to educate, inform and enhance the safety of both staff and offenders. But it remains a taboo subject that is difficult to address.

The interviewing context, by its very nature can be intimate. One-to-one situations, where our role is to establish rapport and trust, can be extremely challenging to navigate with sometimes vulnerable and needy individuals. Add attraction into the mix and this becomes potentially very damaging for both you and the client.

As a young and relatively inexperienced psychologist, I was asked to work with a young man who had previously self-injured and was threatening suicide. 'David' was my age, vulnerable, and undeniably handsome. I was learning the ropes, driven to 'get it right' and largely motivated to rescue people. Weekly support sessions turned into twice weekly sessions and then into frequent ad hoc requests from prison staff for me to see 'David' for fear he would kill himself if I didn't. With the benefit of 20/20 hindsight it is very clear what was going on, but at the time there was no such clarity. It actually took a close friend to wake me up to what was happening when she commented that I talked about this offender 'rather a lot'. Interestingly, colleagues did not address the issue, even though it must have been obvious, and this perhaps reflects an organizational resistance to touch such a sensitive area. I managed to extract myself and keep my professional credibility intact – just. This was achieved through a number of processes, including; reminding myself of what 'David' was capable of (he had committed an armed robbery with a sawn-off shotgun which he held to the heads of (mainly) women); considering the importance of my career to me and others; considering the validity of his expressed feelings in the context (incarcerated offenders can spend many hours considering how to get close to professionals); and considering the persistence of his attentions. (Gavin de Becker (1997), an expert in threat assessment in a range of high-risk settings states that just because a romantic pursuer is relentless does not mean you are special, it means he is troubled and David was clearly troubled).

Footnote: I met David again some two years after my work with him ended. He had been to several different prisons in the interim and had returned to where I was working. I had done a considerable amount of professional 'growing-up'. He immediately put in an application to see me and within five minutes of meeting stated categorically 'you've changed'. I took this to mean he perceived I was no longer susceptible to his attentions, and he was right. It was a defining moment of both my personal and professional development.

TIPS

The following advice is based on scenarios where an offender's attraction to you feels flattering rather than intimidating (decisions are pretty clear cut in the latter situation), or where you find yourself attracted to an offender.

- If you recognize that a client is attracted to you or you are attracted to a client, stop working with them immediately.
- Your motivation to take this action may be compromised by a number of issues including feelings of being special (it can be very rewarding to think you are important and necessary to someone); the magnetic feelings of mutual attraction (which can interfere with rational thinking); fear about how you may be viewed by colleagues or any combination of intense and conflicting emotions. To reinforce the need to take this action think about the following:
  - Your professional code of practice, which prohibits relationships with clients for a number of very good reasons.
  - Your organization's rules regarding relationships with clients.
  - The personal cost to you, including potential loss of job, professional status, future employment prospects, reactions of friends and colleagues and many others.
  - The offence(s) that the client has committed.
  - The depth and genuine nature of the emotion.
  - The reasons you may be reacting in the way that you are. If the situation is feeding a need in you, think about areas of your own life that would benefit from examination.
- As far as possible, discuss the situation with your supervisor or supportive fellow professional. This might be quite easy if an offender is attracted to you, but much harder if it is you who is attracted to the offender.
- If a fellow professional is not an option, find someone outside work who can support you.
- Do NOT keep the situation to yourself.
- If you find yourself defending the situation, to yourself or others, recognize this as a danger signal. It is not professionally defensible to continue working with someone in this context.
- DO NOT underestimate the personal and professional costs of pursuing a romantic relationship with a client – they are incalculable.

A further consideration is the extent to which men and women are able to understand and empathize with gender-specific issues, for example around victimization, sexual abuse and domestic violence. While it is argued that gender need never be a barrier to developing rapport and exploring gender-specific matters, and indeed may sometimes be positively beneficial, sensitivity and awareness on behalf of the interviewer will minimize the risk of gender-associated problems.

As important and relevant as gender is age. It is not unusual, for example, for a young trainee psychologist to be required to interview a long-term life-sentenced prisoner who might be well into their sixties, and these encounters are likely to be fraught with tensions on both sides. From the perspective of the offender, there is likely to be anxiety about the knowledge, experience, skills and training of someone who could potentially be a grandchild or great grandchild! For the interviewer, feeling patronized, experiencing hostility based on their age and perhaps feeling trumped by the offender's comparative experience of the system are inevitably going to influence interview behaviour (let alone interviewing someone who is old enough to be their parent or grandparent). This is just one of an infinite number of potential scenarios around age. Overt acknowledgement of such a dynamic is probably useful, especially if it impacts on the process to the extent that progress is impeded.

CASE STUDY

At the very start of my career in prisons, aged twenty-five, I was sent to prepare a parole report on a life sentence prisoner, aged sixty-five, who had served twenty-five years of his sentence. 'Tony' was old enough to be my grandfather and had considerably more experience of the prison system (and life) than I had. I think it would be fair to say that he managed the process of those early interviews, despite my efforts to appear in control and knowledgeable.

Having one's competence and confidence challenged by offenders who know how to manage the system is a daunting and unsettling experience (and explains why these two elements are central to resilience: see Chapter 14), but it is also a learning experience. We all have to start somewhere and situations such as this are unavoidable.

Be prepared to feel unsettled and doubtful and if you do, use these 'imposters' as learning opportunities. Use supervision to reflect on what you need to learn, both in terms of process and content skills, and how you can develop these, and remember there is no substitute for experience.

Fortunately for me, Tony did not take advantage of his considerably more honed interviewing skills, and in some respects I am indebted to him for what I learned.

Appearance is often a controversial subject in forensic settings (particularly institutions), probably because perception of what is appropriate is so varied. Clearly, appearance designed to be sexually provocative is unacceptable, however it is not always immediately clear what might be found provocative or by whom. Practitioners sometimes express resistance at being required to subdue or change their personal style in some way, but in just the same way an interviewer may be influenced by the appearance of an offender, so an offender will be influenced by the appearance of the interviewer. The problem of course is in understanding what type of appearance has what type of effect. It may be argued that overly formal attire can distance an offender from a practitioner, perhaps perceiving the practitioner as having little in common. However, that might not apply if the offender comes from a background where formal dress was standard. Overly informal appearance may lead an offender to question professionalism, if there is a perception that 'professionals' should present in a certain way. These issues are interesting to explore and, as with nearly all aspects of interpersonal interactions, there is rarely a right or wrong answer.

CASE STUDY

When appointing a psychological assistant to a growing team in a busy local prison, potential candidates were invited to visit. Among the mixed group of men and women was one stunningly beautiful young woman who chose to attend wearing a sarong that revealed a few inches of tanned and toned midriff. I don't think I have ever encountered attire so inappropriate for the occasion. But what was most interesting was not the response of the prisoners, but the response of prison staff, who were universally horrified. In this instance, appearance had revealed a substantial lack of judgement that staff translated into a lack of professionalism. Needless to say this candidate was not invited to interview.

I have also been asked on two occasions to ask male members of my team to get their hair cut. Senior staff perceive long, unkempt hair on males to signify lack of professionalism and also expressed concern that these staff members could easily be mistaken for prisoners if caught in an incident. Putting aside all the political, stereotypical and gender-based debates that these scenarios might provoke, these two examples serve to illustrate the power of appearance.

The personalities of the parties involved in the interview process play an important part in shaping the interaction, independent of the circumstances. So, even though both might be faced with a first-time meeting, an individual with an introverted disposition may respond quite differently from someone more extroverted. Hargie and Tourish propose that the progress of an interview will be shaped by an interaction between the dispositions of both players with the level of skill exercised. As personality is generally stable, in the interviewing context an awareness of one's own personality and its impact on the process is the main consideration.

CONCLUSION

Interviewing is arguably the bedrock of forensic practice. Essentially, every interaction with an offender is a form of interviewing; in that it yields information that can contribute to building a holistic picture of that individual and therefore help make a more informed assessment of their risk and need. It is a complex and nuanced set of skills, requiring mindful application and constant awareness if they are to yield the best return. Like all motor skills, consistent practice, sometimes supervised and regularly reflected on, is required to develop, and although training is important, there is no substitute for experience. It is often said that the actual learning of driving can only happen once a driver has passed their test, when there is a greater opportunity to practice driving in all weather conditions, at night and during the day, on motorways, in towns and on country roads, in new cars and old cars, big cars and small. It is a rich analogy.

RECOMMENDED FURTHER READING

Somers-Flanagan, J. and Sommers-Flanagan, R. (2003). *Clinical Interviewing*, 3rd edn (John Wiley & Sons, New Jersey). This book is packed full with practical tips for interviewing in clinical settings, most of which are highly applicable to forensic settings.

Memon, A. and Bull, R. (eds) (2000). *The Handbook of the Psychology of Interviewing* (John Wiley & Sons, Chichester). In addition to a fuller description of Hargie and Tourish, this book also includes chapters relevant to forensic practice, including cognitive interview and interviewing children.

REFERENCES

De Becker, G. (1997). *The Gift of Fear* (Dell Publishing, USA).

Dougherty, T., Turban, D. and Callender, J. (1994). 'Confirming First Impressions in the Employment Interview: A Field Study of Interviewer Behaviour', *Journal of Applied Psychology*, 79, 659–65.

Gieselman, R. E., Fisher, R. P., MacKinnon, D. P. and Holland, H. L. (1985). 'Eyewitness Memory Enhancement in the Police Interview: Cognitive

Retrieval Mnemonics versus Hypnosis', *Journal of Applied Psychology*, 70, 401–12.

Hargie, O. (2011). *Skilled Interpersonal Communication: Research, Theory and Practice*, 5th edn (London: Routledge).

Hargie, O. and Tourish, D. (2000). 'The Psychology of Interpersonal Skill', in A. Memon and R. Bull (eds) *The Handbook of the Psychology of Interviewing* (John Wiley & Sons, Chichester), 71–88.

Hoaken, P. N. S., Allaby, D. B. and Earle, J. (2007). 'Executive Cognitive Functioning and the Recognition of Facial Expressions of Emotion in Incarcerated Violent Offenders, Non-Violent Offenders, and Control', *Aggressive Behavior* 33(5), 412–21.

Lamb, M. E. and Garretson, M. E. (2003). 'The Effects of Interviewer Gender and Child Gender on the Informativeness of Alleged Child Sexual Abuse Victims in Forensic Interviews', *Law and Human Behavior* 27(2), 157–71.

Memon, A. (2000). 'Interviewing Witnesses: The Cognitive Interview', in A. Memon and R. Bull (eds) *The Handbook of the Psychology of Interviewing* (John Wiley & Sons, Chichester), 343–55.

Miller, W. R., and Rollnick, S. (2002). *Motivational Interviewing: Preparing People for Change*, 2nd edn (Guilford Press, London).

Pollner, M. (1998). 'The Effects of Interviewer Gender in Mental Health Interviews', *The Journal of Mental and Nervous Diseases* 186(6), pp. 369–73.

Sommers-Flanagan, J. and Sommers-Flanagan, R. (2003). *Clinical Interviewing*, 3rd edn (John Wiley & Sons, New Jersey).

Ward, T., Hudson, S. M. and Marshall, W. L. (1995). 'Cognitive Distortions and Affective Deficits in Sex Offenders: A Cognitive Deconstructionist Interpretation', *Sex Abuse* January 7, 67–83.

Wicks (1982). 'Interviewing: Practical aspects', in A. Chapman and A. Gale (eds) *Psychology and People. A Tutorial Text* (London, BPS/Macmillan).

4 Forensic Assessment

Michelle Fletcher

INTRODUCTION

The role of the forensic psychologist has developed significantly over the last ten to fifteen years as the scope of the work and the areas of work within the criminal justice system have changed. Forensic psychologists have started to expand their areas of work from the more traditional area of prisons to family court and mentally disordered offenders, and therefore, as a result, the traditional assessments of a forensic psychologist such as clinical interview have also changed. There are two main aims of an assessment undertaken by that of a forensic psychologist: that of understanding why an individual has committed a criminal offence and that of determining an individual's treatment needs to help ameliorate this risk. As these are the principal aims of an assessment, it follows that an assessment can consist of any aspects that may be related to the risk of an individual reoffending. As other professionals within the criminal justice system become more familiar with the broad scope of psychology, it seems evident that the role of the psychologist will continue to expand. Therefore the purpose of this chapter will be to explore the theoretical perspectives relating to assessment, the purpose of forensic psychological assessment, to introduce the broad categories of assessment methodologies, introduce some of the most influential assessment tools, including their strengths and limitations and finally to highlight ethical issues relating to assessment. Forensic psychologists can work in a variety of areas within the criminal justice system including probation teams, prisons, secure psychiatric facilities and, more recently, independent practice. Depending on the environment the types of assessments used may vary due to the responsive nature of any psychological assessment, this includes being responsive to the environment as well as the individuals being assessed. The basic aim of any forensic assessment is to develop an understanding of the pathway that an offender takes that leads to his or her offending behaviour. It is important that this understanding is developed by the professional even if the offender themselves has little or no insight. If the professional can gain understanding of the offence pathway using the process of offence analysis, then both treatment and management recommendations can be made that will enable both the offender and the professionals to help reduce and minimize any future risk posed. Therefore, any form of data can be considered as relevant to forensic assessment. However, all assessments should be considered within the context of reliability, how replicable and stable an assessment is over time; validity, the extent to which the assessment measures what it claims to measure; and utility which refers to the usefulness of the assessment in answering the questions posed. It should be recognized that no assessment could be said to have 100 per cent reliability, validity or utility and therefore the judgement often of the individual psychologist is to decide which assessment tool they can utilize to aid their risk-assessment knowing and understanding the individual reliability and validity of each assessment they undertake.

CONTEXT AND CONSIDERATIONS

In the majority of cases forensic assessments are utilized to answer questions in formal settings that are of a quasi-legal situation, such as parole board hearings and therefore require consideration of the audience as well as the potential impact of the assessment on the individual's case. The audience often consists of professionals from the criminal justice system, legal representatives, lay people as well as the offender themselves. Therefore, it is best for psychologists to consider the rules of evidence as outlined by court procedures when undertaking a forensic assessment. The main rule that applies to that of forensic assessment is the Hearsay Rule. This rule protects the defendant from unfair or unsafe evidence. It excludes evidence not directly obtained by the witness. When applied to the area of forensic psychology, this rule means that the psychologist should use caution when utilising evidence gathered by an assistant or trainee forensic psychologists. However, this evidentiary rule is often in direct conflict with that of aim of supervised practice which is fundamental to the development of psychological skills, which encourages psychologists in training to undertake assessments while undergoing supervision with a qualified psychologist who may or may not directly observe the full assessment process. It is often common practise in psychology departments to utilize and prioritize all resources within a department while also developing skills in individual learning. Therefore assistant psychologists and forensic psychologists in training are often allocated tasks of gathering data from an individual's files or undertaking psychometric assessments with offenders as a key objective in developing their own psychological skills. This can bring the aims of the psychological profession into conflict with the aims of the formal assessment process. The current British Psychological Society code of conduct and ethics highlights the importance of stating who has carried out any test, examination or interview which has been used for reports and whether it has been carried out under supervision.

The rules guiding the admissibility of evidence include the following concepts: the subject matter must be beyond common understanding of an average juror, the expert must be sufficiently qualified that opinion will aid jury, the evidence must be scientifically reliable and generally accepted and the probative value of evidence must outweigh prejudicial effects. Some of these rules are more compatible with the concepts of applied psychology than others. For example, the idea that evidence must be scientifically reliable and generally accepted is a concept that all areas of applied psychology are comfortable with. One of the key principles of psychology is to undertake and apply research to ensure that work undertaken by an individual psychologist has a body of research evidence that supports it, the principle of evidence-based practice. However, other aspects of admissibility such as those concerning the prejudicial effects of an assessment require much closer consideration. For example, many of the labels used within the area of forensic psychology, such as psychopathy or personality disorder, by their very nature can be considered prejudicial due to the negative connotations assigned by the perception of media and the non-scientific community.

In addition to the rules of admissibility the forensic psychologist has also to consider their own code of conduct and the guidance provided by the British Psychological Society in relation to utilizing a particular assessment tool or 'test'. This advice includes the following guidance: 'the theory or technique must be, and has been, tested – the "Falsifiability" principle, the theory or technique must have been subject to peer review and published in professional journals, there must be general acceptance of the theory and technique in the scientific community, the theory or technique must have a known error rate, there must exist standards to control the techniques operation, the extent to which the technique relies upon the subjective interpretation of the expert must be clear and the extent to which research on the technique extends beyond the courtroom should be clear' (British Psychological Society 2010). These areas of advice should always be considered before an assessment is undertaken in any context. Therefore, it is important that when considering a specific assessment tool to be utilized, the psychologist is clear that the 'tool' has a recognized research base that can be explained to the court, that they are using a test that other psychologists would recognize as a standard procedure, including a full understanding of the benefits and disadvantages to the use of such a tool. All assessments must also follow a standardized procedure that would be replicable by other psychologists.

RISK ASSESSMENT

Risk assessment can be defined as 'the systematic collection of information to determine the degree to which harm (to self and others) is likely, at some point in time' (Dictionary of Forensic Psychology, Towl *et al.*, 2008). If this definition was to be followed, then it could be argued that any assessment, which provides information to help determine a level of harm, collected in a systematic way is a risk assessment. Thus psychological assessments ranging from simple self-report questionnaires used to assess impulsivity to complex interview assessments such as the psychopathy Checklist can all be argued as a form of risk assessment. The key to this area of forensic psychology is that the assessment that is being undertaken must be associated with the risk that an individual poses to others as well as themselves. Although assessments of self-harming behaviour and the risk of suicide are forms of risk assessment generally, it is more widely accepted that the term 'Risk Assessment' in applied forensic psychology applies to the risk an individual poses to others. Therefore, the main aim of risk assessment is to prevent or decrease the likelihood of future offending. This is achieved by several smaller goals including using the assessment to structure and guide interventions and to devise management and supervision strategies to minimize the risk an individual poses. Further aims of assessment in line with more broad ethical aims relating to all psychological assessments include improving consistency in decision making as well as improving transparency in the decision-making process in order to protect the rights of both the public and the individual. Crighton and Towl (2008) argue that the use of appropriate and clear language to describe areas of risk and the criteria against which they are measured is an essential part of any risk assessment, yet it is often poorly addressed in the area of forensic psychology. Often risk assessments are assumed to provide an accurate estimate of risk over an unspecified period of time and across a range of environments both of which are implausible. Therefore, it is the responsibility of each professional to make the limitations of their assessments clear, something that is not often overtly stated but assumed by psychologists to be understood.

In terms of risk assessment there are two main theoretical approaches to undertaking assessments. One approach involves the use of actuarial assessments while the other approach relies on the use of structured professional judgement from the professional.

Actuarial Approaches

In 1974 Steadman and Cocozza's book *Careers of the Criminally Insane* provided a platform for the ensuing discussion and research regarding the predictability of 'dangerousness' of risk of violence. This book suggested that psychologists and psychiatrists demonstrated very low prediction rates for future violence in patients who had been released from a secure psychiatric facility. This natural experiment indicated that professionals were more likely to overpredict the rates of future violence and therefore patients were more likely to remain detained. This conclusion following research by Steadman and Cocozza and Thornberry and Jacoby (1979) led to the assertion that predicting future violence was an almost impossible task and therefore one that should not be undertaken. However, in the early 1980s a different school of thought emerged. Shah (1978) understood that in many arenas within the criminal justice field both forensic psychologists and psychiatrists were expected to provide some assessment of future risk and therefore there was an obligation to improve the rate of prediction rather than state that prediction should not occur. This led to the emergence of actuarial risk assessment tools.

Actuarial approaches involve the use of statistical techniques to provide an assessment of the level of risk an individual poses in terms of reoffending. The most commonly used example of such tools includes the Violence Risk Appraisal Guide (VRAG, Quinsey *et al.*, 2006). Actuarial approaches are commonly used in non-psychology areas such as insurance. For example, when arranging insurance for our cars, we expect to be asked factual questions such as our age, where we live, how many accidents we have had in the past etc. to help determine the cost of the insurance premium. In similar terms actuarial assessments to assess risk of reoffending follow a similar process; they are designed solely to predict outcome, are highly specific, designed for a specific outcome, time period, population and context and are highly structured in terms of the evaluation and decision-making process. For example, a basic risk assessment may indicate that being male, single and under the age of thirty increases the risk of an individual committing a violent act. While this is an overly simplistic example, the basic principles of assessing an individual for the presence of factors statistically related to violence or sexual violence remain in all assessments. Actuarial tools such as the VRAG provide a probability of the individual committing a further offence that in turn indicates whether the offender is high, medium or low risk. The advantages of such an approach include objectivity, as the assessment of the individual cannot be influenced by any bias of the professional or any particular skill of the offender in interviewing techniques, and consistency in decision making, in that all individuals assessed using an actuarial assessment are assessed in the same way. However, this approach also has several limitations: an element of professional judgement is required, including which scale to use and how to interpret the scores; the results tend to be pseudo-scientific and therefore may be easily misinterpreted; and there is also a tendency of over reliance on results due to the assumption that they are always accurate and objective. In reality actuarial assessments require the use of inductive logic, that is, there remains an assumption that the individual being assessed matches the population the original research was undertaken on. Therefore in using a tool like the VRAG, a psychologist based in a prison in England should be confident that applying the assessment to the individual they are assessing will produce replicable and valid results. Often the assessments utilized are designed and developed in North America, with the original research being conducted on offenders within North American prisons or secure facilities. A tool such as the Hare psychopathy Checklist-Revised

(PCL-R, Hare, 1991) struggles against this assumption as research by David Cooke and colleagues (Cooke, 1998) has highlighted potential ethnic differences between populations.

Structured Professional Judgement

The other approach to risk assessment is that of using structured risk assessment guides. The main proponents of this approach are clinicians and researchers linked with Simon Fraser University in Vancouver, Canada, namely, Steve Hart, Christopher Webster, Kevin Douglas and associated colleagues. These authors have been responsible for the majority of risk assessment guides that are most commonly used today including the HCR-20: Assessing Risk for Violence (version 2, Webster *et al.*, 1997), Risk for Sexual Violence Protocol, (Hart *et al.*, 2003) and the Spousal Assault Risk Assessment Guide (Kropp *et al.*, 1999). The process of structured professional judgement asks the psychologist to consider a minimum number of risk factors that are directly related to the type of offending being assessed. These are factors that are statistically significant in predicting the probability of offending occurring in the future. The psychologist is then required to assess if these risk factors are present and relevant to the individual being assessed. Therefore, it combines elements of actuarial assessment with that of professional judgement. The structured judgement approach, like that of actuarial assessments imposes significant structure on evaluation, for example at a minimum, a fixed and explicit set of risk factors must be considered. These are determined by each individual guide, that is, for the HCR-20 a minimum of twenty factors need to considered in each case, however the guide allows for other individual case-specific factors also to be considered by the assessor. These factors have elements of actuarial assessments; in that ten of the factors are historical and therefore static in nature while the other ten are dynamic risk factors. In each guide the risk factors are expressly stated with given definitions that the psychologist is expected to assess the individual against. The structured risk assessment guides also explicitly state the methods used for information gathering, for example the guidance for the HCR-20 states that a combination of clinical interview, collateral file review and third-party information should all be considered. To ensure that the structure for the assessment is consistent, training is provided in each of the separate risk assessment guides along with minimum user qualifications. In contrast to the structured approach on evaluation risk assessment guides such as the HCR-20 impose minor structure on decision making. As the manuals are considered guides rather than specific psychometric assessments, they allow the individual professional to use their own professional judgement in assessing not only the presence of each individual risk factor but also the relevance to the offender's risk of reoffending. The only structure imposed on decision making is that the language used to communicate the findings of the risk assessment is specified.

However, the guides allow the psychologist to determine the importance of each risk factor, for example unlike the VRAG there are no set probability statements, there are no imposed rules regarding how many risk factors should be present to indicate high, medium or low risk with the guides allowing for the possibility that only one or two risk factors may be present but may be so significant that they indicate a high level of risk; for example, one single factor such as psychopathy being present may be enough to indicate high risk of reoffending.

One of the main advantages of tools such as the HCR-20 is that the decisions made using these guides are transparent; it is clear where decisions regarding risk evaluations are made to both professionals working within the criminal justice system such as the Parole Board as well as the offender. This has the advantages of meeting the aim of open reporting that comes with all psychological assessments as well as providing opportunity to challenge and question the decisions made. This transparency and openness to scrutiny works well with the general aims and methods of psychology as a profession. In contrast the actuarial assessments which require complex mathematical equations already determined by the researchers make transparency a difficult aim to achieve, if not impossible.

A further advantage of the structured professional judgement guides comes in terms of outcome following the assessment. The nature of the risk factors and the process of the assessment of each of these factors encourage the psychologist to consider recommendations for future treatment and intervention to try to minimize the risk an individual poses. This action-oriented approach provides the offender with an opportunity to change and reduce their risk. Unlike actuarial assessments there is a clear link between the risk factors rated as relevant and the recommendations made to decrease the impact of the same risk factors, reflecting the concept that risk is a dynamic concept. Actuarial assessments based on risk factors that are static in nature do not measure change over time or acknowledge impact that treatment may have on an individual's risk. Therefore the aims of the structured guides are more consistent with the general aims of forensic psychology and the principles of providing offenders the opportunity to change their future behaviour.

The main limitation of structured professional guides is similar to that of actuarial assessments; in that they still rely on the assumption that the characteristics of the individual being assessed are consistent with the characteristics of the population in which the original research was undertaken. The guides also require a degree of training and 're-tooling' of the assessment process, the rules imposed by each guide must be taught to the professional. In recent years the criminal justice system appears to have accepted that the structured professional judgement approach to risk assessment meets the main requirements for formal proceedings, as evidenced by both Parole Board panels and courts specifically requesting an assessment including a specific risk assessment guide such as the HCR-20 is used. Although, this shows a general acceptance for a psychological model in the assessment of risk, it does pose some further ethical considerations for the professional: what response should the psychologist have in cases where a specific guide is recommended by the hearing that may not be appropriate to the case (e.g., requests for a HCR-20 assessment when the offender has not committed a violent offence as defined by the HCR-20) or a particular assessment is requested that may produce a very pejorative effect without aiding the offender's treatment or management (e.g., a psychopathy assessment being requested for an offender on license in the community). The final limitation to utilizing structured professional judgement over an actuarial assessment is that using a structured risk assessment guide to make a judgement of future risk and future risk management recommendations is often more time consuming and therefore potentially more costly.

GENERAL LIMITATIONS TO RISK ASSESSMENT

Over recent years there has been a focus within forensic assessment on structured guides and assessment tools to ensure both reliability and consistency. However, this has led to potential difficulties as professionals become more proficient in areas of risk of violence and sexual violence to the detriment of other offences such as arson or terrorism etc. for which no reliable and valid risk tools currently exist. At times, this has led to psychologists over generalizing research findings to make conclusions that while based on valid research are limited in accuracy.

Another limitation is based on individual differences that can occur within any profession. The danger of a specific risk assessment guide being used is that it encourages the court to believe in a high degree of consistency between professionals. While it is true that all risk tools and guides currently utilized rely on a specific instructions to be followed, it is also true that some individuals may use different definitions and assumptions to rate both the presence and relevance of an individual risk factor. Therefore, it remains important that the setting in which the risk assessment is being discussed, whether court or a parole board hearing, continues to assess the level of knowledge and credibility of the professional undertaking the assessment. This should include as a minimum the attendance at training events aimed at understanding the risk assessment tool being used.

A final limitation to risk assessment, as the same for many assessments undertaken within the criminal justice system, is that any assessment undertaken is only as good as the information available. It is therefore the responsibility of the psychologist to indicate any limitation to their assessment based on the credibility and amount of information that was used to determine the individual's risk.

ALTERNATIVE ASSESSMENTS

Psychometric Assessment

A Psychometric Test is defined as 'a standardised or systematic form of examination in order to determine the absence or presence of a particular skill, knowledge or characteristic' (Gudjohnson, 2008). They are utilized in two main areas within forensic psychology: to discriminate between personality traits (e.g., psychopathy) seen as relevant to offending behaviour and to identify particular strengths and weaknesses or abilities that are relevant to risk (e.g., intelligence). Psychometrics are frequently used in risk assessments to aid formulation of risk management and treatment plans, which can then be communicated to the formal arenas in which forensic psychologists work. Therefore any test used in a given case must be relevant to the legal question being posed, this relevance to the case must be supported by published validation research as this provides both the professional and the hearing with defensible practice. An example of a psychometric test that is both relevant and validated is that of the PCL-R and the prediction of recidivism. However, an example of a psychometric that is often used where the validation data does not support its use although it is relevant to the question asked is the Wechsler Abbreviated Scale of Intelligence (WASI, Wechsler, 1999). This was originally designed and validated as a research tool but is commonly used by forensic psychologists as an assessment for determining if an individual meets the criteria for attendance at offending behaviour group work programmes. This highlights the balance between using assessments in the forensic context to provide evidence to help assess risk or treatment need with that of ensuring the assessments are fully validated, relevant to the question being posed and that they do not contradict with the rules of evidence or best practice guidance within the field of applied psychology.

Cognitive Functioning Assessments

In the wider context of the criminal justice system psychologists are often requested to undertake other assessments to aid decision making. In the context of court hearings psychologists are often requested to undertake assessments of cognitive functioning to provide evidence to aid the judge in sentencing decisions. The most common assessment used in this area is the Wechsler Adult Intelligence Scale (WAIS), with the WAIS–IV (Wechsler Adult Intelligence Scale – Fourth Edition, Wechsler, 2010) being the most recent version. While the research regarding the WAIS is numerous, it does raise some interesting questions for psychologists. The recognized criteria of Learning Disability as defined by the Department of Health; Mental Health Act (1983) involves set criteria including. A significantly reduced ability to understand complex information or learn new skills, as well as a reduced ability to cope independently on a day-to-day basis with the demands of his/her environment, both of which should have been present prior to adulthood.

Although an assessment such as the WAIS only measures the first of these criteria, the results of the assessment are often used by professionals to determine if an individual should be detained within a specialist learning disability hospital rather than in prison, a decision which can have significant implications for the offender in terms of sentence imposed. Again this is an example of psychological tests becoming over generalized in their usage.

Another aspect of assessments to determine an individuals level of cognitive functioning that raises ethical considerations for the psychology profession is that more recently assessments have been used to exclude offenders from programmes used to address risk of reoffending. In recent months the use of cognitive functioning assessments has led to criticism regarding both offending behaviour programmes and psychological treatment available to offenders to address their assessed level of risk. Where the use of psychological tests to determine an individuals IQ or level of functioning have indicated that the individual does not meet the criteria for the programme, without the prison system having an alternative option to provide to the offender has resulted in restricting the individual the opportunity to decrease their risk of reoffending and therefore reduced their opportunities for parole and other early release schemes. This has resulted in several legal cases challenging the continued detention of an offender who is unable to undertake treatment in prison and therefore demonstrate a reduction in his risk of reoffending. This further highlights another problem with risk assessment in general that has started to occur where professionals (both probation officers and psychologists) have started to consider which offending behaviour group work programmes an individual should undertake as a primary recommendation of the assessment rather than focus on the relevant risk factor and address more general ways in minimizing this risk. There is an argument that once an assessment has been made indicating that an individual requires a specialist intervention, it is the responsibility of criminal justice system to provide an offender the opportunity to undertake an intervention addressing their risk and therefore meet their role of protection of the public and reducing reoffending rates. Otherwise, as has been the case, offenders are left in an impossible situation of being assessed as risky without being able to address or minimize this risk, something that is in direct conflict with the main aims of forensic psychology. It could also be seen as creating conflict with the ethics of psychology as the offender is placed in a position where there are no options for treatment and therefore no chance of reducing their risk to the public.

A similar ethical dilemma exists in the area of personality assessments. Again an assessment of personality disorder can be used for various functions such as sentencing decisions, exclusion criteria for specific treatment programmes or assessments of risk. One of the rules for admissibility of expert testimony is that the probative evidence under consideration must outweigh the prejudicial effects. The term 'Personality Disorder' is a pejorative label and therefore is often prejudicial, particularly with the influence of the media that generally provides a negative portrayal of personality disorder. It is not enough for psychologists to undertake assessments on the understanding that the court has considered these factors; it is the responsibility of all psychologists to ensure that they are not just providing negative labels for individuals without considering possible implications to these assessments.

Physiological Assessments

Physiological measures are used to study the relationship between physiological activity and psychological states. Within the area of forensic psychology the most commonly used methods measure electro dermal activity, heart rate or sexual arousal measured by penile tumescence. Measures are taken during a resting state and as a measure to specific stimuli, following classical conditioning principles. In general methods measuring electro dermal activity or heart rate commonly seen in tests such as 'lie detectors' are not universally accepted within the criminal justice field and are rarely used to predict future behaviour. However, in the assessment of sex offenders physiological assessments are much more widely utilized and accepted as valid measures of future risk of offending. In the main, assessments are made with circumferential gauges; the most commonly used in Britain is the Penile Plethysmograph (PPG) and are used to distinguish between offenders and non-offenders as well as subgroups of offenders such as child offenders and rapists. The link to prediction of recidivism varies between populations. While there appears to be clear evidence that measures such as the PPG can discriminate between offenders who have a sexual preference for children and non-offenders, studies looking at rapists have not found a significantly strong correlation between physiological arousal and sexual recidivism as it may be that offenders who are stimulated by rape images may also be stimulated by images of non-sexual violence. It may be that in these cases arousal measures should be used within the context of assessing other cues to violence and aggression. William Murphy (2001) in the *Handbook of Offender Assessment* (Hollin, 2000) outlines, in more detail, the advantages and disadvantages of using such methods with sex offenders. In general physiological measures appear to have some benefit in assessing sexual recidivism. However, these measures should not be used as the sole criteria for risk assessment but alongside more traditional risk assessment methods to increase the validity of any prediction of future behaviour.

CONCLUSION

Any assessment undertaken within the forensic psychology field is fundamentally concerned with gathering data to enable a specific question or set of questions to be answered. This often requires the use of several different assessment methods such as self-report, structured interviews, scrutiny of file information, collection of data from third parties and direct or indirect observation. Today there is a range of assessment tools that are the most frequently used and generally accepted as valid tools in all areas of forensic assessment. These include risk assessment tools and guides, assessment measures for personality disorder and cognitive functioning assessments. Within these areas a range of psychometric assessments such as self-report questionnaires, actuarial assessments and those that rely on interview schedules can be used. The judgement of the individual psychologist is to determine the most appropriate tool to be used in any given assessment. This needs to include an understanding of the research literature for each assessment tool or approach, an ability to communicate this evidence to other professionals within the criminal justice system, an understanding and communication of the advantages and limitation of each assessment tool used and an ability to effectively communicate findings in a professional non-prejudicial way. Therefore, the role of the psychologist has become crucial not just in predicting future risk of an offender and assessing treatment and management options but also in encouraging an understanding within the wider criminal justice field of risk assessment and management in general.

RECOMMENDED FURTHER READING

Crighton and Towl (2008). *Psychology in Prisons,* 2nd edn. This has two good chapters on assessment. Chapter 5 is a broad summary on Psychological Assessment and Chapter 7 looks specifically at Risk Assessment.

Hollin (2001). *The Handbook of Offender Assessment & Treatment.* This book has a whole section on Risk Assessment including different types of assessment & assessment of different offenders.

REFERENCES

British Psychological Society (2010). *Psychologists as Expert Witnesses: Guidelines and Procedure for England and Wales.* Third Edition.

Cooke, D. J. (1998). 'Psychopathy across Cultures', in D. J. Cooke, A. E. Forth, and R. D. Hare (eds). *Psychopathy: Theory, Research and Implications for Society* (Dordrecht, The Netherlands: Kluwer Academic Publishing).

Crighton, D. A. and Towl, G. J. (2008). *Psychology in Prisons,* 2nd edn (Blackwell Publishing).

Gudjonsson, G. H. (2001). 'Psychometric Assessment', in C. R. Hollin (ed.) *Handbook of Offender Assessment and Treatment* (John Wiley and Sons).

Hare, R. D. (1991). *Manual for the Hare Psychopathy Checklist – Revised* (Toronto, Canada: Multi Health Systems).

Hart, S. D., Kropp, P. R., Laws, D. R., Klaver, J., Logan, C. and Watt, K. A. (2003). *The Risk for Sexual Violence Protocol: Structured Professional Guidelines for Assessing Risk of Sexual Violence* (Vancouver, Canada: Mental Health, Law and Policy Institute, Simon Fraser University).

Kropp, P. R., Hart, S. D., Webster, C. D. and Eaves, D. (1995). *Manual for Spousal Assault Risk Assessment Guide,* 2nd edn (Vancouver, Canada: British Columbia Institute on Family Violence).

Murphy, W. D. (2001). 'Psychophysiology and Risk Assessment', in Hollin, C. R. (ed.) *Handbook of Offender Assessment and Treatment* (John Wiley & Sons Ltd).

Quinsey, V. L., Harris, G. T., Rice, M. E. and Cormier, C. A. (2006). *Violent Offenders: Appraising and Managing Risk.* Second Edition (Washington, DC: American Psychological Association).

Shah, S. A. (1978). 'Dangerousness: A Paradigm for Exploring some Issues in Law and Psychology', *American Psychologist* 33, 224–38

Steadman, H. J. and Cocozza, J. J. (1974). *Careers of the Criminally Insane: Excessive Social Control of Deviance* (Lexington, MA: Lexington Books).

Thornberry T. P. and Jacoby J. E. (1979). *The Criminally Insane: A Community Follow-Up of Mentally Ill Offenders* (Chicago, IL: University of Chicago Press).

Towl, G. J., Farrington, D. P., Crighton D. A. and Hughes, G. (2008). *Dictionary of Forensic Psychology.* (Willan Publishing).

Webster, C. D., Douglas, K. S., Eaves, D. and Hart, S. D. (1997). *HCR-20: Assessing Risk for Violence, Version 2* (Vancouver, Canada: Mental Health, Law and Policy Institute, Simon Fraser University).

Weschler, D. (1999). *Weschler Abbreviated Scale of Intelligence.* (Pearson Assessment, UK).

Weschler, D. (2010). *Weschler Adult Intelligence Scale.* Fourth Edition (Pearson Assessment, UK).

5 Case Formulation

Ruby Bell

INTRODUCTION

A principal component of a forensic psychologist's role is to develop a psychological understanding of the client, usually in relation to offending behaviour. This work further informs us of treatment needs, and enhances risk assessment and management plans. A significant element of work in forensic settings is that of risk assessment, management and prediction. The evidence in relation to risk assessment results in an ever moving, evolving process. All forensic psychologists generally accept Structured Professional Judgement (SPJ) as the best approach to risk assessment. SPJ looks at risk factors both present and relevant to that individual and their offending behaviour. Rather than just identifying what risk factors are present, the practitioner uses this information by developing a formulation and, subsequently, potential scenarios that should be considered when evaluating risk. Given the formulation is based on a wide variety of sources and approaches, it enables the practitioner to engage with defensible decision making when making recommendations in relation to future management and treatment.

FORMULATION

Formulation can itself provide a test of the therapist's understanding of the client. It brings together information from a variety of sources and the multidisciplinary team involved in the service user's care.

The use of formulation is firmly embedded in the work of practitioner clinical psychologists – although formal research into its application and efficacy is somewhat sparse. Increasingly, forensic psychology is looking at utilizing clinical formulation as the basis of assessment and treatment (see Sturmey and McMurran, 2011). To look at how it can be applied in forensic settings, it is helpful to draw on some of the clinical literature.

There is no one 'right' way to carry out a formulation (Harper and Moss, 2003) – this will depend on context, the theoretical model used and also the aim of the formulation.

In recent times, (and this is especially true in forensic settings), there has been an emphasis on the psychosocial aspects of a person's functioning, and other influencing factors – such as the role of biological/organic aspects can be lost (Dexter-Smith, 2010).

Whichever model of formulation is used, it should be seen as a basic framework on which to hang all apparently disparate pieces of information in order to bring it all together in a logical sequence and create a greater understanding of the person one is working with. This will inform assessments of risk, treatment needs and will identify which aspects of the person's functioning are necessary, and amenable, to change.

The use of an agreed model of formulation is useful when working in teams. It allows a common understanding of service users who generally are complex individuals with complex and challenging behaviours and needs. An agreed formulation results in improved understanding and communication across services.

Margison and Brown (2007) summarize the advantages of formulation as follows:

a. Conceptualization, i.e., the formulation 'draws together descriptive, evaluative, causative and predictive factors' (box 1.7, p. 18). Information is brought together under different headings thereby facilitating a conceptual overview. This will lead to recommendations for treatment and management.
b. Stable Focus – it allows the therapist and client to retain focus. Especially with such a complex client group, it is easy for 'therapeutic drift' to occur.
c. Sets Limits – attempting to (or being coerced to) achieve unrealistic therapeutic demands is damaging to both the therapist and client. Here, the agreed formulation acts as a 'reference point to avoid extending the therapy in response to countertransference pressures' (Margison and Brown, 2007).
d. Predicts, blocks resistance and likely transference – the formulation helps the therapist to identify potential areas of difficulty.
e. Sets goals – formulation can help specify treatment goals – these should be agreed by the therapist **and** client – although this can prove challenging in forensic settings.

DEFINITION OF FORMULATION

So, what is formulation? There is no one agreed definition – although those who have attempted to define this concept tend to draw on similar themes – differing only on theoretical underpinnings and therapeutic focus.

Formulation has developed in forensic psychology, moving from a simplistic behavioural analysis, ABC (antecedents, behaviour, consequences) through extended functional analysis, to a much more comprehensive framework capturing a great deal of information.

The word 'formulation' is frequently used interchangeably with case formulation, clinical formulation and case conceptualization. Hence there are many definitions on which to draw, and these vary according to which theoretical approach one adopts (e.g., Cognitive Behavioural Therapy – CBT and Cognitive Analytic Therapy – CAT).

Eells (2007, p. 1) defines case formulation in psychotherapy as 'a hypothesis about the causes, precipitants and maintaining influences of a persons psychological, interpersonal and behavioural problems'.

In a recent paper, Hart, Sturmey, Logan and McMurran (2011) define formulation as 'the process or product of gathering and integrating diverse information to develop a concise account of the nature and aetiology of the problems affecting a person's mental health to guide ideographic treatment design and other decision making' (p. 118).

Despite the current focus, formulation is not new; it has featured across the literature for decades. Previous definitions include 'a provisional explanation or hypothesis of how an individual comes to present with a certain disorder or circumstance at a particular point in time' (Weerasekera, 1996, p. 4).

Kuyken, Padesky and Dudley (2005) offer a definition of CBT case conceptualization as

> a process whereby therapist and client work collaboratively first to describe and then to explain the issues a client presents in therapy. Its primary function is to guide therapy in order to relieve client distress and build client resilience.
>
> (p. 3)

Whatever definition is utilized, it remains that a case formulation is a framework designed to help the therapist make sense of a large amount of information, identifying what the current problems are, how they developed and how they are maintained. The forensic psychologist aims to offer informed 'ideas' about causal or functional relationships between variables/issues and the presenting problem. From this, treatment needs can be identified and management plans devised.

HOW TO CREATE A FORMULATION

It is not possible to detail all components contributing to a comprehensive formulation within the constraints of this chapter. The reader is advised to seek further information in some of the texts referenced later. Practitioners using case formulation are 'guided more by principles and less by the manual' (Persons *et al.*, 2006, p. 1048).

Most therapeutic approaches (e.g., cognitive behavioural therapy, CBT; Cognitive Analytic therapy, CAT; Psychodynamic Psychotherapy, Family therapy) have formulation as central to the therapeutic process. These differ, sometimes in very subtle ways, in where the focus lies. It remains the case that most work on formulation has been produced in non-forensic settings. However, Hart *et al.* (2011) in a helpful article examining the issues in relation to the practice and evaluation of forensic case formulation have identified certain key features required when developing formulation. These are summarized as:

1. Inferential – i.e., providing an explanation rather than just describing situations, facts and so on. They view formulation as a form of 'Abductive Inference'. Abduction utilizes observations in order to make informed explanations and predictions of future behaviour. The therapist does not know the level of its accuracy, and these explanations are only a few of many potential scenarios.

2. Action centred – here, the formulation provides a basis of understanding of the client's problems and allows the therapist to prioritize treatment and management strategies. Eells and Lombart (2011) concur – stating that formulation must have treatment utility.

   Increasingly, when developing sentence plans and care pathways, this aspect is of particular appeal to Courts, Parole Board, Mental Health Review Tribunals and so on. In addition, with the introduction of Key Performance Indicators (KPIs), and Payments by Results (PBR), the formulation and identified treatment needs can only be of increasing focus and attention.

3. Theory Driven – as stated above, different theoretical approaches will identify different behaviours to target. All are valid (Sturmey, 2009) and helpful in aiding the therapist. The fact is the forensic and clinical issues that clients bring are often too complex to identify easily, hence having a therapeutic model helps make the process more manageable.

   The American Psychological Association Task Force (2006) on evidence-based practice in psychology state that formulations must be evidence-based. As stated earlier, there is a lack of evidence and research generally in this area and there is even no agreement as what would constitute evidence!

4. Individualized – while the formulation is based on a specific theory, it also focuses on the client's personal life and history. Should the therapist move to a more general non-individualized focus, interventions are chosen to deal with the average person with this sort of problem. The purpose of formulation is to decide 'what will work best for this particular problem, in light of this person's unique history, current situation, and possible futures?' (Hart, 2003, p. 120).

5. Narrative – i.e., the information in a formulation is based on language and is not a numeric calculation or formula. The authors further identify what makes a good narrative, i.e., it has two important features:
   a. It compares information, making clear the motivation and emotional meaning of the behaviour.
   b. It has a plot that helps to give structure to the narrative – influencing what is in the formulation and how it is structured.

   Hart (2003) states that formulation should be viewed as an 'anchored narrative' in terms of the theoretical framework and the facts pertaining to an individual case. In other words, the formulation in many ways can be seen as a story, but one that is based on facts and reasonably accurate information that centres on the problem the individual presents. This information can provide a (one of several) rationale or explanation of how the problem came about, and using this information, combined with a grounding in psychological theory, the psychologist can offer potential scenarios that may be played out in the future. All aspects of the formulation provide the basis for treatment targets.

6. Diachronic – much of our assessment in forensic psychology is based on the old adage that the best predictor of future behaviour is past behaviour. While it is essential we have as much historical information as possible – it is not a given that people will do the same thing again. People do change and mature and are not necessarily subject to the same environmental factors as previously. Formulation must, however, span time, including the past, present and future.

7. Testable – any formulation is developed in order to offer an explanation of problems, and how and why they developed and also to identify areas to target for change (treatment targets). This means that the formulation is testable. If expected results do not ensue, then the information should be reviewed in order to offer an alternative formulation.

In their review of the literature, Eells and Lombard (2011) suggest that for any formulation to positively contribute to an individual and the problems they experience, it must meet five goals:

(i) It should aim to be as accurate as possible for the individual being assessed.
(ii) It should have treatment utility.
(iii) It should be comprehensive **enough** – and represent enough information in order to be clinically beneficial. They refer to the formulation as being 'parsimonious' (p. 6).
(iv) It should offer a balance between description and explanation, i.e., it should do more than just summarize biographical information.
(v) It should be evidence-based.

They go on to say that should these goals be met, the therapist is more likely to be developing an effective and useful tool in order to progress treatment.

BASIC FORMULATION

In practice, the forensic psychologist will choose an orientation and develop a formulation based on their preferred model of treatment (for example CBT, CAT). Across most forensic services, clinicians are introduced at an early stage to the 4 Ps (or 5Ps) model of formulation. It is simple but can capture a significant amount of information.

Weerasekara's (1996) 4P model is devised from Cognitive Therapy and offers an integrative approach to formulation. This simple model facilitates a structured and systematic approach to the collation of information and helps generate a process of how it all fits together. It draws on the functional analysis approach, that is, looking at past events and current momentary factors, but also looking at the coping style of the individual. The 4 Ps are:

a. Predisposing Factors – i.e. these are factors that result in the client being more vulnerable to certain things. Here we are looking at childhood abuse/trauma, inconsistent parenting, family history of mental illness etc.
b. Precipitating Factors – these can be seen as the triggers of the problem/event that occurred near to the problem, e.g., divorce, bereavement, illegal substance use, assault.
c. Perpetuating Factors – these are the factors that maintain the problem and keep it going. Examples here include the client's beliefs, substance misuse or secondary gains from the presenting problem/offending behaviour.
d. Protective Factors – these factors are more helpful and can offer some protection from the problem in providing the client with a level of resilience to the problem developing. These may be internal or external, e.g., family support, good social skills or sense of humour.

The fifth 'P' is the 'Presenting Problem' – this may be a particular type of offending behaviour, or drug use or aspects of mental illness. Weerasekara (1996) also includes 'coping styles' – that is, identifying the specific ways/characteristics a client uses to deal with problems. These can be complex and variable and the model draws a distinction between dispositional and episodic coping styles.

We all have identifiable ways of reacting to stress and distress. In the 4 Ps model this is broken down in to four areas:

(i) Dispositional – i.e., enduring personal style that identifies the client's general style of coping with events.
(ii) Episodic – more variable styles of coping with different situations.

(iii) Individual – including biological, cognitive and behavioural influences.
(iv) Systemic – i.e., patterns of interpersonal or family relationships; social and occupational aspects.

Figure 5.1 illustrates a potential formulation based on this model.

For this client, in terms of coping style, it seems the individual relies on drugs, (both legal and illegal), which indicates he is more accepting of a biological approach. The client maintains contact with family (father) and it may be that there are unresolved problems which when exposed result in violence. Some coping mechanisms can be regarded as systemic – violence as a means of resolution of family conflicts has been present since early childhood.

This offers only some potential explanations or aspects of the formulation. Dallos *et al.* (2006) suggest the 4 (5) Ps model is helpful; in that it allows a systematic and comprehensive analysis but that there are many limitations to the approach. Increasingly, the role of the psychologist is seen as an essential element of therapeutic success. The psychologist as reflective practitioner is at the core of clinical and forensic psychology training. The model described places little emphasis in the therapeutic alliance – which is essential if both the therapist and client are going to be able to progress in treatment. In addition, it does not allow for reflection or reformulation as therapy continues. The model also refers to different aspects (e.g., individual, systemic and so on) but whichever explanation is chosen influences the treatment offered. It is unclear as to whether the approaches can or should be combined in furthering treatment. One of the main issues is that it offers a somewhat simplistic, linear formulation with the assumption that an effective outcome will naturally progress when targeting specific areas. The model does not allow for lapse, relapse etc. It is also clear that the formulation is psychologist driven (albeit based on the client's information); there is little evidence of collaboration or client input in to the process.

Figure 5.1 *A potential formulation*

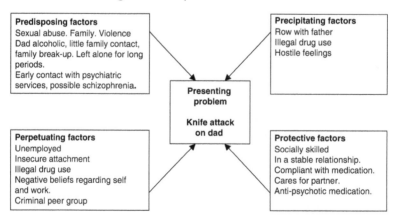

LONGITUDINAL FORMULATION

The 4 Ps model has evolved into a longitudinal form. While still somewhat basic, it allows the forensic psychologist more scope for identifying core beliefs and rules for living – and is based on the work of Judith Beck (1995; 2005). The incorporation of schemas, core beliefs and rules is especially helpful in forensic situations where there are frequently very strong rules underlying the client's behaviour. Beck emphasizes the need for the formulation to make logical sense to the client and that it is an ever-changing process subject to repeated updates and revision.

Grosse, Holtforth and Castonguay (2005) assert that any repeated behaviour by an organism is an attempt to meet a need within it. They divide these motivations into approach or avoidance goals – approach goals being those the individual seeks out and avoidance goals – as the name suggests – those that the individual avoids. Approach goals may include such things as intimacy, control, status etc. and avoidance – humiliation, helplessness, vulnerability etc. The identification of these goals can be helpful in identifying treatment targets. However, these are not easy to access – most core beliefs and subsequent goals are not immediately near the individual's conscious thoughts.

Formulation again helps the client to understand the developmental processes involved and links made as to why the problem recurs – rather than 'it just happens – it's nothing to do with me'.

A simple longitudinal formulation may look like the diagram overleaf. Already the information is presented in such a way as to identify potential targets for treatment.

ISSUES SURROUNDING FORMULATIONS

I sometimes think that 99 per cent of the suffering that comes in through my door has to do with how devalued people feel by the labels that have been applied to them or the derogatory opinions they hold about themselves.

(Hoffman, 1993, p. 79)

This view is particularly true with the client group we work with in forensic services. All through life they have been labelled 'troublemaker, bad, abused, victim, personality disordered, psychopathic, treatment resistant' and so on. For years, behaviours have been pathologized which when reviewed using case formulation, results in a very different opinion. An extreme example of this is the 'disease' drapetomania, identified in the 1850s by a well-respected doctor at the time, Dr. Samuel Cartwright. A medic who had published widely, based in the University of Louisiana, Dr. Cartwright identified this disease diagnosed only in the black slave population – characterized by a repeated desire to run

Figure 5.2 *A longitudinal formulation*

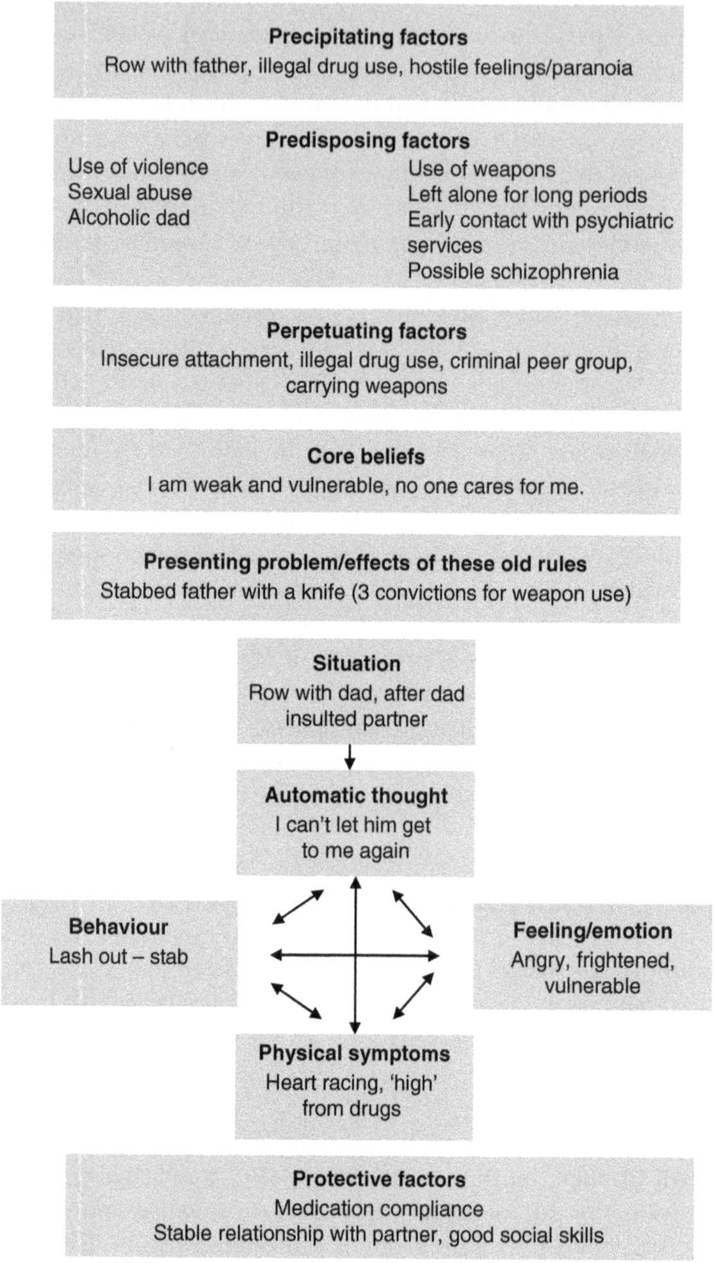

Precipitating factors
Row with father, illegal drug use, hostile feelings/paranoia

Predisposing factors

Use of violence	Use of weapons
Sexual abuse	Left alone for long periods
Alcoholic dad	Early contact with psychiatric services
	Possible schizophrenia

Perpetuating factors
Insecure attachment, illegal drug use, criminal peer group, carrying weapons

Core beliefs
I am weak and vulnerable, no one cares for me.

Presenting problem/effects of these old rules
Stabbed father with a knife (3 convictions for weapon use)

Situation
Row with dad, after dad insulted partner

Automatic thought
I can't let him get to me again

Behaviour
Lash out – stab

Feeling/emotion
Angry, frightened, vulnerable

Physical symptoms
Heart racing, 'high' from drugs

Protective factors
Medication compliance
Stable relationship with partner, good social skills

away usually from abusive masters. The other disease he identified at this time was 'dysaethesia aethiopica', a disease causing 'rascality' in black people, both free and enslaved. While this is derisible now – there are lessons to be learnt. The person we see before us is not just an offender or mentally disordered.

There are many contributory factors that result in why that person presents in the manner they currently do. All have a story that we need to make sense of. Formulation is clearly integral to providing such understanding.

However hard the therapist tries, no one formulation will be fully inclusive and explanatory of all issues the client brings. The process of formulation is so complex, not least because all involved have differing views, opinions and agendas. In forensic settings, we aim to produce a formulation within differing systems (health, criminal justice, social etc.) which have different agendas, and which do not apply or regard to all models equally. The first major issue is agreeing what, if anything, the problem actually is. Our clients, in reality, do not present with one problem – however, the therapist is often compelled to focus on one, and this is frequently chosen for us (e.g., offending behaviour).

It remains the case that there is a dearth of research looking at the validity and efficacy of formulation. Bieling and Kuyken (2003), when reviewing the research, suggest 'current evidence for the reliability of the cognitive case formulation method is modest at best' and is often contradictory (Kuyken, 2006). The formulation(s) the therapist (or therapist and client) devises offers only potential explanations of a specific set of observations. The fact is that we do not know if the formulation is complete or correct, but it is our best professional judgement at that time. Eells (1997) identifies several functions of formulation – in organizing vast amounts of information; providing a 'blueprint' for treatment and allowing the therapist to identify future risks (such as resistance, therapy-interfering behaviours and risk behaviours). Additionally, formulation allows us to measure change and, by facilitating understanding of the client's issues, promotes empathy and enhances the therapeutic alliance. The latter is increasingly being shown to be a significant factor in effective psychological interventions.

This chapter has deliberately focussed on the basic structure of formulation that is usually common to all theoretical approaches. As the practitioner develops, there is a move to a different, apparently more refined, model of formulation (see Figure 5.3 as an example).

While adhering to a theoretical model allows the therapist to maintain focus, adhering rigidly to a formulation can be counter-productive. This frequently occurs when the therapist is using an evidence base relevant to the client group that serves only to identify what cannot be done or provided. Dallos *et al.* (2006) suggest that the pressure to focus on evidence-based interventions has actually resulted in more constraints as to what is regarded as legitimate therapeutic activity. While this can be a challenge ethically, unless we adapt to the constraints

Figure 5.3 *A more refined model of formulation*

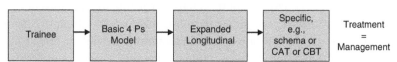

of the system in which the client is being treated, we are likely to become frustrated and demoralized when producing a broad, all-inclusive formulation.

Other authors advocate a more eclectic approach. Eells and Lambert (2004) suggest that multiple theoretic models can offer a great deal to formulation. They suggest several separate formulations each impacting on identified treatment needs. Others aim for an integrated formulation, incorporating different approaches (behavioural, cognitive, psychodynamic etc.), which allows the therapist to choose a variety of interventions and approaches throughout the treatment (e.g., Weerasekera, 1996).

There is a danger when completing the initial formulation, that this conceptualization is locked into and that there is selection of evidence and information that supports the formulation. Formulation is not a quick and easy skill; it takes a great deal of time, thought and reflection.

One of the major issues with such formulations, particularly when working with incarcerated populations, is that both the client and therapist are frequently not working with current behaviours and scenarios – and are attempting to work on state-dependant ways of thinking and behaviour which proves challenging in the extreme – especially when someone is working on issues that were evident many years prior to the intervention. And yet one of the requirements of a formulation is that it is testable. The work of Lawrence Jones, at Rampton Hospital, on Offence Paralleling Behaviours (OPB) – see Daffern, Jones and Shine (2010) – may help improve the reliability and validity of the formulation in this respect. Jones (2004, p. 38) defines OPB as 'Any form of offence related behavioural (or fantasized behaviour) pattern that emerges at any point before or after an offence. It does not have to result in an offence, it simply needs to resemble, in some significant respect, the sequence of behaviours leading up to the offence'. Daffern *et al.* (2007) advocate the inclusion of OPBs in case formulation which can be measured and, as such, evaluated as to their utility, reliability and validity. Should this be demonstrated, it can serve only to increase the accuracy of the formulation.

CONCLUSION

Forensic psychology as a discipline is increasingly prominent in mental health settings. Here, there is frequently a (incorrect) logic applied that purports that mental illness is the root cause of all problems (including risk). Hence, at its most simplistic, if the mental illness is treated and stabilized, the risk is reduced. The link between mental illness and violence is more complex and cannot be reviewed within the constraints of this chapter. Clearly, the therapist does need to look at how and if the symptoms have impacted on the client's decision to offend, and the role of delusions and hallucinations in violent offending has been supported (Bentall and Taylor, 2006). However, Sturmey and McMurran

(2011) advise that while 'symptoms of mental illness do ... have relevance in case formulation ... care should be taken not to ignore other risk factors that apply more generally' (p. 291).

However the therapist approaches formulation, the fact remains there is little evidence as to its efficacy in the forensic arena. There is much to learn from clinical practitioners in non-forensic settings. Despite the limited evidence base, formulation allows us to go beyond a mere description, diagnosis, or statistic; it facilitates explanation, identifies origins of the problems and addresses individual needs. The problems lie not with formulation itself but rather with the empirical research underpinning its utility. Forensic populations, specifically those with mental illness and/or personality disorders have complex histories and complex needs – formulation is the most effective way of presenting, agreeing and making sense of the individual.

RECOMMENDED FURTHER READING

Dallos, R., Wright, J., Stedman, J. and Johnstone, L. (2006). 'Integrative Formulation', in L. Johnstone and R. Dallos eds *Formulation in Psychology and Psychotherapy: Making Sense of People's Problems* (London: Routledge). This is a good introduction to formulation for the novice practitioner. It guides the reader through a variety of psychological models of formulation to aid application and practice in understanding clients' problems and identified treatment goals, 154–81.

Division of Clinical Psychology (2011). 'Good Practice Guidelines on the use of psychological formulation', *The British Psychological Society*, Leicester.

Hart, S., Sturmey, P., Logan, C. and McMurran, M. (2011). 'Forensic Case Formulation', *International Journal of Forensic Mental Health* 10, 118–26. There is a dearth of literature regarding the use of formulation with forensic clients. This is an excellent summary of current practice and issues.

REFERENCES

Adshead, G. and Brown, C. (2003). *Ethical Issues in Forensic Mental Health Research* (London: Jessica Kingsley Publishers Ltd).

American Psychological Association Presidential Task Force (2006). 'Evidence-Based Practice in Psychology', *American Psychologist* 61(4), 271–85.

Beck, J. S. (1995). *Cognitive Therapy: Basics and Beyond* (New York: Guilford Press).

Beck, J. S. (2005). *Cognitive Therapy for Challenging Problems* (New York: Guilford Press).

Bentall, R. P and Taylor, J. L. (2006). 'Psychological Processes and Paranoia: Implications for Forensic Behavioural Science', *Behavioural Sciences and the Law* 24, 123–42.

Bieling, P. J. and Kuyken, W. (2003). 'Is Cognitive Case Formulation Science or Science Fiction?', *Clinical Psychology: Science and Practice* 10(1), 52–69.

Daffern, M., Jones, L., Howells, K., Shine, J., Mikton, C. and Tunbridge, V. (2007). 'Editorial – Refining the Definition of Offence Paralleling Behaviour', *Criminal Behaviour and Mental Health* 17, 265–73.

Daffern, M., Jones, L. and Shine, J. (2010). *Offence Paralleling Behaviour: A Case Formulation Approach to Offender Assessment and Intervention* (Chichester: John Wiley & Sons).

Dallos, R., Wright, J., Stedman, J. and Johnstone, L. (2006). 'Integrative Formulation', in L. Johnstone and R. Dallos (eds) *Formulation is Psychology and Psychotherapy: Making Sense of People's Problems* (London: Routledge).

Dexter-Smith, S. (2010) 'Integrating Psychological Formulations in to Older People's Services – Three Years On (Part 1)', PSIGE Newsletter, 112, October Pub.: The British Psychological Society, 8–11.

Eells, T. D. (1997). 'Psychotherapy Case Formulation: History and Current Status',. In T. D. Eells (ed.) *Handbook of Psychotherapy Case Formulation,* 2nd edn (New York: Guilford Press).

Eells, T. D. and Lombart, K. G. (2004). 'Case Formulation: Determining the Focus in Brief Dynamic Psychohterapy', in D. P. Charman (ed.) *Core Processes in Brief Psychodynamic psychotherapy,* (Lawrence Erlbaum Associates: Mahwah, NJ), 119–44.

Eells, T. D. and Lombart, K. G. (2011) 'Theoretical and Evidence-Based Approaches to Case Formulation' in P. Sturmey and M. McMurran (eds) *Forensic Case Formulation* (Chichester: John Wiley & Sons).

Graham, H. L. (2004). *Cognitive-Behavioural Integrated Treatment (C-BIT): A Treatment Manual for Substance Misuse in People with Severe Mental Health Problems* (Chichester: John Wiley & Sons).

Grosse Holtforth, M. and Castonguay, L. G. (2005). 'Relationship and Techniques in Cognitive-Behavioral Therapy – A Motivational Approach', *Psychotherapy Theory Research Practice Training* 42(4), 443–55.

Harper R. and Moss, G. (2003). 'A Different Kind of Chemistry? Reformulating "Formulation"', *Clinical Psychology* 25, 6–10.

Hart, S. (2003). 'Violence Risk Assessment, an Anchored Narrative Approach', in M. Vanderhallen, G. Vervaeke, P. J. Van Koppen and J. Gaethals (eds) *Much Ado About Crime: Chapters on Psychology and Law* (Brussels: Vitgeverij Politeia, NV), 209–30.

Hart, S., Sturmey, P., Logan, C. and McMurran, M. (2011). 'Forensic Case Formulation', *International Journal of Forensic Mental Health*, 10, 118–26.

Hoffman, L. (1993). *Exchanging Voices: A Collaborative Approach to Family Therapy* (London: Karnac).

Johnstone, L. and Dallos, R. (2006). *Formulation in Psychology and Psychotherapy: Making Sense of People's Problems* (Hove: Routledge).

Jones, L. (2004). 'Offence Paralleling Behaviour (OPB) as a Framework for Assessment and Interventions with Offenders', in A. Needs and G. Towl (eds) *Applying Psychology to Forensic Practice* (Oxford: Blackwell).

Kuyken, W. (2006). 'Evidence-Based Case Formulation: Is the Emperor Clothed?', in A. Tarrier (ed.) *Case Formulation in Cognitive Behaviour Therapy* (Hove: Brumner – Routledge).

Margison, F. and Brown, P. (2007). 'Assessment in Psychotherapy', in J. Naismith and S. Grant (eds) *Seminars in the Psychotherapies* (London: Royal College of Psychiatrists).

Persons, J. B., Roberts, N. A., Zalecki, C. A. and Brechwald, W. A. G. (2006). 'Naturalistic Outcome of Case Formulation-Driven Cognitive-Behavior Therapy for Anxious Depressed Outpatients', *Behaviour Reaearch & Therapy* 44, 1041–51.

Sturmey, P. (2009). *Varieties of Case Formulation* (Chichester, UK: Wiley).

Sturmey, P. and McMurran, M. (2011). 'Forensic Case Formulation: Emerging Issues', in P. Sturmey and M. McMurran (eds) *Forensic Case Formulation* (Chichester: John Wiley & Sons).

Weerasekera, P. (1996). *Mulitperspective Case Formulation: A Step Towards Treatment Integration* (Florida: Malabar).

6 Report Writing

Sue Evershed

INTRODUCTION

Report writing is fundamental to the work of a forensic psychologist. Reports may be required for a variety of different reasons and in different settings, but the ultimate purpose of all reports remains the same. It is to provide 'information, advice, guidance and feedback to personnel, agencies and organisations to enable effective problem solving and decision making, formulation and implementation of policy and practice' (BPS, 2011).

Report writing is a complex skill requiring the assimilation of different types of information into an integrated whole. Reports have to inform, explain and frequently persuade a variety of different readers, and assist them to reach a well-researched and well-argued conclusion. Evidence suggests that well-presented solution-based information affects readers' expectations about the ability of the offender to change, and can influence their views about their potential to misbehave. Well-communicated explanatory information, on the other hand, affects the readers' emotional reactions and the degree of exceptionality they will allow the offender. Reports also form a significant part of the historical record that will follow offenders for the duration of their engagement with the criminal justice system, if not for the rest of their lives. Hence a good report should be comprehensive, logical, balanced and clear.

Although research in this area is limited, there is evidence to suggest that reports do influence perception and expectations (Greenfield and Gottschalk, 2009). Unfortunately there is also evidence demonstrating that poor-quality reports have an impact on the opinions of readers and can be dangerous (Mertens, 1976).

The process of report writing should also involve the offender in a meaningful and collaborative way, to ensure that they can understand and utilize the information and that they will be inclined to engage in a similar process in the future. Meeting the needs of both the offender and the professional bodies requiring the report can be a difficult feat for the forensic psychologist, who often has to balance a clear communication of risk with the need to maintain a therapeutic relationship with the offender.

It is therefore not surprising to discover that psychologists often find report writing difficult, and that consumers are frequently dissatisfied with the results. While this chapter is far from an exhaustive list of report writing 'dos and don'ts', it introduces some of the issues to consider when planning and executing reports. It also gives some guidance to forensic psychologists about the disclosure of reports to offenders.

LEGAL, PROFESSIONAL AND ETHICAL CONSIDERATIONS

Prior to engaging the offender in the assessment process and even before planning a forensic report, the report writer has a number of important processes and complex issues to consider.

Professional Guidelines

The British Psychological Society (BPS) and the Health Professions Council (HPC) are the professional bodies that regulate the work of forensic psychologists. Both organizations have issued codes of conduct and guidelines regarding the work of psychologists (BPS, 2008 and 2009; HPC, 2008). Forensic psychologists should be familiar with and abide by these standards in all the professional work they undertake.

The HPC *Standards of Conduct, Performance and Ethics* (2008), and the BPS *Code of Ethics and Conduct* (2009) both direct psychologists to treat clients with respect, to act within their areas of competence and to perform their duties with honesty and integrity. Along with the BPS *Generic Professional Practice Guidelines* (2008), they include some specific guidelines which are relevant to the writing of reports in areas such as confidentiality and its limits, obtaining informed consent, disclosure and open reporting, keeping accurate records and communicating effectively. There are references to the guidelines throughout this chapter, but it is not possible to incorporate all the relevant guidelines here. It is recommended that psychologists familiarize themselves with these guidelines before embarking on assessment or report writing activity.

Legal Considerations

Several aspects of the report writing process are governed by legal requirements. For offenders who are subject to the Mental Health Act (2007) there is guidance for the preparation and disclosure of reports to Mental Health Review Tribunals. These are outlined in the chapter.

The Mental Capacity Act (2005) has laid out requirements for psychologists who work with vulnerable offenders in matters of gaining informed consent. The Act specifies the criteria for judging an offender's capacity to make informed decisions and stipulates what psychologists should do if the offender lacks capacity. In general, the Act states that psychologists should assume capacity unless all practicable steps have been taken to assist in appropriate decision making. While the Act is more relevant to obtaining consent for the process of assessment and evaluation, it is worth becoming familiar with the basic tenets in order to guide the process of informing the offender about the process of report writing.

The Data Protection Act (1998) gives individuals the right to know what information is held about them and provides a framework to ensure that personal information is handled properly. With regard to report writing this means that psychologists must ensure that any personal information they collect is (among other things) accurate, kept securely and not kept for longer than is necessary. It also requires that individuals have the right to find out what personal information is held on them within forty days of making a formal request.

With respect to reports for court proceedings, any notes made as a part of an assessment or evaluation can be called upon as evidence along with the report. Thus it is important to make them as legible and transparent as possible.

Confidentiality

The BPS and HPC professional guidelines and codes of conduct state that information given to psychologists should remain confidential unless the client gives consent to disclose. However, there are recognized exceptions to this if the safety or welfare of the client, or of others, is at risk. With a view to the evaluation or assessment of risk, this is almost always the case, and is the purpose of the report. Thus, psychologists should not promise full confidentiality in these contexts and should inform the offender of the limits. However, psychologists should not disclose confidential information outside of the parties and organizations involved in the reporting process. They should also only disclose information relevant to the issues in hand.

Multiple Roles and Biases

The mixing of roles is an issue that is frequently raised as a concern when psychologists work with offenders, particularly when there is a mixing of therapy and assessment roles with the same offender (Evans and Hearn, 1997; Knapp and VandeCreek, 2001). This commonly occurs when a psychologist who has worked with an offender in a treatment role is asked to prepare an end-of-treatment report that includes an assessment of continuing risk.

There is a view that as the treatment provider, the psychologist is the most knowledgeable source of information about the offender. However, combining the objective and detached approach required of a risk assessor with the supportive and non-judgemental approach of the therapist is a difficult task. Strasburger, Gutheil and Brodsky (1997) argue that to take on either role compromises capacity to fulfil the other. As a treatment provider, taking on an additional risk-assessment role could jeopardize the therapeutic alliance with the offender. As a risk assessor, it is difficult to evaluate evidence of risk objectively while trying to maintain a non-judgemental stance. Most writers advise against mixing the two roles, especially in forensic settings and suggest that separate psychologists perform separate roles (Haag, 2006; Iverson 2000).

However, although dual roles should *generally* be avoided, it cannot be assumed that they *always* impair objectivity, competence and effectiveness. Strous (2009) makes the case, especially when working with children and vulnerable offenders, that there may be good reasons to mix roles. For example, some offenders may be more willing to enter into therapy when the therapist is a psychologist with whom they have established rapport during an assessment; and others offenders may be less resistant to providing assessment information when the assessor is a psychologist whom he or she has come to trust in therapy. He argues that many therapists are able to accept offenders in a non-judgemental manner, yet still challenge them on objective facts. There are also circumstances where resources do not allow the separation of the two roles.

Regardless of the reasons, psychologists do find themselves in a position where the production of a report inevitably causes a mixing of the two roles. In these circumstances, they should state this explicitly in the report (Haag, 2006) and seek supervision in the preparation and execution of the report from a source who has not been involved in the case.

Who is the Client?

In the UK the vast majority of reports prepared by forensic psychologists concern individuals accused of or already convicted of an offence. Writing forensic reports on accused or convicted individuals begs the question: 'who is the client?' In most areas of applied psychology, the answer to this question is usually straightforward: the client is typically the person with whom the psychologist is working and this person has generally sought the help of psychologist in addressing some acknowledged difficulties in functioning. In forensic psychology, however, where the person referred often has not sought help and sometimes does not acknowledge the existence of any difficulties, the question is more complex. In this arena, where a key aim of the work is to protect the public, it can be argued that the offender is not the only client. Brodsky (1980) argues that the court, or the government department, working on behalf of society in requesting the report, is also a client.

Some writers suggest that the role undertaken by the psychologist in relation to the offender determines the identity of the client. They propose that when writing a risk assessment report (to assess the danger of future harm to the public) the decision-making body (e.g., Parole Board, Mental Health Tribunal, court) is the client. However, when a psychologist's role is that of treatment provider, then the offender should be viewed as the client (Haag, 2006; Ogloff, 1995).

In practice the distinction is not so clear-cut, since psychologists are often required to fulfil multiple roles with offenders. It may be more helpful if the psychologist considers both the individual and the public (as represented by the decision-making body) as clients, and attempts to address the agenda for both clients: defining the ongoing risk posed, but also outlining their associated needs and explaining the tasks required of the offender to ameliorate their risk.

Whether one takes this view or believes that the client alters according to the role undertaken, in all circumstances, there remains a duty of care to the offender to preserve their rights with regard to consent, confidentiality and the avoidance of harm (BPS, 2008).

Informed Consent

The BPS *Code of Ethics and Conduct* states that psychologists should 'seek to obtain the informed consent of all clients to whom professional services or research participation are offered' (BPS, 2009, p. 12, sec 1.3 (iii)). The BPS *Professional Practice Guidelines* (2008) give advice on the type of information that should be provided to allow this to happen. In this context, the psychologist will ask for the offender's consent to engage in the assessment or intervention process, about which the report is to be written. Information therefore needs to be given to the offender about the assessment or intervention process in order to make a properly informed choice about whether to engage in the process or whether to decline.

Information also needs to be given about the report writing process itself. The offender should be made aware of the role, function and competency of the report writer, and the extent of their power and responsibilities. They should be given information about the nature and purpose of the report and the likely outcomes (benefits and risks). The report writer should also explain the use of information from other parties (e.g., police), the offender's rights of access to the report, as well as those of any other party and the limits of confidentiality. The Mental Capacity Act (2005) stipulates how psychologists should judge whether or not offenders have the capacity to make informed decisions. Its relevance lies primarily to the process of obtaining informed consent to engage in the assessment or evaluation process, but the spirit of the Act is a useful guide when the psychologist provides information about the report writing process.

Should the offender choose not to give consent, it is important to remember that the offender is refusing to engage in the process of assessment or intervention, rather than refusing permission for the report to be written. If the offender declines to give consent, the psychologist can still write a report based on information available from other sources. However, the report should acknowledge that the offender has declined to engage in the process (explaining their reasons for doing so); and it must clearly point out the resulting limitations of fact and application.

It is good practice to seek the offender's opinions of the report in final draft (whether they have engaged or not) and to note in the report any comments, challenges or disagreements.

Writing in a Forensic Environment

Unusual ethical dilemmas arise when practising in a forensic environment. A recurring issue facing forensic psychologists is the issue of consent, given of free will. The culture within forensic environments rewards the offender for compliance with assessment and treatment. Offenders who comply are likely to progress through the system towards release more easily and earn the right to greater freedom and privileges. Given these consequences, it could be argued that a forensic psychologist, especially one working in a secure setting, can rarely obtain genuine consent, given of free will. *The Code of Ethics and Conduct* (BPS, 2009) cautions psychologists to take particular care when seeking the informed consent of detained persons, given that the circumstances of the detention may affect their ability to consent freely.

Ethical considerations in psychology involve cooperation and collaboration, and the notion of working for the best interests of the client. However forensic assessment and reporting is undertaken in an environment which is both 'adversarial and has a unique social microcosm' (Haag, 2006). Haag describes this social microcosm as characterized by a paramilitary staff hierarchy: an 'us versus them' attitude between offenders and staff, long-term separation from society and a subculture among offenders which places pressure to conform to antisocial values. When writing reports in such a system, the psychologist must be aware, not just of their own values and those of the offender, but also of the environment in which the report is to be written. The forensic psychologist should take the time to consider the impact of these issues, in reflection and supervision, prior to preparing reports in environments such as prisons and secure hospitals.

PLANNING

After taking account of the issues and processes above, the writer is in a position to start planning. Designing the nature of the assessment or intervention required will not be addressed here, but the chapter does address the process of planning the outline and structure of the report itself to maximize the value of the report to its commissioner.

Who are the Readers?

The purpose of any report is to communicate information to its readers. An ideal report must, then, be both understandable and useful to the readers. According to Ackerman (2006) there are three types of reader that the author of a psychological report should consider: mental health professionals, non-mental health professionals and non professionals (including the offender). In a forensic setting most reports will be read by all three groups. It is also worth considering that reports, especially in a forensic context, follow the offender throughout his journey through the criminal justice and mental health systems. It is not unusual for a professional, when appraising an offender, to review historical reports, some dating back to childhood. Thus the report writer should keep in mind the possibility that the report will be read by other professionals many years into the future, for many different purposes.

The challenges for the report writer are twofold: to write comprehensively, incorporating all relevant information past and present, but to write concisely such that the information is accessible but not overwhelming; and to write at a level which will be accessible to all readers. Consumers of forensic reports prefer reports that are brief, use headings and simple language, answer the referral questions and provide a summary. An ideal approach assumes little specialist knowledge in forensic psychology, but provides enough detail and explanation to be useful to a fellow professional. This often requires the psychologist to distinguish the key information, summarize it and to communicate complex concepts in the most simple of terms (Benn and Brady, 1994).

Communicating psychological information to both the offender and commissioner of the report is a difficult balance to reach. While the risks posed by the offender must be communicated clearly, this may cause distress to the offender, who will be aware of the potential impact of the report, and may reject the conclusions. Harvey (2006, p. 5) recognized this difficulty when she suggested that the purpose of psychological reports was 'to increase others' understanding of clients, communicate interventions in such a way that they are understood, appreciated, and implemented, and ultimately result in clients manifesting improved functioning'.

The use of language may help to make difficult conclusions more acceptable to the offender. For example, Mann and Shingler (2001) note that reporting problematic sexual fantasies as 'fantasies about sexual activity with children' rather than 'deviant sexual fantasies' may increase the likelihood of acceptance of the conclusions.

What are the Questions to be Addressed?

Reports may be commissioned to answer a variety of different questions depending upon the business of the decision-making body: what would be the best disposal for an offender; whether the offender is ready for release; whether the offender's risk of reoffending has reduced; what treatment progress has been made etc. On occasions, the report's commissioner will clearly elaborate questions to be addressed. For Mental Health Review Tribunals the Mental Health

Act (2007) specifies that reports must give details of the mental state, behaviour and any treatment undertaken; give details of any neglect, harm to self or others; outline the risk and risk management if the offender were to be discharged; and outline the offender's strengths. However, this level of clarity is not always present and, even when specific questions are outlined, they are often very broad in scope. The report writer still needs to consider exactly what the commissioner and the various clients need to know (the 'ultimate issues') to reach the most effective decisions. It should also not be assumed that commissioners of reports know the full extent of the information they require in order to make a decision. It is sometimes the case that information comes to light during the course of an assessment or intervention, which is unexpected or has not been requested by the commissioner. Where this has a bearing on the 'ultimate issues', such information should be included in the report. Thus, rather than simply attempting to answer the questions posed by the commissioner, the report writer should be trying to provide all the information required by the commissioner to enable effective decision making.

It is therefore important to understand the role of the decision-making body, its powers and limitations, and the interests of the different clients. Almost all reports in a forensic setting will need to address issues of risk, need and responsivity: what level of risk the offender poses; what needs they have now and in the future; and how best to match services to needs in order to maximize their response.

Research has found that approximately 75 per cent of American psychologists believe that psychologists should address the 'ultimate issues' (Ackerman et al., 2004). In the current risk-adverse climate however, it is tempting to give ambiguous or non-committal statements about risk, need and responsivity. Nevertheless, it is important to provide evidence-based opinion and direction on the key issues to enable the decision-making bodies to make defensible recommendations to protect the public and the rights of the individual.

Domains of Information

Having decided upon the information required to address the key questions, the psychologist must decide how best to try to glean the information. Information available for use can be categorized into different domains including demographic and life-history information, usually obtained through file review and interview; cognitive, attitudinal, affective and behavioural functioning, usually obtained through psychometric assessment, interview and observation; information about particular events such as the context, the person's thoughts, feelings and behaviour and the outcome, usually obtained through interview and file review; and the person's current presentation and responses to the assessment, obtained through interview and observation. A comprehensive report should contain information relating to each of these domains for each topic heading (Thompson and Webster, 2003). When forming an opinion about risk, information from all domains should be incorporated along with a structured risk assessment.

Psychological Focus

Forensic psychologists 'are concerned with the application of psychological knowledge and skills in relation to the full range of legal and judicial processes' (BPS, 2011, p. 4, sec 2(2.i)). The report writer should bear in mind that the report has been requested either because the commissioner of the report values a psychological perspective on the case, or because the information required can be best obtained through the use of skills specific to a psychological approach. Thus, when writing reports, forensic psychologists should employ psychological meaning to explain events and apply their psychological skills to obtain and analyse information. Without this emphasis, the report will offer no added value to the commissioner.

A comprehensive report should include information gleaned from interview, psychometrics and risk assessment, observational information and file review. The report should also link the information gathered from these sources to psychological theory, and to the relevant empirical evidence. McMain and Webster (1990) recommend that clinicians should be able to defend expressed opinions in a way that reflects a high degree of reliability and validity. This is generally achieved through formulation or functional analysis, particularly with respect to offending patterns.

Balanced and Comprehensive Reporting

Most forensic psychology reports are likely to include issues of risk, needs and responsivity. These issues are commonly dealt with in reports by listing those factors that place the person at risk of reoffending (such as situations, activities or people that should be avoided); those deficits or weaknesses that could be addressed through treatment or intervention (such as medication, supervision or psychological treatment); and any difficulties that may inhibit the person from engaging with recommended systems, treatments or interventions. Inevitably, this list is likely to seem very negative, and by itself is unlikely to present an unbiased or comprehensive picture of the person (Snyder *et al.*, 2006).

Most modern-day risk appraisal systems and models for formulation and functional analysis (De Ruiter and Nicholls, 2011; Hart & Logan, 2011; Whitehead, Ward and Collie, 2007) emphasize the importance of determining not just weaknesses, but also strengths; not just risk factors but also protective factors (those factors that reduce the risk of reoffending). Neglecting protective factors can have important negative social and political implications such as restricting civil liberties unnecessarily, or assigning limited resources to the wrong offenders. It should also be remembered that although risk assessment is the process by which the report writer gathers information on the likely risk of the offender, the commissioner of the report is more often interested in how to manage this risk. The inclusion of strengths will assist treatment or intervention planning by highlighting priorities and helping to formulate conditions of placement and supervision, and release planning (Ingram and Snyder, 2006; McMain and Webster, 1990). Similarly, if the protective factors are specified, they may be promoted or encouraged to further the overall objective of reducing future risky behaviour (Borum, Bartel and Forth, 2006).

PREPARATION

Having determined the readership of the report and the key questions to be addressed, the report writer will carry out the assessment or collect the information required. The means by which the information is gathered is not addressed here but has been covered in Chapter 4. Once the information is assembled, the writer must prepare to address the relevant questions in a comprehensive and meaningful way within a report.

What am I Planning to Say?

A comprehensive assessment is likely to generate a great deal of information. Sattler (2001, p. 677) makes the fundamental point that a psychological assessment is not complete until 'the obtained information has been organized, synthesized, and integrated'. Often there will be inconsistent stories, conflicts of opinion and missing details within the obtained information. The task of the report writer at this point is to collate and come to an opinion about the case and the 'ultimate issues'. If the wrier can come to a decision at this stage, about what they are planning to recommend, and why, it will assist in the structuring of the report. The danger if this is not done is that the resulting report will fail to link a consistent argument to the recommendations (Benn and Brady, 1994; Brown and Steger, 1988).

   This process is normally achieved through collation of the information, analysis and subsequent hypothesizing about the meaning of the results. The links to psychological theory are explored through functional analysis or formulation to find the best 'fit' for the information gleaned. At this point the writer is able to form opinions and decide what is to be said and can structure the report to include the relevant evidence (both for and against the argument).

Organizing the Report

Once the writer has decided what they are planning to say, the next task is to organize the report in a way that outlines the evidence for the opinions to be presented. A number of authors have made suggestions in relation to the organization of a report (Benn and Brady, 1994; Lichtenberger *et al.*, 2004;

Ownby, 1997). Most recommend that a report should fall into four parts. An introduction should give information about the writer and the writer's competence (personal qualifications and the sources of information); and an outline of the purpose of the report (the context of the referral and details of the questions to be answered). The background information forms the basis of the evidence in support of the writer's recommendations. It should give details about the person (their personal, educational, work, psychiatric and offending history). It is important to outline the evidence for and against the recommendations made, so that the reader can form their own opinion about the strength and appropriateness of the same. Further evidence will be presented in the third part of the report that should focus on current information. This will likely include any psychometric or risk assessments and the person's current thoughts, emotions and attitudes. Formulation or functional analysis is often included here. Finally the report should make recommendations regarding the questions to be answered, referring back to the key facts as evidence.

PRESENTATION

A forensic psychology report is the end product of a period of intervention or an assessment. The report will be scrutinized by decision makers, legal representatives, case supervisors, treatment providers and the offender. It is the single most important opportunity to communicate the writer's opinions and recommendations to others. A poorly written report has the potential to undermine the assessment, mis-communicate opinion or alienate the offender. Thus it is worth considering exactly how to present the report to maximize the desired impact.

Language

Research suggests that consumers (especially non psychologists) find forensic psychological reports cumbersome to read. The overuse of psychological terminology was the most frequent complaint of mental health professionals as well as other consumers (Brenner, 2003). However, Harvey (2006) also found that psychological reports are often written at a level that is difficult to understand, requiring reading skills above year 12 (A level). Unfortunately Winslow and Jacobson's (1998) study showed that the average reading skill in adults is around year 8 and that a fifth of adults have reading skills at year 5 or below.

Harvey (2006) offers a number of suggestions such as shortening sentence length, minimizing the number of difficult words, reducing jargon, increasing the use of subheadings, using everyday descriptions of behaviour and making treatment recommendations as specific and concrete as possible. Since most computer software now has the facility to review readability levels, the process of checking readability has become easier.

In addition to psychological jargon, the use of acronyms and technical terms, or slang and colloquialisms can also be dangerous since they assume knowledge in the reader.

Length

Feedback from consumers of reports frequently emphasizes problems with the content of the report (Tallent, 1993). This includes unnecessary duplication, the inclusion of raw data in the main text (rather than an appendix), improper emphasis of information, and the omission of important information. Short deadlines for reports mean less available time to review drafts and the paradox 'if I had more time, I would have written less' is relevant here. Writing succinctly, while still including all the relevant information is a skill that needs to be honed through practice. However taking the time to edit duplication, remove extraneous detail and reduce the word count does increase the ease of reading and will enhance the efficacy of the report.

Ambiguity and Interpretation

Additionally, consumers have criticized psychological reports on the grounds that they give vague explanations of how results were reached, often focussing on numbers rather than the interpretation of facts, and ultimately giving unclear recommendations (Ownby, 1997; Sattler, 2001; Tallent, 1993).

Readers of a report should not have to work hard to see the links between the facts presented and the recommendations made. A well-argued report would do this for the reader by ensuring that, for each topic area, the report refers back to the questions to be answered, presents the relevant facts, and interprets them to formulate their meaning with respect to the questions. However, this process involves a degree of interpretation on the part of the report writer and it is essential to differentiate between fact and opinion, clarifying what is reality and what is speculation.

It is also important that readers are made aware of the confidence that the writer has in the recommendations given. This is usually achieved by ensuring that the report outlines any contradictory or missing information within each topic area. Report writers should avoid over interpretation if the evidence is limited.

Cohesion

Within each part of the report the information should be presented in a logical sequence. Often this is done as a chronological sequence within each subheading of the report. When presenting information, the report writer should start with simple descriptions and basic test scores and move to an outline of any discrepancies in the data and what these might mean. Finally the writer should attempt to integrate the different types and sources of information and any discrepancies (test scores, observations, historical data) and explain what these mean for the offender.

Where possible, information of different types and sources (historical information, psychometric tests results and interviews) should be integrated rather than placed in separate sections. If there is a wealth of information, it can sometimes be easier for the reader if these are placed in separate sections, but then the writer must work harder to elaborate the links between the different types of information. Where the information is complex, summaries are useful, especially if these can be linked back to the referral questions, and the resulting recommendations.

Psychometric Test Scores

Psychological testing is a core component of clinical practice in forensic psychology (Camara, Nathan and Puente, 2000), and of forensic assessment in particular (Carlin, 2010). Incorporating test results in a forensic psychology report is a challenge because the information is often specialized and inherently technical. A number of writers give advice about communicating and integrating psychological test results. First, they recommend that the report should outline the justifications for using a particular test (including its relevance to the issue at hand, the tests strengths and its limitations (Sattler, 2001), and that it should acknowledge any factors that could influence the validity of the test results such as cultural, linguistic, motivational and situational factors (Haag, 2006; Heilbrun, 1992).

When reporting results from multiple tests, or from complex tests that have multiple components or subtests, the results may be better presented in an appendix rather than in the main body of the report (Groth-Marnat, 2006; Sattler, 2001; Tallent, 1993). However, the report writer should always explain, interpret and integrate the test results into the text, rather than simply list test scores (Benn and Brady, 1994; Ownby, 1997).

Report writers should note that the BPS advises that raw scores should not be included in report unless there is an explanation of their context and appropriate interpretation of the results. The inclusion of blank test material or scoring strategies is also inadvisable because many assessments are invalidated by prior knowledge of their specific content and objectives (PTC, 2007). While a court can legally request access to test materials through the Data Protection Act, psychologists should not release such data and materials to unqualified individuals without adequate interpretation.

Test results should be reported and interpreted in a manner that is easily understood by the reader, avoiding statistical jargon (Sattler, 2001; Tallent, 1993). Finally, the report should include any results indicating strengths or low risk, as well as those indicating weaknesses. Such results are frequently overlooked because they generally appear as 'non significant' results (Sattler, 2001).

Disclosure

Reports written within the Mental Health system must be disclosed to the offender (Mental Health Act, 2007) unless there is a view that this would be detrimental to the offender's well-being or place another person at risk (e.g., third-party information). Whether a legal requirement or not, there are distinct advantages to the sharing of reports with offenders. First, the disclosure and discussion of a draft report allows the offender to challenge areas of disagreement, and to comment on the report. The offender's comments can be incorporated into the report. This allows for any inaccuracies and misunderstandings to be amended and conflicts of opinions to be noted and managed. In addition, disclosure allows offenders to collaborate rather than experience the process as something that is done to them (Miller and Rollnick, 2001).

The report itself can be used as a further assessment of how the offender understands the risk, and can facilitate their awareness of their risk factors and treatment needs. Thus disclosure affords an opportunity for offenders to acknowledge and take ownership of their risk, and it maximizes the probability that they will engage in future psychological activity. In this respect, report writing can be seen as an integral part of the assessment and treatment of an offender. Facilitating offenders to understand their risk factors, engaging them in the process of understanding how and why a risk statement is being made is fundamental in helping to change the risk behaviour of an individual. The next chapter will consider further the practice of motivational report disclosure.

CONCLUSION

A psychological evaluation or assessment is only as good as the written report that conveys the findings. The task is complex and even experienced psychologists find it challenging. Given the importance of the task and the high level of skills required, it is worth spending time reviewing and honing the report, and seeking opinions from others. Supervision or peer review is recommended but it may also be helpful to seek views from the commissioner and other readers (including during the disclosure process with offenders) on both the content and style of reports.

RECOMMENDED FURTHER READING

Lichtenberger, E. O., Mather, N., Kaufman, N. L. and Kaufman, A. S. (2004). *Essentials of Assessment Report Writing* (New York: Wiley & Sons). A comprehensive but accessible guide to writing professional psychology reports and although not specific to forensic psychology, it covers all of the general issues about writing competent reports.

Snyder, C. R., Ritschel, L. A., Rand, K. L. and Berg, C. J. (2006). 'Balancing Psychological Assessments: Including Human Strengths and Hope in Client Reports'. *Journal of Clinical Psychology* 62(1), 33–46. This is an essential book in the current risk-averse climate where it is all too easy to focus entirely on the negative aspects and deficits of clients, overlooking the protective factors and client strengths.

REFERENCES

Ackerman, M. J. (2006). *Clinician's Guide to Child Custody Evaluations,* 3rd edn (New York: Wiley).

Ackerman, M. J., Ackerman, M. C., Steffen, L. J. and Kelly-Poulos, S. (2004). 'Psychologists' Practices Compared to the Expectations of Family Law Judges and Attorneys in Child Custody Cases', *Journal of Child Custody* 1, 41–60.

British Psychological Society (BPS) (2008). *Generic Professional Practice Guidelines* (Leicester: British Psychological Society).

BPS (2009). *Code of Ethics and Conduct* (Leicester: British Psychological Society).

BPS (2011). *Qualification in Forensic Psychology* (Stage 2) *Candidate Handbook* (Leicester: British Psychological Society).

Benn, A. and Brady, C. (1994). 'Forensic Report Writing', in M. McMurran and J. E. Hodge (eds) *The Assessment of Criminal Behaviours of Clients in Secure Settings* (London: Jessica Kingsley), 127–45.

Borum, R, Bartel, P. and Forth, A. (2006). *Manual for the Structured Assessment for Violence Risk in Youth (SAVRY)*. Odessa, FL: Psychological Assessment Resources.

Brenner, E. (2003). 'Consumer-Focused Psychological Assessment', *Professional Psychology: Research and Practice,* 34, 240–7.

Brodsky, S. L. (1980). 'Ethical Issues for Psychologists in Corrections', in J. Monahan (ed.) *Who is the Client? The Ethics of Psychological Intervention in the Criminal Justice System* (Washington, DC: American Psychological Association), 63–92.

Brown, P. F. and Steger, C. M. (1988). *Evaluations of Pre-Sentence Reports in Victoria by Legal Professionals* (Melbourne, Victoria: Attorney-General's Department).

Camara, W. J., Nathan, J. S. and Puente, A. E. (2000). 'Psychological Test Usage: Implications in Professional Psychology', *Professional Psychology: Research and Practice,* 31(2), 141–54.

Carlin, M. (2010). 'The Psychologist as Expert Witness in Criminal Cases', in J. M. Brown and E. A. Campbell (eds) *The Cambridge Handbook of Forensic Psychology* (Cambridge: Cambridge University Press), 766–82.

De Ruiter, C. and Nicholls, T. L. (2011). 'Protective Factors in Forensic Mental Health: A New Frontier', *International Journal of Forensic Mental Health,* 10, 160–70.

Evans, D. R. and Hearn, M. T. (1997). 'Sexual and Non-Sexual Dual Relationships: Managing the Boundaries', in D. R. Evans (ed.), *The Law, Standards of Practice, and Ethics in the Practice of Psychology* (Toronto, Ontario: Edmond Montgomery), 53–83.

Greenfield, D. P. and Gottschalk, J. A. (2009). *Writing Forensic Reports: A Guide for Mental Health Professionals* (New York: Springer).

Groth-Marnat, G. (2006). 'The Psychological Report: A Review of Current Controversies', *Journal of Clinical Psychology*, 62, 73–81.

Haag, A. M. (2006). 'Ethical Dilemmas Faced by Correctional Psychologists in Canada', *Criminal Justice and Behaviour*, 33, 93.

Hart, S. D. and Logan, C. (2011). 'Formulation of Violence Risk Using Evidence-Based Assessments: The Structured Professional Judgment Approach', In P. Sturmey and M. McMurran (eds) *Forensic Case Formulation* (Chichester UK: Wiley-Blackwell), 83–106.

Harvey, V. S. (2006). 'Variables Affecting the Clarity of Psychological Reports', *Journal of Clinical Psychology*, 62(1), 5–18.

Heilbrun, K. (1992). 'The Role of Psychological Testing in Forensic Assessment', *Law and Human Behaviour*, 16, 3, 257–72.

Health Professions Council (HPC) (2008). *Standards of Conduct, Performance and Ethics* (London: Health Professions Council).

Ingram, R. E. and Snyder, C. R (2006). 'Blending the Good with the Bad: Integrating Positive Psychology and Cognitive Psychotherapy', *Journal of Cognitive Psychotherapy*, 20(2), 117–22.

Iverson, G. L. (2000). 'Dual Relationships in Psycholegal Evaluations: Treating Psychologists Serving as Expert Witnesses', *American Journal of Forensic Psychology*, 18(2), 79–87.

Knapp, S. and VandeCreek, L. (2001). 'Psychotherapists' Legal Responsibility to Third Parties: Does it Extend to Alleged Perpetrators of Childhood Abuse?', *Professional Psychology: Research and Practice*, 32(5), 479–83.

Lichtenberger, E. O., Mather, N., Kaufman, N. L. and Kaufman, A. S. (2004). *Essentials of Assessment Report Writing* (New York: Wiley & Sons).

Mann, R. E. and Shingler, J. (2001). Collaborative Risk Assessment with Sexual Offenders. Paper presented at the National Organization for the Treatment of Abusers, Cardiff.

McMain, S. F. and Webster, C. D. (1990). 'Youth Workers in the Courts', *Child & Youth Services*, 13, 83–94.

Mertens, D. M. (1976). 'Expectations of Teachers in Training', *Journal of School Psychology*, 14(3), 222–9.

Miller, W. R. and Rollnick, S. (2001). *Motivational Interviewing: Preparing People For Change* (New York: Guilford Press).

Ogloff, J. R. P. (1995). 'Information Sharing and Related Ethical and Legal Issues for Psychologists Working in Corrections', in J. R. P. Ogloff (ed.) *Forensic*

Psychology: Policy and Practice in Corrections (Ottawa, Ontario: Correctional Service of Canada), 15–23.

Ownby, R. L. (1997). *Psychological Reports: A Guide to Report Writing in Professional Psychology*, 3rd edn (New York: John Wiley).

Psychological Testing Centre (PTC) (2007) *Statement on the Conduct of Psychologists providing Expert Psychometric Evidence to Courts and Lawyers* (Leicester: British Psychological Society).

Sattler, J. M. (2001). *Assessment of Children. Cognitive Applications*, 4th edn (San Diego, CA: Jerome Sattler).

Snyder, C. R., Ritschel, L. A., Rand, K. L. and Berg, C. J. (2006). 'Balancing Psychological Assessments: Including Human Strengths and Hope in Client Reports', *Journal of Clinical Psychology*, 62(1), 33–46.

Strasburger, L. H., Gutheil, T. G. and Brodsky, A. (1997). 'On Wearing Two Hats: Role Conflict in Serving as Both Psychotherapist and Expert Witness', *American Journal of Psychiatry*, 154, 448–56.

Strous, M. (2009). 'Do Dual Forensic and Therapy Roles Damage Children?', *Journal of Child and Adolescent Mental Health*, 21(2), 185–6.

Tallent, N. (1993). *Psychological Report Writing* (New Jersey: Englewood Cliffs: Prentice-Hall).

Thompson, A. and Webster, M. (2003). 'An Analysis of Psychological Forensic Reports for Juvenile Offenders', CRU Monograph Series – Number 3, Collaborative Research Unit, Department of Juvenile Justice, New South Wales Department of Juvenile Justice.

Whitehead, P. R., Ward, T. and Collie, R. M. (2007). 'Time for a Change: Applying the Good Lives Model of Rehabilitation to a High-Risk Violent Offender', *International Journal of Offender Therapy and Comparative Criminology* 51, 578–98.

Winslow, E. H. and Jacobson, A. F. (1998). 'Research for Practice', *American Journal of Nursing*, 98(7), 55–7.

7 Motivational Report Disclosure

Rebecca Milner and Tracy Brookes

INTRODUCTION

Preparing and disclosing psychological reports to offenders has historically been a process in which the offender himself has little say or opportunity to influence. It has been a process that has been done 'to' offenders, rather than 'with' them. In this chapter we will explore the move towards a more collaborative approach, and the features and benefits of this type of working. Using a case study we will try to illustrate the strategies that could be utilized to build a positive environment and collaborative relationship in order to facilitate motivational report disclosure.

COLLABORATIVE WORKING

Collaborative working with offenders has started to attract more attention in the rehabilitation literature reflecting the general shift towards a strength-based approach and the use of positive psychology. However establishing a therapeutic alliance between the therapist and the client is a technique that has long underpinned rehabilitation, specifically psychotherapy. Research indicates that therapy outcome is related to the strength of the therapeutic alliance, or the bond between client and therapist; the stronger the bond the better the treatment outcome (e.g., Martin, Garske and Davis, 2000). Importantly, a lack of therapeutic alliance is related to client non-compliance (Eisenthal *et al.*, 1979). Hence, in order to maximize potential client engagement it is important that therapeutic alliance is considered at all stages of treatment.

One definition of a therapeutic alliance is that it reflects a collaborative relationship that facilitates positive change for the client (Ross, Polaschek and Ward, 2008). As such collaborative working can be seen as an element within therapeutic alliance. For the purposes of this chapter we will borrow a definition from Shingler and Mann (2006) who define collaboration as 'a practice in which the therapist works with the client to define together the nature of the client's problems and to agree on a process for working towards solutions to the problem' (p. 226).

The ultimate aim of collaborative working is that it helps the offender engage in the therapeutic process and become his own agent of change. Collaboration can be used at all points in the treatment process including assessment, treatment, report writing and disclosure. We argue that disclosing risk assessment or other psychological reports should be seen as an integral part of the treatment process.

Features of Collaborative Working

Key features of collaborative working include treating clients with respect and using a flexible, individualized approach. Shingler and Mann (2006) give a detailed overview of the features of collaboration with sexual offenders, which could usefully be generalized to other client subgroups, and to the processes involved during report preparation and disclosure. These include being open with the offender about all aspects of treatment, promoting a sense of teamwork, consulting with the offender about treatment decisions and hearing any objections about the therapy. Collaboration is not just about agreeing with the client, especially if his views or goals are inappropriate, and Shingler and Mann highlight the importance of the equality of the roles between client and therapist in deciding on the content and structure of the therapy.

In terms of report disclosure the report writer would need to be open to hearing the offender's views and consulting with him on the report recommendations. It is useful to view the offender as the 'expert' in his case. Only the offender has in-depth knowledge about his own internal processes, motivators and experiences. Collaborative working respects this knowledge and attempts to help the offender access and use this to understand his thinking and behaviour and engage in the process of change.

Therapist Characteristics

Research has attempted to identify features of the therapist that are important in creating a strong therapeutic alliance and therefore are fundamental in collaborative working. Serran and Marshall (2010) summarize the key skills necessary to help the client build a belief that he can change and benefit from treatment, increase client hope, provide an opportunity to learn and motivate him to maintain treatment gains and engage on an emotional level with clients. Use of humour, an encouraging and flexible approach and a confident and credible therapist style have all found to be linked with good therapeutic outcome and a positive alliance. In addition to skills, the personal characteristics of effective therapists have been well researched. Ackerman and Hilsenroth (2003) conducted an extensive review of the literature and found that the therapist personal attributes that contribute to a positive alliance are flexibility, experience, honesty, being respectful, trustworthy, confident, interested, alert, friendly, warm and open. Therapist features and behaviours that have been shown to have a negative impact on treatment include aggressive confrontation, rejection of the client, manipulation of the client to meet the needs of the therapist, low levels of (positive) therapist skills and low interest in the client (Marshall *et al.*, 2003).

Challenges to Collaborative Working

While there are advantages to collaborative working, there are also challenges to be overcome. Shingler and Mann (2006) provide an in-depth review of the barriers to working collaboratively with sexual offenders. To summarize, they highlight issues such as the client and/or therapist lacking the skills to be collaborative, negative environmental factors such as unsupportive peers or family, the client's belief that he/she will fail in therapy and the client's fear of losing important relationships if he/she engages/changes in therapy. A lack of intrinsic motivation, frustration at lack of progress and statutory barriers such as the sharing of risk information are also highlighted as hurdles.

In terms of collaborative report disclosure another issue to consider is the power dynamics operating within a forensic setting, as discussed in previous chapters. Conducting any type of treatment in a forensic setting is not ideal due to the hierarchical structure, 'them and us' attitudes and the difference in power between offenders and treatment providers. Preparing and disclosing reports in these settings can be viewed as the battleground where offenders fight the system and report writers defend their reports and recommendations. Report writers are likely to have the upper hand given their position of authority and the offender's lack of influence. Hence it is often the case that offenders engage legal representatives to take forward their complaints and arguments, and the battle continues. In collaborative working, the battle is removed and the offender and report writer operate as a team to try and reach agreed recommendations and treatment targets. While this may not be easy in practice, it is worth pursuing if the end result is an offender who takes responsibility for his own treatment goals.

Another issue is that collaboration during report disclosure may seem more time consuming. It might appear quicker to compile a report and send a finished copy to the offender. In contrast the collaborative report writer would work through the report with the offender, asking for input and agreeing on final recommendations. If the offender is consulted, then it is more likely that he will continue to engage in the treatment process. In contrast if he receives a finished report which he disagrees with, it may result in more correspondence to try and re-engage him in the process. In terms of resources, we would argue that the collaborative approach saves more time in the long term, and with more positive results.

THEORETICAL CONCEPTS

If we consider that one of the aims of report writing is to engage the client and support them to change the problem behaviour (i.e., offending), then the report writer needs to consider the perspective of the client when disclosing the report. One strategy that supports this collaborative approach to disclosure is Motivational Interviewing (MI). This approach recognizes that the therapist/report writer and client may have a very different definition of what the 'problem' is and gives practical suggestions in how to manage this discrepancy.

Historical Perspective

Interestingly, MI was not born out of an empirically supported theoretical concept. William R. Miller, the founder of this approach (1983) was lecturing to a group of psychologists about behavioural treatment of alcohol problems when he was asked to demonstrate how he would engage with some of the psychologist's clients. Miller began articulating a model of his clinical practice, which was different to the therapies he was lecturing on. Rather than seeing motivation as a personality *trait*, which was present or not, Miller conceptualized motivation as a more changeable *state*, linked to the interaction between the client and therapist. It was from this position that he built his theory.

MI can be logically linked to a number of theoretical approaches. The approach draws on Carl Rogers' work (1959) on a non-directive counselling[1] approach, in its emphasis on the clients' understanding of their internal world and the discrepancies between the values clients have and their behaviours. The focus of MI was to respond to the client in an empathic client-centred manner. Leon Festinger's cognitive dissonance theory (1957) and Daryl Bem's self-perception theory (1972) can also be seen within the concept of creating discrepancy, and which will be discussed later in the chapter.

THE SPIRIT OF MOTIVATIONAL INTERVIEWING (MILLER AND ROLLNICK, 1991; 2002)

Any training in MI will allude to the 'spirit' of the approach and the importance of understanding the principles that lie behind the techniques. Without this understanding the therapist does not have meaning driving his/her interactions that will impact upon the fundamentally important relationship that needs to be developed between the therapist and client. The process has been summarized as collaboration, evocation and autonomy. Therefore, the treatment (or feedback) needs to be seen as a journey that the client and therapist engage in together; the client taking the lead in articulating his/her ambivalence to change

---

[1] C. R. Rogers (1951). *Client-Centred Therapy* (New York: Houghton Mifflin Company).

and doing most of the work in resolving the dissonance. The therapist is seen as facilitating this process through supporting the client in his/her examination of ambivalence and avoiding any direct persuasion which may cause resistance.

Principles of Motivational Interviewing

Using the 'spirit' of MI as a fundamental underlying value, Miller and Rollnick (2002) propose four guiding principles to be used in the MI approach.

Develop empathy

It is through reflective listening that the therapist seeks to understand the experience of the client. This does not equate to agreement, but to a respectful acknowledgement of the client's perspective. The therapist needs to manage his/her own expectations, recognizing that ambivalence is an understandable state for the client and that reluctance to change is expected.

Develop discrepancy

This principle highlights a clear difference between MI and Rogerian style counselling; in that MI is intentionally directive towards resolution of the ambivalence to change towards more positive behaviour. This is achieved through developing or amplifying the discrepancy between the client's problematic behaviour and his/her broader goals. Miller and Rollnick note that it can be the case that the client is 'stuck' in a position of approach/avoidance conflict, which can keep him in this ambivalent state. The therapist focuses upon the discrepancies that are internal to the client, rather than external. This enables the process to proceed without the sense of coercion, as the client is focusing on the goals important to him/her and not imposed goals (e.g., pressure from partner, lack of employment). This hopefully results in the client presenting his/her reason for change. This is in keeping with the spirit of MI being about clients creating their own journey with the therapist guiding the process.

Roll with resistance

In MI the idea of arguing against resistance is counter-productive and can often strengthen the client's arguments against change. The therapist presents new ideas and perspectives only when it is invited. Resistance can be used by the therapist to pose a question or turn the issue back to the client, as the client is seen as the primary resource in finding the solutions. Persistent resistance should be a signal to the therapist to respond differently to the client.

Support self-efficacy

The therapist needs to instil confidence in the client that change is possible. A therapist's belief in a client can develop into a self-fulfilling prophecy, in which the client then believes in his/her own ability to change. This impacts significantly on his/her personal responsibility for change, again reinforcing that the process of MI is about the client pursuing a change in behaviour with the therapist enabling the change process.

These MI principles can be seen as a fundamental underlying concept in collaborative working, informing and influencing the manner in which the therapist or report writer builds and manages the therapeutic relationship.

CASE STUDY

This chapter will aim to discuss the strategies that could be employed to support motivational report disclosure, including building a positive environment, overcoming barriers and collaborative working. This will be aided by the presentation of a case study.

Mr. Colins is a fifty-two-year-old man who is ten years into a life sentence for the rape and murder of a nineteen-year-old woman. While he admits to having sexual intercourse with the victim, he states this was consensual. He describes the murder as an accident that occurred when trying to calm the victim down after an argument. Official documentation reports that Mr. Colins attacked the victim on her way home from work.

Mr. Colins has previously served a six-year sentence for rape, which he accepts responsibility for and states that he worked through his issues during therapy prior to his release. As a result, he states he is unwilling to engage in any treatment programmes during his current sentence, often deriding the treatment and the specialist member of staff offering it.

While he does not present with control or security issues in prison, Mr. Colins does demand a significant amount of resources. He uses the prison's internal complaints procedures significantly more that other prisoners and refuses to discuss any matters with Wing-based officers or trainee psychologists, instead making demands to speak directly to the Heads of Departments. During interview, Mr. Colins regularly attends with his case file including all the reports and letters he has accumulated over his sentence and refers to them throughout the meeting. This can often distract from the aim of the interview. Staff working closely with Mr. Colins state that he can speak 'down' to them and report finding him to be challenging over even the smallest things.

A trainee psychologist had to disclose a Risk Assessment report. She has assessed him as being 'High' risk and has recommended that he remain in high security conditions until he has completed a range of treatment programmes, including a treatment group to address his sexual offending.

Practical Considerations

Ideally the trainee psychologist should have prepared a draft report for Mr. Colins. The interview would then be about reviewing the draft collaboratively rather than him being presented with a 'finished' copy, which may well cause immediate resistance and disengagement from the process. One option would be to attend the interview without the recommendations written, allowing for an open discussion about the treatment options available. This does not mean that the trainee psychologist should not have thought about her recommendations; rather that this work be finalized with the client, not without him. This transparent approach would aids collaborative working and hopefully help to motivate and engage the client, giving him a sense of responsibility and ownership of his treatment and future. However there is a balance to be struck between the report writer needing to get her clinical recommendations and opinions across and hearing and incorporating those from Mr. Colins. The trainee psychologist will need to attend to this balance during the disclosure session.

APPLICATION OF MI TECHNIQUES

Clear themes of resistance to engagement and denial of any ongoing areas of treatment need are present in Mr. Colins' case and are likely to present during the process of Risk Assessment disclosure. Applying MI techniques may support the process. It is clear that Mr. Colins is in a pattern of working *against* others and therefore, in order to create the spirit behind MI, a collaborative relationship is required.

Using the technique of 'rolling with the resistance' may allow Mr. Colins to step out of the pattern of defensive/attack mode. In the disclosure of the report to Mr. Colins, the trainee psychologist would not aim to challenge his denial of the offence, rather 'roll with this' and discuss areas he does acknowledge first, such as the previous offence. Pointing out his previous success of completing a treatment programme may provide a starting point for a discussion about treatment. The trainee psychologist will need to try and help develop a 'discrepancy' for Mr. Colins between where he is now and where he wants to be. Rather than demanding or insisting that he completes treatment, this report disclosure should be the start of trying to help him make the decision that treatment may help achieve goals in life, such as gaining a relationship. The report disclosure should be seen as a small step towards this rather than trying to achieve this in one sitting. Hence the disclosure is seen as a part of the treatment process itself.

Developing Rapport

When disclosing the Risk Assessment report to Mr. Colins, it would be essential to start to build a therapeutic alliance. It does not appear that this has been easy for previous staff working with Mr. Colins. We know from the literature that the key therapist features include being flexible, credible, respectful, interested, friendly and open (Ackerman and Hilsenroth, 2003)). It would be important in this disclosure session for the trainee psychologist to show that she is friendly, warm and non-threatening. This does not need to be exaggerated in case it increases suspicion, but allowing natural warmth and smiling upon meeting the client and throughout the interview would be important. The trainee psychologist will need to present as credible and confident. This may be difficult in this situation, as Mr. Colins has previously expressed that he does not like speaking to trainees. The trainee psychologist will need to be confident in her knowledge of the report and in the procedure of disclosure to help Mr. Colins start to build confidence in the assessment and treatment process. There would be no need to dwell on or apologize for trainee status, but to focus on the fact that she is appropriately trained and competent in this particular area.

Other attributes include being interested and alert. It would be important to attend to Mr. Colins' perspective and opinions on the report, for example, '*I am interested in what you think about these recommendations, is there anything that you think I have missed that would help us to understand you?*' The trainee psychologist would need to be alert to changes in mood/behaviour and show that she is aware and interested, '*you seem to be agitated when we talk about this area? Can you tell me why so I can try and understand/help you?*'

Openness, honesty and transparency would be critically important in this situation. It would be important to provide Mr. Colins with a copy of the report, preferably before the session, thus giving chance for him to read and digest it. Any scoring guidelines or psychological terms should be clearly explained. Listening to Mr. Colins' opinions would be key, even if these were challenging of the report writer. It would be very disarming for the trainee psychologist to respond to criticism and challenge with '*I hear what you are saying, I am listening*', '*what are your thoughts on this?*' rather than to try and defend and justify her own opinions. Once the client feels he has been heard, this can often open doors to other areas of discussion.

Humour allows two people to laugh at the same thing and increase a common bond. It may help to release tension (Falk and Hill 1992). While humour may not seem like it would be the obvious technique here, if the interview progresses well and an opportunity arises for appropriate humour, this may help to strengthen any bond through common experience. It may be about something as simple as the latest TV reality show but should never be personally directed at the client's expense.

True collaborative working is about working as a team and facing the issue together. In this report disclosure it would help if Mr. Colins could start to see the report writer as someone who can help him. Statements such as '*we need to work as a team on this*', '*how can we work on this together*' may help Mr. Colins to view the disclosure session as work that is being done 'with him' rather than 'to him'.

Modelling

Prosocial modelling is important when working with offenders; as within the context of many offenders' lives, it is often the case that there are limited examples of managing problems and challenges in a prosocial manner. The therapist or report writer can take the opportunity to model appropriate methods of dealing with challenges that arise in the therapeutic relationship.

Mr. Colins is likely to be resistant to much of the content within the report and the trainee psychologist may find it difficult to develop rapport with him for most of the meeting. She could try modelling and building rapport in the following way:

Mr. Colins: You've written it wrong. The system is always against you. Everyone is a fool here, they defend their own mistakes. Reports are always written with things wrong in them and no one owns up to it.

Trainee: *That sounds frustrating. It looks like I may have made some mistakes in this report. Can you tell me what they are and I will check?*

Mr Colins: ... well ... I can but you won't change them will you.

Trainee: *If I've made a mistake, I would like to alter it. I'll go back and check out where I got the information and correct the report if it is wrong. People make mistakes and I make mistakes too.*

Mr Colins: ... OK.

Here the trainee psychologist modelled the process of responding to making a possible mistake. This appears to have worked in two ways. It reassures Mr. Colins that he is being listened to and that mistakes will not be repeated in the report. It also demonstrates that responsibility can be taken for our actions that are wrong, without it diminishing the 'wrong doer'.

Use of Language

Consideration of the type of language used by the trainee psychologist in this disclosure interview will be crucial. There are two main issues for consideration; language which promotes transparency and readability, and avoiding of labels.

Readability

Psychological reports need to be written at a level by which the reader can interpret the information and make use of it. Harvey (2006) suggests ways in which reports can be made more readable. These include using shorter sentences, reducing jargon and acronyms, omitting passive verbs, using more subheadings, using everyday descriptions of the client's behaviour and making treatment recommendations as specific and concrete as possible. During preparation of the report for Mr. Colins the trainee psychologist should attend to these suggestions and use supervision to discuss the issue of readability in this case. The trainee psychologist will also need to be 'transparent' throughout the report and the report disclosure in terms of the type of language used and the recommendations discussed and made. This means using open and clear language with no hidden meanings or psychological terms left unexplained, such as his risk level. This would be particularly important in Mr. Colins' case given his tendency to challenge issues in reports. Supervision should also be the venue to consider responsivity issues in terms of the language used, for example, thinking about the language and terms used in relation to Mr. Colins' education, background and learning style.

Labelling

According to labelling theory (Becker, 1963), crime is a consequence of labelling individuals as criminal. While the fundamental content of labelling theory is concerned with those in power, labelling those who are less powerful, the theoretical concept which proposes that labelling a person as criminal leads to a self-fulfilling prophecy is useful here (for an overview of labelling theory, see Chapter 1).

The labelling and stigmatization of offenders, and in particular men who have committed sexual offences, is observed regularly throughout the media and popular press. In terms of a psychological impact this is not helpful and can serve to reinforce a self-fulfilling prophecy.

Mann and Shingler (2001) note that reporting problematic sexual fantasies as 'fantasies about sexual activity with children' rather than 'deviant sexual fantasies' may reduce the possibility that the offender will see himself as 'deviant' and therefore untreatable or certain to reoffend. They report that by employing this principle they have found less dissatisfaction from the offender client as evidenced by a reduction of complaints from lawyers acting for offenders in prison.

In terms of the case study there is a wealth of difference between the statements, '*Mr. Colins is a rapist*' and '*Mr. Colins is a man who has committed a rape*', with the first statement making a direct assertion about Mr. Colins as a person and the second statement distinguishing between Mr. Colins' behaviour and his core self. The second type of statement is likely to be more acceptable to clients and help to preserve a sense of their core self being worthy, rather than 'deviant'. It would be important for the trainee psychologist to be mindful of her language and choose phrases that avoid labelling and promote a positive sense of self.

MANAGING SELF SCHEMAS

When working in any respect with clients, it is important to remember that there are two people in an interview; in this case the client and the report writer. Much of this chapter has been about the different techniques that can be used in order to engage the client, however there is a need for the report writer to also be aware of their own schemas. These can be defined as fundamental underlying patterns of beliefs about oneself, which the report writer brings into this context.

In this case, Mr. Colins presents with a superior attitude towards people he works with and the trainee psychologist may experience comments directed at her that reflect this attitude. She will need to be able to recognize and manage the automatic reciprocal response she may have to this dynamic of the relationship, based on her own schemas. For example, the therapist may have a schema relating to self-inferiority and while disclosing the report to Mr. Colins this schema may be triggered. Monitoring her own thinking and responses would be key to ensure that a defensive response was not offered as this would run counter to the development of a collaborative relationship with Mr. Colins and reinforce his beliefs about engaging in treatment. Working through these issues in supervision prior to the interview would be of paramount importance. In the supervision environment, strategies for recognizing and managing schemas and the accompanying emotional response could be developed. This is a useful approach prior to working with offenders in any treatment context.

In his 2006 paper James Bennett-Levy argues the therapist should not only focus on the client's state, and how it impacts on the relationship, but importantly upon his/her own internal state. An awareness of the therapist's own emotional reactions can be the best indicator that something is happening within the client-therapist relationship. Safran and Muran (2000) report that it is this awareness that allows the therapist to change his/her treatment or feedback approach.

Other factors may also impact upon a therapist/report writer that are external to the client-therapist relationship. Life events which the therapist/report writer has experienced, such as bereavement, divorce or becoming a parent may impact upon what the report writer brings to the interview internally, and are open to being triggered by the offender. Again supervision is the venue to review such issues and note if current events are likely to impact on the development of the collaborative relationship.

Therefore the skilled therapist/report writer will be self-aware. Reflecting upon practice and being open to constructive criticism allows for self-awareness to develop. While there is limited research within this area, self-awareness is believed to be one of the most important mechanisms in the development of learning (Bennett-Levy, 2003; Staudinger 1999). This strongly supports the notion of supervision and debrief as an instrumental part of an individual's practice. Eventually, through supervision the therapist/report writer will become competent in reflection-in-action, that is, reflection *during* the session with the client, rather than reflecting upon the action post-session

(Bennett-Levy 2006). It is this reflective practice that the trainee psychologist should return to following the disclosure session, in order to review and learn from the process.

CONCLUSION

This chapter reviews the use of collaborative working in order to facilitate motivational report disclosure, and practical techniques and strategies to engage an offender in the report-disclosure process are suggested. We propose that the risk assessment and report writing disclosure procedure be seen as part of the continuing process of management and treatment of the offender, not as an add-on. Hence the report writer should prepare for, engage in and reflect on the process with the same enthusiasm and commitment as during treatment.

There are challenges with collaborative approach, especially where resources and deadlines are tight, however we would argue that an approach which helps an offender take responsibility for his own risk management and engage in the process of change is one that is worth investing in.

RECOMMENDED FURTHER READING

Bennett-Levy, J. (2006). 'Therapist Skills: A Cognitive Model of their Acquisition and Refinement', *Behavioural and Cognitive Psychotherapy* 34, 57–78. A useful paper that focuses on the cognitive model and relates issues to consider as a therapist.

Miller, W. R. and Rollnick, S. (2002). *Motivational Interviewing: Preparing People for Change,* 2nd edn (Guilford Press, London). The leaders in the field of motivational interviewing, this book describes the philosophy and techniques of this extremely effective style of interviewing. It is no substitute for training though.

Shingler, J. and Mann, R. E. (2006). 'Collaboration in Clinical Work with Sexual Offenders: Treatment and Risk Assessment', in W. L. Marshall, Y. M. Fernandez, L. E. Marshall and G. Serran (eds) *Sexual Offender Treatment: Controversial Issues* (John Wiley & Sons Chichester, England). This chapter outlines the basics of collaborative working with a specialist population.

REFERENCES

Ackerman, S. J. and Hilsenroth, M. J. (2003). 'A Review of Therapist Characteristics and Techniques Positively Impacting the Therapeutic Alliance', *Clinical Psychology Review* 23(1), 1–33.

Becker, H. S. (1963). *Outsiders: Studies in the Sociology of Deviance* (New York, NY: The Free Press).

Bem, D. J. (1972). 'Self-Perception Theory', in L. Berkowitz (ed.) *Advances in Experimental Social Psychology,* vol. 6 (New York: Academic Press), 1–62.

Bennett-Levy, J. (2006). 'Therapist Skills: A Cognitive Model of their Acquisition and Refinement', *Behavioural and Cognitive Psychotherapy* 34, 57–78

Bennett-Levy, J. (2003). 'Reflection: A Blind Spot in Psychology?', *Clinical Psychology* July, 16–19.

Eisenthal, S., Emery, R., Lazare, A. and Udin, H. (1979). 'Adherence and the Negotiated Approach to Patienthood', *Arch Gen Psychiatry,* 36(4), 393–8.

Falk, D. R. and Hill, C. E. (1992). 'Counselor Interventions Preceding Client Laughter in Brief Therapy', *Journal of Counseling Psychology,* 39, 39–45.

Festinger, L. (1957). *A Theory of Cognitive Dissonance* (Stanford, CA: Stanford University Press).

Harvey, V. S. (2006). 'Variables Affecting the Clarity of Psychological Reports', *Journal of Clinical Psychology* 62(1), 5–18.

Mann, R. E. and Shingler, J. (2001). Collaborative Risk Assessment with Sexual Offenders. Paper presented at the National Organisation for the Treatment of Abusers, Cardiff, Wales.

Martin, D. J., Garske, J. P. and Davis, K. M. (2000). 'Relation of the Therapeutic Alliance with Outcome and Other Variables: A Meta-Analytic Review', *Journal of Consulting and Clinical Psychology,* 68(3), 438–50.

Marshall, W. L., Fernandez, Y. M., Serran, G. A., Mulloy, R., Thornton, D., Mann, R. E. and Anderson, D. (2003). 'Process Variables in the Treatment of Sexual Offenders: A Review of the Relevant Literature', *Aggression and Violent Behaviour* 8(2) 205–34.

Miller, W. R. (1983). 'Motivational Interviewing with Problem Drinkers', *Behavioural Psychotherapy* 11, 147–72.

Miller, W. R. and Rollnick, S. (1991). *Motivational Interviewing: Preparing People to Change Addictive Behaviour* (New York: Guildford Press).

Miller, W. R. and Rollnick, S. (2002) *Motivational Interviewing: Preparing People to Change,* 2nd edn (New York: Guildford).

Prochaska, J. O. and DiClemente, C. C. (2005). 'The Trans-Theoretical Approach', in J. C. Norcross and M. R. Goldfried (eds) *Handbook of Psychotherapy Integration,* 2nd edn (New York: Oxford University Press), 147–71.

Rogers, C. R. (1951). *Client-Centred Therapy. It's Current Practice, Implications and Theory* (Boston: Houghton Mifflin).

Rogers, C. R. (1959). A Theory of Therapy, Personality, and Interpersonal Relationships as Developed in the Client-Centred Framework', in S. Koch (ed.) *Psychology: The Study of a Science. Vol. 3. Formulations of the Person and the Social Contexts* (New York: McGraw-Hill), 184–256.

Ross, E. C., Polaschek, D. L. L. and Ward, T. (2008). 'The Therapeutic Alliance: A Theoretical Revision for Offender Rehabilitation', *Aggression and Violent Behaviour,* 13(6), 462–80.

Safran, J. D. and Muran, C. J. (2000). *Negotiating the Therapeutic Alliance: A Relational Treatment Guide* (New York, NY, US: Guilford Press).

Serran, G. A. and Marshall, W. L. (2010). 'Therapeutic Process in the Treatment of Sexual Offenders: A Review Article', *The British Journal of Forensic Practice,* 12, 3.

Shingler, J. and Mann, R. E. (2006). 'Collaboration in Clinical Work with Sexual Offenders: Treatment and Risk Assessment', in W. L. Marshall and Y. M. Fernandez, L. E. Marshall and G. Serran (eds) *Sexual Offender Treatment: Controversial Issues* (Chichester: John Wiley & Sons).

Staudinger, U. M. (1999). 'Older and Wiser? Integrating Results on the Relationship between Age and Wisdom-related Performance', *International Journal of Behavioral Development* 23(3), 641–64.

Part II   Application of Skills to Forensic Populations

8 Working with Juvenile Offenders

Kirstin Barnes and Ruby Fitter

INTRODUCTION

In recent years, juvenile offenders (aged ten to eighteen years) have been in the spotlight within the Government and public domain. Issues have been highlighted by the media's focus on the most serious offences committed by the very young, rare though these are (Blom-Cooper, 2003).

In 2008–9 there were 244,583 proven offences resulting in a disposal committed by children and young people between the ages of ten to seventeen years (Youth Justice Annual Workload Data, 2008–10). In 2008–9, most offending committed by young people was by young men, and 142,507 offences were committed by young men between the ages of fifteen and seventeen years, accounting for 58 per cent of all offences (Youth Justice Annual Workload Data, 2010). The main offences committed by this age group are theft and handling, violence against the person and criminal damage (Youth Justice Annual Workload Data, 2010). For those serving custodial sentences, the main offences committed are violence against the person, robbery and burglary (Ministry of Justice, 2010). Unlike adult offenders, research suggests juvenile offenders are generalist rather than specialist, and many have committed a variety of offences (Campbell and Harrington, 2000). However, there are a growing number of juvenile offenders who are committing more serious crimes, such as violent and sexual offences, including grievous bodily harm, murder, rape and child molestation. As a consequence of juveniles committing serious crimes, many juvenile offenders are being given custodial sentences. In August 2010, there were 1198 young males in custody serving custodial sentences, and 433 young males on remand (Ministry of Justice, 2010). The focus of this chapter is on juvenile males in custody and therefore does not cover females or community interventions.

The regime within the Prison Service for the management of juveniles has significantly changed in recent years as a result of government initiatives and changes in legislation (Blom-Cooper, 2003). In England and Wales, the current prison system now provides distinct and separate regimes for juvenile offenders aged between fifteen and seventeen years. The Youth Justice Board for England

and Wales (YJB) is an executive non-departmental public body that has over-seen the youth justice system in England and Wales since 1999. Prior to the YJB overseeing the youth justice system, little research had been undertaken to investigate the most effective way of assessing and treating these young people, and many approaches and programmes currently used with adult offenders were employed within the juvenile prison estate. However juveniles are significantly different to adults and the characteristics of adolescent behaviour must be taken into account in order for the regime to be effective in treating these young people (Prison Service Order 4950, 1999). Therefore, in the last decade, there has been an increase in research to look at what works with juvenile offenders and developments in assessments and interventions with young people.

PSYCHOLOGICAL THEORIES OF JUVENILE OFFENDING

Before exploring the assessments and interventions carried out with juvenile offenders, it is important to consider the various psychological theories of juvenile offending. There are numerous theories, some of which cannot be covered in this summary, although it is important to note that most theories and research in general psychology have frequently been used when trying to understand criminal and antisocial behaviour in juveniles. The theories covered here in this chapter are some of the most commonly used when formulating interventions with young people in custody.

Cognitive Theories

Cognitive theories of offending propose offenders think differently than those who do not offend. Ross and Fabiano (1985) distinguished between impersonal cognition and interpersonal cognition. Impersonal cognition can be described as intelligence and interpersonal cognition concerns understanding other people and their behaviour. Considering impersonal cognition first, the relationship between intelligence and criminal behaviour is one of the long-est running debates. Studies using measures of intelligence suggested young offenders scored lower on IQ measures than non-offenders (Glueck and Glueck, 1950). Studies, such as The Cambridge Study, found that 'low non-verbal intelligence was highly correlated with low verbal intelligence ... and with low school attainment, and all of these measures predicted juvenile convictions to much the same extent' (Farrington 1996, p. 9). Lipsitt, Buka, and Lipsitt (1990) carried out a longitudinal study of young people from the age of seven until eighteen. The IQ scores between the offenders and non-offenders were compared and the data showed a lower level of intellectual performance in the juvenile offenders. There are some doubts about the links between IQ and criminality, as lower IQ scores may in fact reflect social disadvantage rather than intellectual ability, but there is a general acceptance that there is some link between intelligence and criminality.

When considering interpersonal cognition, Ross and Fabiano (1985) argue that this type of cognition may be more important when trying to understand offending behaviour. Ross and Fabiano described different styles of cognition that are frequently associated with offending and antisocial behaviour. These cognitive styles include self-control, locus of control, perspective taking, moral development and social problem solving. Many interventions designed for both adults and juvenile offenders have been formulated to address these cognitive styles described by Ross and Fabiano. These interventions are based on the idea that thinking influences behaviour and therefore if thinking can be changed, this will result in a change in behaviour.

Social Learning Theory

While understanding cognition is important, it is vital to consider how cognition links to behaviour. Social learning theory (Bandura, 1977, 1986) has frequently been applied by psychologists and criminologists to the study of offending behaviour, as described in Chapter 2. Social learning theory suggests that behaviour can be learnt at a cognitive level by observing the behaviour of other people and then once it has been learnt, when it is then performed, the behaviour is either reinforced by others or by the individual themselves. Criminal behaviour is then maintained through further rewards such as financial gain or enhanced status within a peer group. There may also be internal rewards for the individual such as excitement when committing the crime.

Social learning theories have been considered when developing interventions for young people in custody. They suggest that young people who offend may be encouraged to behave differently by modelling or observing prosocial adults and peers and by developing internal reinforcement for such non-offending behaviours.

Moral Reasoning

It is generally accepted that behaviour is related in some way to the way in which an individual reasons and therefore behaviour can be linked to our moral reasoning (Blasi, 1980). Kohlberg (1976) adapted the famous studies by Piaget (1932) and described three levels of moral development in children. The first level is the *pre-conventional level*, which consists of the individual considering obedience based on punishment and what is in it for them. The second level is *conventional level* in which the individual considers social norms and obeys rules in order to be 'a good boy/girl' in order to live up to expectations both for maintaining relationships and society. The third level is *post-conventional level* and this is when the individual understands the rules of society and the principles underlying such rules. There is further research supporting the theory that people do progress through such stages and the theory has been further revised, for example Gibbs, Basinger and Fuller (1992) in response to criticism of some aspects of Kohlberg's theory. It has been suggested that the moral reasoning of young people who offend is less developed than those that do not offend and a number of studies have demonstrated a link between delinquency and lower levels of moral reasoning. For example, Eisenberg and Mussen (1989) found in a number of studies, low levels of moral reasoning predicted delinquency and dishonesty (Nichols and Mitchell, 2004).

The link between moral reasoning and offending, however, should not be considered in isolation, as there are a number of other explanations for offending behaviour. Research is beginning to demonstrate how moral reasoning may interact with other factors to increase the likelihood of offending (Nichols and Mitchell, 2004).

Pathways and Persistence

Some researchers have suggested that there are a number of pathways that juveniles experience with regards to offending. Many feel that this approach helps in explaining how some young people go from quite minor antisocial or criminal acts to much more serious acts of crime. Loeber *et al.* (1993) suggested three pathways: overt, covert and authority conflict pathways. The overt pathway deals with behaviour that begins as minor aggressive behaviour such as bullying, which then further intensifies resulting in more violent behaviour such as fighting, and ultimately escalates to offences such as assault, robbery or rape. The second pathway, covert, involves behaviour escalating from lying and acts of vandalism to more serious acts of theft and damage, possibly including offences such as arson. The third and final pathway is authority conflict typically begins with a young person being involved in minor disobedience and results in more serious disobedience such as truanting from school or running away. There are a number of authors who support the idea of juveniles experiencing different pathways in offending and there is some evidence to suggest when a young person experiences more than one pathway, there is an increased likelihood of higher rates of offending behaviour (Nichols and Mitchell, 2004).

There have been other longitudinal studies that have demonstrated that antisocial or criminal behaviour by some young people can be temporary and situational and by others it is more stable and persistent. One of the most prominent studies is by Moffitt (1993) who examined a representative sample of boys from their New Zealand study proposing that temporary and situational antisocial behaviour is relatively common in young adolescents, whereas persistent antisocial behaviour is found in quite a small number of males. In this study Moffitt (1993) found that approximately 5 per cent of the boys showed antisocial behaviour before starting school and another 33 per cent who had not previously shown antisocial behaviour began to get involved in offending behaviour between the ages of eleven and fifteen. This 33 per cent, who had not previously been involved in offending behaviour before this point, were starting to offend as frequently and as seriously as the 5 per cent who had started to offend and behave antisocially early on in their life. Furthermore, the latter group of young males tended to show a decrease in their offending as they entered into late adolescence and early adulthood, whereas the early starters were more likely to not desist.

Moffitt suggests there are two types of offenders, *adolescent limited* and *life course persistent* offenders. Adolescent limited offenders are those that begin offending during adolescence and then desist when entering early adulthood whereas life course persistent offenders are those that begin early in life and then continue throughout. Moffitt suggests these are two qualitatively different categories of adolescent offenders and therefore gives distinct theoretical explanations for each.

A more recent study by Stattin, Kerr and Bergman (2010) examined Moffitt's adolescent limited and life course persistent theory. Stattin, Kerr and Bergman used data from three time periods that were before age fifteen years, between fifteen and twenty years and then from twenty-one to thirty-five years. They confirmed similar findings to Moffitt with both adolescent limited and life course persistent males being present in the research. However, they also suggested a group of childhood onset desister group that was not present in Moffitt's study. It was suggested that this group had a number of similar problems to those in Moffitt's life course persistent group in early childhood and adolescence, but that they did not differ much from the adolescent limited in the next two time periods. Stattin, Kerr and Bergman (2010) also highlighted a group that began to offend in adolescence and then continued into adulthood.

ASSESSMENT OF JUVENILE OFFENDERS

Forensic psychologists in prison settings and in the community are frequently required to carry out assessments in order to establish the likelihood of a young person reoffending in the future. Such assessments allow practitioners to make decisions and recommendations for sentence plans and parole, and also to aid in the identifying of appropriate interventions. Perhaps the most common applications of risk assessments carried out with young people most recently are with those serving mandatory or ISPP (Indeterminate Sentence for Public Protection) life sentences. In August 2010, there were forty-seven males between fifteen and seventeen years of age in custody serving indeterminate sentences. Forensic psychologists working with juvenile offenders serving indeterminate sentences are typically involved in preparing the sentence plan that includes a risk assessment. This risk assessment allows appropriate interventions to be identified and an intervention plan developed in order to reduce the risk the young person poses. However, risk assessments are not limited to assessing the risk a young person poses in terms of future reoffending. Forensic psychologists are also frequently involved in assessing an individual's cognitive functioning, the risk of suicide or self-harm or the risk of other target behaviours occurring.

There are a number of general assessments that can be used with juvenile offenders, which are not necessarily specific to offending, but can assist in assessing a young person. For example, the following assessments are frequently used:

- WAIS IV (Wechsler, 1997)
- Locus of Control Scale (Nowicki and Strickland, 1973)
- Self Esteem Questionnaire (Rosenberg, 1965)
- Emotional Control Questionnaire (Roger and Najarian, 1989)
- Becks Youth Inventory (Steer *et al.*, 2005)
- Problem Solving Inventory (D'Zurilla, Nezu, and Maydeu-Olivares, 2000)

Whether using the above assessments, or the ones described later in this section, there are a number of considerations that must be taken into account such as learning difficulties, low motivation to engage with psychological services and attention difficulties. Another consideration concerns the limited number of assessments available for young people, as the majority are adult-focussed with norms only available for over eighteen years. It is not appropriate to use adult assessments on young people and therefore clinical judgement is vital in assessing a young persons risk and need. Other considerations for both assessments and interventions with young people are highlighted later in this chapter.

There are some limitations when it comes to assessing juvenile offenders, particularly with regards to the risk of the young person reoffending, due to the limited available research and data considering juveniles. However, there has been some significant progress over recent years in this area, especially when assessing violent and sexual juvenile offenders.

ISSUES RELATED TO INTERVENTION WITH JUVENILE OFFENDERS

There are a significant number of individual contributory factors in relation to a young person's offending behaviour and it is unlikely that there will be one singular cause of offending. Interventions that are designed to be used with young people are most effective when they follow a holistic approach which take account of an individual's areas of risk and need but which also seek to identify and build on protective factors and strengths (Youth Justice Board, 2008–10).

Interventions with young people are most effective when they are relevant to their own lives and when they use methods and techniques that are of interest to them and can help to engage, motivate and interest them. Prior to any form of intervention being undertaken, much thought and consideration needs to have taken place with regards the formulation of the intervention and to ultimately ensure that the individual needs of the young person have been met.

CURRENT FORMS OF INTERVENTION IN CUSTODIAL SETTINGS

Structured Offending Behaviour Programmes

Evidence indicates that structured programmes are more effective at reducing reoffending than other types of intervention (Whyte, 2001). Lipsey and Wilson (1998) reviewed several different types of interventions offered to young people (majority males aged between ten and twenty-one years) who were institutionalized and non-institutionalized. The interventions that were strongest in terms of reducing reoffending were those that focussed on interpersonal skills training, individual structured counselling and behaviour programmes. Interventions that were least effective or not effective in reducing reoffending were 'challenge' programmes, deterrence programmes and vocational programmes. One disadvantage to group work is that it tends to have a 'one size fits all approach'. This could be addressed by programmes for young people being more tailored to individual needs in their design. However, it is the case that programmes designed specifically for a juvenile population do include individual sessions in addition to the group work sessions.

Individual Work

Given the heterogeneity of adolescent offenders and the complexities of their offending behaviour, individual work with a young person is often more appropriate and effective. With individual work, interventions can be targeted specifically at the principles of risk and need but also responsivity. Cooke and Philip (2000) suggest that for interventions to be effective, all three principles should be present. There are disadvantages to individual work. It can be less cost effective, time consuming and generally resources to undertake such work will be limited. For the practitioner, the work can at times be isolated and challenging.

SPECIAL CONSIDERATIONS WHEN WORKING WITH YOUNG PEOPLE WHO HAVE OFFENDED

There are a number of considerations that should be taken into account when carrying out assessment and intervention with young people. Some of the issues that need to be considered will be historical but may still have an impact on any assessment or intervention process.

Low Motivation to Engage with Psychological Services

Low motivation is a common issue that arises when working with young people. They often have difficulty, especially in the early stages of work, appreciating the importance and use of offending behaviour work in the long and short term. For some young people their motivation is low because they do not have faith or trust in 'professionals' or 'people in authority'. Low motivation can be influenced by external situations such as lack of parental or caregiver support or current difficult life events, such as the breakdown of a relationship or a bereavement. In order to manage fluctuating levels of motivation with a young person, it is important not to become demotivated as motivation levels are not constant and it is human nature to become demotivated from time to time. Motivation is not a stable factor and can change according to time and situations (Lopez-Viets, Walker and Miller, 2002). Being open and honest with the young person is useful to determine the reasons for the drop in motivation. It is important to explore any current barriers or obstacles that may be preventing the person from engaging in the work.

Overall, helping an individual to recognize that they have the capability to change is recognized as a valuable approach that focusses on a person's strengths (Seligman, 2006).

The Issue of Informed Consent

Gaining informed consent within a psychological context can be difficult especially if the young person has learning difficulties. Here it is important that clear and easy-to-understand consent forms are used as well as discussing points in clear language. Asking the young person to paraphrase or reflect what they have been told is useful to determine whether they have understood what they are consenting to do. As a practitioner, attempt to structure expectations about the nature of the work and how long the work will take (within reason). Discuss the aspects of the work that may be challenging, your experience and qualifications and if the involvement on the part of the young person is voluntary, although at the same time being clear about the benefits about engaging in psychological work.

Current or Previous Use of Self Harm/Poor Coping Strategies While in Custody

Young people with a history of self-harm may use this coping strategy during any stage on your work. It may also arise for those who have no history. It is important to allow the young person time to address whatever issue is affecting them at this time, which may mean deviating from your planned sessions. This approach demonstrates responsivity to your client.

Bullying

If a young person is being bullied while working with you, this may affect their ability to engage with the work. It is important to address how the young person is feeling with regards to being bullied and to explore what support they are being offered and whether there are other forms of help and support that they would benefit from.

Fear and Anxiety about Engaging with a Psychologist

Previous negative involvement with a psychology service where there were no favourable outcomes can be a barrier to a young person engaging. Developing a positive therapeutic relationship can be the initial process that can help a young person to feel able to trust, talk and disclose. There are many ways that this can be done, from taking time to get to know their likes and dislikes so that beginnings and endings of sessions can be more light hearted. Using appropriate self-disclosure can help as can incorporating humour where appropriate. Offering positive reinforcement in other settings can help, such as attending sentence planning meetings and talking honestly about progress in front of other staff and family members.

Mental Health Issues

If a young person is experiencing current and significant mental health issues, it is more than likely that they will be engaged with the Child and Adolescent Mental Health Service (CAMHS). In certain circumstances it may be appropriate for forensic psychologists and CAMHS services to undertake joint work if it is the best interests of the young person.

Current Problematic Relationships

This relates to the family, peer and intimate relationship difficulties that young people may face. Generally the types of situations are parents not showing any support or care towards their children in custody, bereavements of significant others, intimate relationships ending, discovering a partner has been unfaithful, loss of peer relationships and breakdown of parental relationships. For young parents in custody, there is the issue of not having sufficient access to their child. The majority of these situations are common challenges that people face; however, for young people in custody, they feel a sense of powerlessness and do not feel they have any level of control over the situations. Feelings of guilt, depression and upset may arise and these may need to be explored and the young person supported to manage these feelings appropriately.

Disclosure of Historical Abuse

Child protection measures should follow any disclosure of historical abuse. Making a disclosure of this type can cause the young person to feel anxious about what would happen next and any possible outcomes. These feelings can have an impact on how well the young person engages with any type of assessment or intervention. Motivation and attention levels may decrease and you may have to think of some strategies to re-engage the young person taking account of their current feelings but enabling them to appreciate the importance of continuing with the work. The young person may want to speak with you about the disclosure, however it is important to stress your limitations in doing this with them, but offering reassurance that the matter is being dealt with and feedback will be given from the appropriate staff involved.

Learning Difficulties

Many young people in custody have some form of learning difficulty that can limit their ability to undertake psychological work. Those with learning difficulties can experience feelings of shame, embarrassment and anxiety, which contribute to feelings of low self-esteem. These feelings can manifest in behavioural difficulties such as frustration and annoyance with tasks or questions, avoiding tasks, encouraging others to misbehave or not engage with work or being withdrawn and unresponsive. The use of creativity within sessions is one method to ensure young people with learning difficulties are not disadvantaged. The use of clear and simple language as well as pictures, diagrams and cartoons cannot be underestimated. Importantly, young people often are aware of what helps them to learn, so discussing what methods will help them and incorporating these into session plans is a good start.

WHAT CAN HELP?

There are some practical tips for completing assessments and interventions with young people and also aspects of a practitioner's style of working that contribute towards more effective working with young people.

TIPS

- Spend as much time building a rapport as possible
- Employ a motivational style of interviewing
- Be collaborative
- Encourage and use positive reinforcement

- Try to involve other staff to 'co-facilitate' some sessions where appropriate
- Use a motivational report writing style
- Empower the young person to make their own informed decisions
- Be flexible and adaptable to respond to individual needs
- Be creative, and where appropriate use humour in sessions
- Use simple analogies
- Use appropriate self-disclosure
- Be realistic and prepare for challenges and difficulties along the way

CASE STUDY

It is useful to consider the types of assessment and intervention that a forensic psychology practitioner may undertake given the following information. It is important to note that this case study provides a framework for guidance purposes.

John[1] presents as a 17-year-old male at the time of the offence. He is serving an Indeterminate Sentence for Public Protection (five-year tariff) for the offence of Rape and Grievous Bodily Harm (GBH). The victim of the offence was a stranger (known less than twenty-four hours) and was aged ten years at the time of the offence. John lived in Kent with his mother, his mother's partner and his two half siblings. John's mother and father are divorced but he has frequent visits with his father. John has an offending history with two previous convictions for Burglary and one for Violence against the Person. He was having a sexual relationship with a seventeen-year-old female at the time of the offence.

Information from Custodial Sources

Information indicates that John has had many conflicts with staff and in particular with officers. He has refused all contact with his mother and his siblings, however prefers to have contact with his father. John works well in education although he lacks confidence in his own abilities. He has had a part-time job in the stores department, where he initially worked to a high standard then lost his job. John is isolated on the residential unit and is isolated generally. He does have a positive relationship with his caseworker. John attends gym sessions and enjoys taking part in weights sessions, as he is keen to develop his muscle.

---

[1] Case example of John is a hypothetical example and bears no reference to any person in particular.

He has engaged with the psychology department for the purposes of completing the Life Sentence Plan Risk Assessment Report (LSP 2D) but this was limited and he chose to not attend many of the sessions.

Assessments Undertaken

- Structured Assessment of Violence Risk in Youth (Borum, Bartel and Forth, 2006)
- Estimate of Risk of Adolescence Sexual Offence Recidivism (Worling and Curwen, 2001)
- Locus of Control Scale (Nowicki and Strickland, 1973)
- Self Esteem Questionnaire (Rosenberg, 1965)
- Emotional Control Questionnaire (Roger and Najarian, 1989)
- Wechsler Adult Intelligent Scale (Wechsler, 1997)

Outcomes from Assessments

- Deficits in understanding what is meant by a healthy sexual relationship
- Antisocial behaviours towards others
- Lack of peer relationships
- Emotional loneliness
- Poor self-regulation
- Negative attitudes towards women
- Negative ruminations
- Low self-esteem and some issues with self-image
- Slightly above average IQ

Intervention Plan

Given the outcomes from the assessments and taking account of psychological theory of adolescent sexual and violent offending, the following intervention plan has been formulated.

Once the intervention plan has been designed, the next stage is to consider what specific sessions can be developed for each of the different stages of the intervention. Some of the questions that forensic psychology practitioners should be asking themselves are:

- What mode of learning suits John the most?
- What are his interests?
- Is he suited to group work or would his needs be met more effectively via individual work?
- Has he been involved with psychological services previously and if yes, what were his views about it?
- How much time remains in custody in order to complete the work?
- Where will he be transferring to after he leaves his current establishment?

- What services (Psychology) are available at the receiving establishment?
- What are the views of his Youth Offending Team (YOT) Officer with regards the intervention plan?
- What can the YOT offer in terms of supporting him during the intervention?

SUGGESTIONS FOR SESSION PLANS FOR JOHN

Self-Esteem/Self-Confidence

A challenge when working with young people who have offended is how to raise their self-esteem in cases where this has been assessed as low. Research has indicated that in young people, low self-esteem in adolescent sexual offenders has been linked to non-sexual recidivism (Worling and Curwen, 2001). During intervention with a young person, their levels of self-esteem may fluctuate for a time depending of the situations they find themselves. Ideas to help develop self-esteem are to initially determine what level of self-esteem a person currently has. Then to explore what would be the ideal level that the young person aspires to. What are their goals, aims and expectations in life? Are these realistic or could some of the goals be reframed to be more realistic and consequently more achievable? What challenges and difficulties has the young person come across in life and how have they dealt with such situations? Can they reflect on their methods and consider more effective ways to deal with their challenges? Furthermore, enabling a young person to appreciate that life in general is a constant series of positive experiences and negative experiences (highs and lows) and learning to accept this and manage feelings when disappointments or rejections occur is all part of the process of everyday life and becoming an adult, however difficult or upsetting it can be.

In terms of your style as a practitioner working with a young person, the use of praise and positive reinforcement where applicable is useful as are tangible examples of reinforcements such as small prizes or certificates. Attending relevant meetings and being honest about developments is also a useful strategy. The use of self-disclosure can be helpful as long as it is used appropriately and within the correct context. As a practitioner, being realistic about your expectations for the young person is a fundamental aspect.

Coping Strategies

There is evidence that points to stressful life events being associated with a greater degree of the use of violence in young people (Guerra *et al.*, 1995). Addressing how a young person copes with difficult and challenging situations in their life is an important aspect of intervention.

Explore what the different styles of coping are for different people. Why do some people react differently to others in the same situation? What coping styles has the young person used to date to manage challenging situations and have these proven to be effective or have they led to further difficulties? A comparison between the positive ways of coping and the negative ways of coping is a useful technique. Have any of these techniques ever been employed by the young person, and if so to what effect? How can the young person try to incorporate the use of more positive coping in their own life?

Interpersonal Problem Solving

Currently there is one accredited offending behaviour programme that focuses on thinking and behaviour of young people, called JETS. Addressing the thinking and behaviour styles associated with offending has been found to be effective with young people. The JETS programme incorporates a number of different modes of learning that are tailored to suit different learning styles (Nichols and Mitchell, 2004; McGuire, 2002). This could provide the young person with a break from the individual work and allow for some development of social skills, as they will be attending the programme with other peers.

Relationship Skills

Research suggests that adolescents who are unable to form intimate peer relationships and who are socially isolated are at a higher risk of reoffending sexually. As well as being intimate, evidence indicates that where there is a lack of mutual respect, warmth, affection and closeness in relationships, this too can increase the risk of sexual reoffending (Epps, 1997, Langstrom and Grann, 2000). Some useful strategies are to explore with the young person their current family, peer and intimate relationships. What networks do they have currently and what is the quality of their relationships with these different groups? What relationships (either current or historical) have been positive and why is this? What relationships have been negative and why?

Another aspect of this area is to develop skills in maintaining positive relationships with new people that enter a young person's life. What can the young person do to increase the probability of maintaining positive relationships? Learning some techniques of how one can deal with rejection may also be useful; and equally useful will be learning techniques for how to deal with the situation where a relationship appears to be negative or unhealthy.

Healthy Sexual Interests

Current evidence indicates that adolescents who are sexually aroused by younger children are more likely to commit further sexual offences (Worling and Curwen, 2000). It would be useful to note that for many young people convicted for a sexual offence, engaging in offence-focussed work can be extremely challenging and stressful and one suggestion is to carry out this work last.

Suggestions for sessions that could be undertaken for this part of the intervention could be to explore initially what is meant by abusive behaviour first in a general context and then in as sexual offending context? At this stage explore with the young person their own sexual abusive behaviours and why they understand their behaviours to be abusive. Explore the benefits of being able to identify the behaviours that are abusive.

Before carrying out sessions that focus on what constitutes a healthy and appropriate sexual relationship, it is useful to determine sexual knowledge and to fill in any gaps in knowledge. It would be useful here to revisit the earlier discussions about relationships in general before exploring with the young person what their beliefs are about healthy sexual relationships and what factors constitute a healthy sexual relationship. Having this awareness can enable the young person to acknowledge what was positive about their relationships with sexual partners previously and what was not. Explore what the young person can do or say should they be faced with a sexual relationship that is becoming unhealthy.

Discuss the importance of gaining consent from a potential sexual partner and furthermore enabling the young person to understand that decisions that are made about sex should be made in collaboration with their partner and not singularly.

CONCLUSION

This chapter has focussed on both the theory underpinning juvenile offending as well as providing some practical guidelines. Working with offenders to address their offending behaviour can be challenging at the best of times and this is certainly the case with a juvenile offender. That said the practical aspects of this chapter hopefully have provided some guidelines and strategies to ensure that psychological work can be completed effectively and responsively.

RECOMMENDED FURTHER READING

Farrington, D. P. (1997). 'Human Development and Criminal Careers', in M. McGuire, R. Morgan and R. Reiner (eds) *The Oxford Handbook of Criminology* (Oxford: Oxford University Press), 361–95. As above, one of the more influential studies and based on longitudinal evidence.

Moffitt, T. E. (1993). 'Adolescence Limited and Life Course Persistent Anti Social Behaviour: A Developmental Taxonomy', *Psychological Review* 100, 625–9. One of the most influential studies with regards juvenile offending.

Worling, J. R. and Curwen, T. (2000). *ERASOR: Estimate of the Risk of Sexual Recidivism. Version 1.2*. Ontario Ministry of community and social services. Original manual and rating guide.

Youth Justice Board (2002–3). *The Key Elements of Effective Practice*. Youth Justice Board for England and Wales, London. Sets out what the YJB expect in terms of effective offending practice with young people.

Youth, R., Borum, R., Bartel, and Forth, A. (2006). 'SAVRY: Structured Assessment of Violence Risk'. Psychological Assessments Resources Inc. This is the original manual and user guide. Current research is now available with regards to SAVRY and its predictive validity.

REFERENCES

Bandura, A. (1977). *Social Learning Theory* (New York: Prentice Hall).

Bandura, A. (1986). *Social Foundations of Thought and Action: A Social Cognitive Theory* (Englewood Cliffs, NJ: Prentice Hall).

Blasi, A. (1980). 'Bridging Moral Cognition and Moral Action: A Critical Review of the Literature', *Psychological Bulletin* 88, 1–45.

Blom-Cooper, M. (2003). 'Working with Young Offenders and Juveniles', in G. Towl (ed.) *Psychology in Prisons* (Oxford: British Psychological Society and Blackwell Publishing Ltd).

Borum, R., Bartel, R., and Forth, A. (2006). *Structured Assessment of Violence Risk in Youth* (Tampa, FL: Psychological Assessment Resources, Inc.).

S. Campbell and V. Harrington, (2000). *Youth Crime: Findings from the 1998/99 Youth Life-Styles Survey* (Home Office Research Findings no. 126. London: Home Office).

Cooke, D. J. and Philip, L. (2000). 'To Treat or Not to Treat; an Empirical Perspective', in C. R. Hollin (ed.) *The Handbook of Offender Assessment and Treatment* (Chichester: John Wiley and Son).

D'Zurilla, T. J., Nezu, A. M. and Maydeu-Olivares, A. (2000). *Manual for the Social Problem Solving Inventory – Revised* (North Tonawanda, NY: Multi-Health Systems, Inc.).

Eisenburg. N. and Mussen, P. H. (1989). *The Roots of Prosocial Behaviour in Children* (Cambridge: Cambridge University Press).

Epps, K. J. (1997). 'Managing Risk', in M. S. Hoghughi, S. R. Bhate and F. Graham (eds) *Working with Sexually Abusive Adolescents* (London: Sage), 35–51.

Farrington, D. P. (1996). 'Criminological Psychology: Individual and Family Factors in the Explanation and Prevention of Offending', in C. R. Hollin (ed.) *Working with Offenders: Psychological Practice in Offender Rehabilitation* (Wiley and Sons).

Gibbs, J. C., Basinger, K. S. and Fuller, D. (1992). *Moral Maturity Measuring the Development of Sociomoral Reflection* (Hillsdale, New Jersey. Lawrence Erlbaum Associates Inc.).

Glueck, S. and Glueck, E. (1950). *Unraveling Juvenile Delinquency* (New York: Simon and Schuster).

Guerra, N. G., Huesmann, L. R., Tolan, P. H., Van Acker, R. and Eron, L. D. (1995). 'Stressful Events and Individual Beliefs as Correlates of Economic Disadvantage of Aggression among Urban Children', *Journal of Consulting and Clinical Psychology* 63(4), 518–28.

Kohlberg, L. (1976). 'Moral Stage and Moralization: The Cognitive-Behavioural Model Approach', in T. Likona (ed.) *Moral Development and Behaviour: Theory, Research and Social Issues* (New York: Holt, Reinhart and Winston).

Langstrom, N. and Grann, M. (2000). 'Risk of Criminal Recidivism Among Young Sex Offenders', *Journal of Interpersonal Violence* 15(8), 855–71.

Lipsitt, P. D., Buka, S. L. and Lipsitt, L. P. (1990). 'Early Intelligence Scores and Subsequent Delinquency: A Prospective Study', *The American Journal of Family Therapy* 18, 197–208.

Lipsey, M. W. and Wilson, D. B. (1998). 'Effective Intervention for Serious Juvenile Offenders: A Synthesis of Research', in R. Loeber and D. Farrington (eds) *Serious and Violent Juvenile Offenders; Risk Factors and Successful Interventions* (Thousand Oaks: Sage Publications).

Loeber, R., Wung, P., Keenan, K., Giroux, B., Stouthamer-Loeber, M., Van Kammen, W. B. and Maughan, B. (1993). Developmental Pathways in Disruptive Child Behaviour', *Development and Psychopathology* 5, 101–31.

Lopez-Viets, V., Walker, D. D. and Miller, W. R. (2002). 'What is Motivation to Change? A Scientific Analysis', in M. McMurran (ed.) *Motivating Offenders to Change: A Guide to Enhancing Engagement in Therapy* (Chichester: Wiley), 15–30.

McGuire, J. (2002). *Elements of Effective Practice in Offending Behaviour Programmes; Final Report* (London: University of Liverpool).

Ministry of Justice (2010). *Population in Custody Monthly Tables, August 2010 England and Wales*. Retrieved from: www.justice.gov.uk/populationincustody. htm, Accessed 5/10/11.

Moffitt, T. E. (1993). 'Adolescence-Limited and Life-Course Persistent Antisocial Behaviour: A Developmental Taxonomy', *Psychological Review* 100, 644–701.

Nichols, C. and Mitchell, J. (2004). JETS – An Integrated Living Skills Programme for Younger Offenders. Theory manual.

Nowicki, S. and Strickland, B. (1973). 'Locus of Control. A Locus of Control Scale for Children', *Journal of Counselling and Clinical Psychology* 42, 148–55.

Piaget, J. (1932). *The Moral Judgement of the Child* (London: Routledge and Kegan Paul).

Prison Service Order 4950 (1999). *Regimes for Prisoners Under 18 Years Old* (Home Office).

Roger, D. and Najarian, B. (1989). 'The Construction and Validation of a New Scale for Measuring Emotional Control', *Personality and Individual Differences* 10(8), 845–53. (Adapted version)

Rosenberg, M. (1965). *Society and the Adolescent Self-Image* (NJ: Princeton University Press).

Ross, R. R. and Fabiano, E. A. (1985). *Time to Think: A Cognitive Model of Delinquency Prevention and Offender Rehabilitation* (Johnson City, TN: Institute of Social Sciences and Arts).

Seligman, M. E. P. (2006). *Learned Optimism* (London: Nicholas Brealey Publishing).

Stattin, H., Kerr, M. and Bergman, L. R. (2010). 'On the Utility of Moffitt's Typology Trajectories in Long-Term Perspective', *European Journal of Criminology* October 21, 7(6), 521–45.

Steer, R., Beck, A., Beck., J. S. and Jolly, J. (2005). *Becks Youth Inventories*, 2nd edn for Children and Adolescents (BYI-II). PsychCorp.

Wechsler, D. (1997). *WAIS III Administration and Scoring Manual* (San Antonio, TX: The Psychological Corporation).

Whyte, B. (2001). *Effective Intervention for Serious and Violent Young Offenders* (Criminal Justice Social Work Development Centre for Scotland).

Worling, J. R. and Curwen, T. (2000). 'Adolescent Sexual Offender Recidivism: Success of Specialised Treatment and Implications for Risk Prediction', *Child Abuse and Neglect* 24, 965–82.

Worling, J. R. and Curwen,T. (2001). *Estimate of Risk of Adolescent Sexual Offence Recidivism. Version 2.0.* (Ontario: SAFE-T Program).

Youth Justice Board (2008–10). *Youth Justice Annual Workload Data2008/09 England and Wales.* Retrieved from: www.justice.gov.uk/publications/youth-justice statistics.htm, Accessed 12/11/11.

9 Internet Sex Offenders

Matthew Shirley

INTRODUCTION

The aim of this chapter is to address some of the key issues in working with internet sex offenders. This begins with a discussion of the term 'internet sex offender', considering the range of behaviours it covers, before exploring the response of the criminal justice system in England and Wales to this new phenomenon. Treatment programmes, risk assessment (static and dynamic), interviews and interventions (internal and external) are addressed in turn, before concluding with a reminder of the importance of collaborative working to motivationally disclose reports to offenders.

INTERNET SEX OFFENDERS – WHO ARE THEY AND WHAT HAVE WE DONE WITH THEM?

The term 'internet offender' typically refers to someone who has been convicted of 'accessing, downloading and possessing indecent images or pseudo-images, depicting the sexual abuse of children' (Middleton *et al.*, 2006). However, this only captures part of the range of offending behaviour that needs to be considered under this label. The above definition excludes those offenders involved in the production and distribution of indecent images of children, where the internet was the principle media used. Krone (2004) identified a typology of nine different forms of online child abuse, which ranged from the 'browser', to the 'physical abuser', who uses child abuse images to facilitate sexual activity with children. Any definition of the term 'internet sex offender' would also have to include those people guilty of accessing and possessing 'extreme pornography' (sexually explicit material that features bestiality, necrophilia and serious violence) under the Criminal Justice and Immigration Act, 2008 (http://www.cps.gov.uk/legal/d_to_g/extreme_pornography/index.html#a02), which recognizes adult victims of internet offending.

A WORD ABOUT PORNOGRAPHY

Often in the literature on this subject, the images in focus are referred to as 'child pornography'. It would be remiss of any practitioner-oriented publication not to highlight this issue, as Tim Tate explains:

> 'Child Pornography' is a misleading term. This is not the tawdry glamour of *Playboy* centrefolds, nor yet the gory gynaecology of hard-core. In fact it is not pornography in any real sense: simply the evidence – recorded on film or videotape – of serious sexual assaults on young children.
>
> (Tate, 1993, p. 203)

As Middleton and Hayes (2006) highlight, this term should be challenged when working with offenders, as the word 'pornography' could reinforce distorted cognitions legitimizing the material in the mind of the offender. As an alternative, the term child abuse images (CAI) ensures the context of the images is not lost on the offenders. The term also can be applied across the full range of images categorized by Combating Online Paedophile Networks In Europe (COPINE) (Taylor, Holland and Quayle, 2001, in O'Brien and Webster, 2011), from the least sexually explicit, to the most abusive. This term is also applicable to offenders who have not used the internet to commit their offences, using older forms of technology (print media, VHS).

Additionally, other forms of offending behaviour are committed via the internet which would also qualify under the internet sex offender label, such as using web cam technology to cause or incite children to perform or watch sexual acts (Card, 2004). Bourke and Hernandez (2009) refer to these behaviours as 'cybervoyeurism' and 'cyberexhibitionism'. 'Online sexual offending' is another term that has been used which has a broad meaning, but again does not distinguish between offending behaviours and the qualitative differences that may exist between downloaders of child abuse images and those attempting to groom children online.

The main response to this new phenomenon in sexual offending in the criminal justice system in England and Wales has been the development of the internet Sexual Offences Treatment Programme (i-SOTP, Middleton and Hayes, 2006). Middleton (2008) outlines the need for a 'second generation' programme to move beyond the 'one size fits all' approach of the previous raft of accredited sex offender programmes, established throughout the probation and prison estates. While these programmes demonstrated some encouraging evidencing of their effectiveness in reducing the risk of reconviction for programme completers (Middleton, 2008), they did not discriminate between offence types; so concerns remained regarding less risky and deviant group members becoming contaminated by other offenders.

The i-SOTP was designed to be delivered in the community setting in individual or group format, catering for offences defined as making, distributing and producing indecent images of children (Middleton and Hayes, 2006). Furthermore, candidates must also be assessed as between 'low' to 'high' risk on Risk Matrix 2000(S) (Thornton, 2010) and 'low' deviance according to a battery of psychometric tests. Those offenders deemed 'very high' risk of reconviction and 'high' deviance would be expected to complete the more intensive community programmes, 'as such assessments are indicative of a predisposition to commit contact offences' (Middleton and Hayes, 2006, p. 5). Thus those offenders convicted of Meeting a Child Following Sexual Grooming, or Causing/Inciting a Child to Watch a Sexual Act or Engaging in Sexual Activity were more appropriately allocated to the longer programmes (Community Sex Offender Groupwork Programme, Northumbria Sex Offender Groupwork Programme, Thames Valley Sex Offender Groupwork Programme in the community, Sexual Offender Treatment Programme in custody, Brown, 2005), despite the internet featuring in their offending behaviour.

The i-SOTP was developed combining the 'model of change' from the previous accredited programmes; the 'Model of Problematic Internet Use' and the 'Good Lives Model' (Fisher and Beech, 1998; Quayle and Taylor, 2003; and Ward and Stewart, 2003, in Middleton and Hayes, 2006). The new i-SOTP model of change thus comprised six components:

1. Increase motivation, decrease denial and identify and reduce discrepancy between perceived prosocial values and behaviour (addressing distorted attitudes).
2. Challenge offence-supportive attitudes and behaviours (addressing distorted attitudes).
3. Build an empathic response to identifying that all children depicted in the indecent images are real victims of child abuse (addressing distorted attitudes and socio-affective functioning).
4. Reduce use of sex as a coping strategy and emotional avoidance, replacing it with effective problem-solving strategies (addressing socio-affective functioning and self-management).
5. Develop adequate relationship intimacy and coping skills; improve self-esteem and internal locus of control (social adequacy factors and self-management).
6. Develop realistic relapse prevention strategies and new prosocial lifestyle goals (addressing self-management and socio-affective functioning).

These elements broadly correspond with the six modules within the i-SOTP, which also include collecting, compulsivity and online communities (O'Brien and Webster, 2011).

Early research indicated that where internet offenders were concerned, reconviction levels for sexual offences were relatively low (<10%) but more likely where the offenders had previous convictions – especially for violent and/or previous contact sexual offending (Seto and Eke, 2005). In extended follow-up research, Eke, Seto and Williams (2011) again found that previous convictions (including violent offences) were one of the most predictive factors of violent (including contact sexual) offences. Other research indicated that internet offenders tended to have low levels of prior convictions for sexual offences against children (Wolak, Finkelhor and Mitchell, 2005; Webb, Craissati and Keen, 2007, both in Middleton, 2008). Given this risk profile, the rationale for providing a (comparatively) shorter programme of intervention for this offender group was justified on the risk principle (Chapman and Hough, 1998), as those internet offenders with prior convictions were more likely to score higher on Risk Matrix 2000 and be assessed as better suited to the more intensive programmes.

The i-SOTP was accredited in 2006 and what little follow-up research has been undertaken to gauge its effectiveness concluded that the programme performed well. In it's first two years in employment with the (then) National Probation Service, more than half of the 264 sampled offenders were assessed as having a treated psychometric profile, meaning their responses to attitudinal questionnaires were indistinguishable from a non-offender normative sample (Middleton *et al.*, 2009).

At the time of going to press, the National Offender Management Service (NOMS) has formulated two new programmes that are intended to replace all but one of the ten existing accredited sex offender treatment programmes delivered in both the custodial and community settings. Few details have so far been released but the Adapted Sex Offender Programme remains, alongside the new Low Intensity and High Intensity Programmes. It is envisaged that those offenders previously receiving the i-SOTP would be suitable for the Low Intensity Programme, with higher risk and deviance offenders being subject to the considerably lengthier High Intensity Programme.

The underpinning theory has been revised from the previous programmes to take greater account of the Bio-Psycho-Social (BPS) model of change (Mann, Carter and Thornton, 2011). While the specific approach to treating internet offenders has gone, much of this model is familiar – it still addresses the key dynamic risk areas of sexual interests, offence-supportive attitudes, social and emotional functioning and self-management, as well as retaining the risk and responsivity principles that applied previously (Andrews and Bonta, 2006 in Mann, Carter and Thornton, 2011). For this reason, the Correctional Services Accreditation Panel considered that other non-contact offenders (assessed as low-high risk on Risk Matrix 2000) and low-risk contact offenders are suitable for this intervention.

What appears to be new is the greater influence of neurobiology, hence medication, diet and exercise now feature, although it is claimed that the model of change is still consistent with the Good Lives Model (Ward, Mann and Gannon, 2007, in Mann, Carter and Thornton, 2011).

SPECIAL CONSIDERATIONS WHEN ASSESSING INTERNET OFFENDERS

Beech, Fisher and Thornton (2003) suggest that a thorough risk assessment of a convicted sex-offender requires four components to be addressed: (1) a functional analysis to assess the modus operandi of the offender and underlying problems, (2) the application of a static risk predictor, (3) identification of stable dynamic risk factors to generate treatment targets and (4) monitoring of acute dynamic risk factors. When it comes to assessing internet offenders, this model would be appropriate to replicate.

In terms of this model, in working with sex offenders under the auspices of the criminal justice system, it would be most common for actuarial and dynamic risk assessment to precede the functional analysis. The accredited programmes account for assessing the modus operandi of the offending, but this then forms part of the intervention, ensuring the offender understands how they came to offend. In terms of risk assessment, it would contribute greatly to the ongoing monitoring of established treatment targets, as well as highlight the existence of potential risk factors previously un-scored. Quayle, Erooga, Wright, Taylor and Harbinson (2006) provide a range of models to undertake this type of analysis, including decision chains, Wolf's multi-factorial model and an adapted version of Sullivan's Spiral of Abuse (2002, cited in Quayle *et al.*, 2006).

Actuarial Risk Assessment

Caution needs to be applied even in the most ideal of circumstances when using actuarial risk assessment tools, with some understanding of the limitations of the tool and the methodology behind it being a prerequisite (Craig and Beech, 2009). This is especially the case when using these tools with internet offenders, as the most commonly used examples were not devised and formulated with these offenders among the original research sample. A case in point, the Risk Matrix 2000 (RM2000) devised by David Thornton, was developed using data on convicted offenders that largely predated the proliferation of access to the World Wide Web in the mid to late 1990s (Calder, 2004; Thornton, 2010). Subsequently, in response to the growing demand for risk assessment systems for use with internet offenders, a number of additional caveats and cautions were issued to adapt the application of the RM2000 (S) to this offender group. The most recently revised version of the Scoring Guide for Risk Matrix 2000 (Thornton, 2010) clarifies the following points in relation to three of the aggravating risk factors as they pertain to internet offending:

■ **Sexual Offence against a Male**
This should only be scored in cases of possession/making indecent images if there is evidence the offender had deliberately sought images of males.

■ **Sexual Offences against a Stranger**
Should not be scored in cases limited to accessing, viewing and possessing indecent images of children. Where the offending behaviour involved the offender communicating with the victim via a web cam, they can be considered as 'knowing' each other as it can be argued that they have conversed and can recognize each other.

■ **Non-Contact Sex Offence**
This requires more consideration. Thornton advises we count indecent images of children as non-contact offences, *but* makes separate provision for internet offenders. Presumably this scoring item relates to procuring non-internet sourced forms of pornographic image, such as photographs and VHS (as well as DVDs), as it is likely that representatives of the older forms of media were likely to have featured in the original validating data set. Thornton advises that this item should not be scored if the offender's only sexual offence relates to downloading indecent images of children, but if there is another (non-internet) sexual conviction (past or present), then the scoring item would apply.

Other researchers have explored the suitability of the RM2000 with internet offenders. Osborn and Beech (2006, in Elliott and Beech, 2009) removed the aggravating factors of Non-Contact Offences and Stranger Victim, but still concluded that the levels of risk may have been overstated. More recently, Wakeling, Howard and Barnett (2011) examined the predictive validity of all three of the RM2000 scales (S, V and C) and the Offender Group Reconviction Scale (OGRS) 3. The results indicate that all four tools had moderate to very good predictive accuracy. The reoffending rates were very low with the majority of further proven reoffending being a repetition of internet-specific offending. While these findings appear to support the idea that internet-only offenders pose little risk of reconviction, the authors point out that the very low recidivism rates make comparisons with offenders with contact and internet offending history difficult (Wakeling, Howard and Barnett, 2011).

Dynamic Risk Assessment

While static risk factors cannot be influenced by treatment, those risk factors that can be prone to change (dynamic risk factors) form the basis of treatment targets for interventions. Drawing on the works of Hanson and Morton-Bourgon (2004), Craissati and Beech (2003) (both quoted in Offending Behaviour Programmes Unit, 2004), the Structured Assessment of Risk and Need (SARN,

Offending Behaviour Programmes Unit, 2004) concludes that dynamic risk factors fall broadly into four areas:

1. Deviant sexual interests,
2. Offence supportive attitudes,
3. Poor emotional functioning
4. Self-management

This model forms the basis for assessing dynamic risk factors, and hence treatment targets for accredited sex offender programmes in the Prison and Probation Services in England and Wales. For those unfamiliar with this instrument it would share some similarities with the Static and Acute 07 (Hanson *et al.*, 2007, in Elliott and Beech, 2009), in that clinical scores are given to evidence of dynamic risk factors. The SARN also distinguishes between evidence of risk factors in the offender's life generally as well as in the offence chain, thus enabling clinicians to identify which areas are essential or merely desirable to treat.

O'Brien and Webster (2011) point out that the Stable and Acute 07 instrument, which although seen as a reliable instrument and well received when piloted in Police and Probation services across England and Wales, has not been evaluated for efficacy with online offenders. To some extent the same is true with the SARN, as this was compiled prior to much of the work exploring online-offending-specific risk assessment. An update to the scoring guide (NOMS, 2009) states that there is sufficient commonality in the known literature between internet offenders and other types of offenders for the SARN to remain a valid risk assessment tool.

More recently, a number of research articles have attempted to fill the void where internet offenders and risk are concerned. Earlier research tended to conclude that there was little evidence to conclude that all collectors of online child abuse images would escalate to committing contact offences against children, but *some* would (Middleton, 2008). The study by Bourke and Hernandez (2009) raised some alarm when it claimed that 85 per cent of online-only offenders (downloading child abuse images) had a history of contact offending that had gone unreported. This study used the polygraph as a means of scrutinizing self-report measures, as previous studies reliant on reconviction data and self-report alone have arguably underestimated the degree of 'cross-over', or 'dual offending' (Seto and Eke, 2005; Webb, Craissati and Keen, 2007 and O'Brien and Webster, 2005, cited in Middleton, 2008). Furthermore, Buschman *et al.* (2010) also compared self-report data with information derived through an interview schedule using the polygraph, to investigate potential differences between internet and contact offenders, in terms of key dynamic risk factors. They found that, typically, internet offenders were:

- More sexually deviant than they admitted to in self-report alone (as judged by masturbating to images of children).

- More sexually interested in younger (pre-pubescent) children than they admitted to.
- More likely to have undisclosed contact offences in their histories.

The notion that internet offenders may not be entirely forthcoming with information that pertains to the more socially unacceptable elements of their offence-related behaviour may not surprise some, but the implications this would have for risk assessment echoes the need to 'triangulate' risk assessment methods, just as you would with contact offenders (O'Brien and Marshall, 2004, cited in O'Brien and Webster, 2011).

Towards this aim, Glasgow highlights the utility in using the Affinity computer programme to gauge the time offenders spent observing images of people (all ages from pre-pubescent to adult). The greater the amount of time the offender dwells on an image, the greater interest she/he has in the person in the image. This would be compared against their self-report of how sexually attractive they rate the person, all of which provides additional evidence for assessing sexual interest in children (Glasgow, Osborne and Croxon, 2003, Glasgow, 2010).

McCarthy (2010) attempted to identify a range of online sexual behaviours which could be used to predict which internet offenders are likely to have an unknown history of, or will progress to commit, contact offending. The findings indicate that those offenders with both internet offences and contact offences are more likely than internet-only offenders to engage in the following online behaviours:

- Viewing (non-pornographic) child-centred web sites.
- Using the internet to engage children in sexualized chat.
- Sending children sexually explicit material (both child abuse images and adult pornography).
- Attempting to contact those children they have communicated with online.
- Communicating with other adults in connection with their deviant sexual interests, both online and in person.
- Engaging in cyber-sex with other adults.
- Having larger collections of child abuse images, as well as a higher ratio of child abuse images to adult pornographic images in their collection.

Other researchers have concluded that there may be evidence of new typologies of internet offender emerging. Briggs, Simon and Simonsen (2011) contend that there might be two distinct forms of internet offenders who have used online chat rooms to engage in sexualized communication with children – the contact-driven offender and the fantasy-driven offender. The former is compelled to use this behaviour to seek physical sexual contact with the children, whereas the latter group seem more content for the online seduction process to remain a fantasy. The researchers claim that both types of offenders have fewer severe criminogenic risk factors than other sex offenders (rapists, child molesters).

In overall terms, a reasonable approach to risk assessment would be to 'treat as you find'. internet offenders are capable of having histories of contact offending, as well as being online-only voyeurs. Explore all avenues of information, use as many methods at your disposal as possible, be motivational to increase compliance and lessen resistance and shame, to aid your assessment. It would be wise to consider internet offenders as being located on a continuum of risk and deviance and determine the quantity and quality of treatment accordingly.

SPECIAL CONSIDERATIONS WHEN INTERVIEWING INTERNET OFFENDERS

Many clinicians are likely to find themselves without the additional resources described above (polygraph testing or Affinity software), and so are likely to be basing their assessment on an analysis of documents and interviewing the offender.

As for any interview undertaken with a sex offender or child abuser, preparation and forethought is essential to ensure that personal discomfort, distaste or other strong emotions are held in check and do not 'leak' into the interview through spoken or other behaviour. Willmot (Chapter 11) reminds us that many life events can impact on our capacity to cope with the emotional demands of working in this field. Specialist counselling, supportive supervision and line-management are important to ensure staff working with sex offenders (of any type) can do so effectively and safely. Joanna Clarke has written extensively on this subject (see Chapter 14).

Those clinicians trained in the use of SARN will be familiar with the Treatment Need Analysis (TNA) Interview Schedule, contained in the training manual appendices (Offending Behaviour Programmes Unit, 2004). This schedule of suggested questions is organized to enable assessment of dynamic risk domains/treatment needs (sexual interests, distorted attitudes, management of relationships and self-management). However, it does not specifically address some of the intricacies concerning online offending. For this reason the semi-structured interview provided by Quayle and Taylor (2002, in Calder, 2004) and a framework provided by COPINE (which can be requested by email at copine@ucc.ie) would be useful documents to add to the assessment process for internet offenders. These interview schedules directly target information relevant to assessing dynamic risk factors, as well as generating information relating to online and computer-based behaviour, necessary to fully assessing the risks posed by internet offenders, of reoffending and escalating to contact offences (Glasgow, 2010; McCarthy, 2010).

In addition to utilizing interview schedules such as those above, clinicians need to ensure that the information they gather enables them to complete the Risk Matrix 2000. This tool has many caveats that need to be explored before risk factors can be scored, giving the overall level of risk of reconviction.

While interviewing can be a highly effective means of gathering essential information for the purposes of assessing risk and treatment needs, the research from Buschman *et al.* (2010) draws attention to the notion that internet offenders may not be entirely forthcoming with salient details about their sexual interests and offending histories. For this reason, additional measures such as the polygraph, David Glasgow's Internet Sex Offender Profiling System (ISOPS) computer-based evidence analysis or Affinity viewing time assessment programme (Glasgow, Osborne and Croxen, 2003) could offer greater confidence in your assessment, *should* they be available to you.

SPECIAL CONSIDERATIONS WHEN PLANNING INTERVENTIONS FOR INTERNET OFFENDERS

Internal Measures/Treatment

As discussed earlier in this chapter, functional analysis is key aspect of a thorough risk assessment (Beech, Fisher and Thornton, 2003). The Spiral of Abuse (Sullivan, 2003, cited in Quayle *et al.*, 2006) is the model chosen for the i-SOTP in preference to an exercise based on Finkelhor's Four Preconditions to Abuse model, due to the difficulty applying the fourth precondition (securing victim compliance) to indirect offenders (i.e., those convicted of downloading preexisting child abuse images). It was also deemed to better encapsulate the sense of escalation that many internet offenders experience, where thoughts, feelings and (sexual) behaviour start to feel out of their control and gravitate towards more explicit or abusive images, featuring younger children (Middleton and Hayes, 2006), or as we have seen, contact offending.

For those unfamiliar with the model, the Spiral appears to contain some elements of both the Wolf and Finkelhor models, in that the starting place remains the motivation of the offender. Subsequent areas for exploration include the justifications used to bypass any sense of guilt, fear or shame experienced by the offender. Cognitive distortions are also listed, along with details over developing fantasies, masturbation habits, the planning and preparation in order to offend and the offence itself. This model is flexible, in that it can address the first, or another significant, offence (e.g., the first time images were paid for) (Middleton and Hayes, 2006). Flexibility is a concept inherent in the design of the i-SOTP, which ensures that the treatment needs of offenders can be met in terms of the four pathways for internet offending – intimacy deficits; emotional dysregulation; distorted sexual scripts and antisocial cognitions (Middleton and Hayes, 2006).

The two dominant pathways, according to Middleton *et al.* (2006) are emotional dysregulation and intimacy deficits, which account for 70 per cent of the internet offenders in their research. The i-SOTP, as with other accredited community-based sex offender programmes, primarily uses role plays to address social skills deficits, or mono-dramas to rehearse and refine self-talk strategies (Middleton and Hayes, 2006). Group members' coping styles are also reviewed, fostering an increased recognition of the benefits of problem-focused strategies, over emotion-focused or avoidant coping. Following the CBT format, group members explore which feelings are the most difficult to cope with, before being encouraged to formulate new, positive, self-talk. New skills are then practised that will assist the offender, such as problem solving, conflict resolution and ways to avoid acting on impulse.

Thought-control strategies are discussed and practised, so group members can feel empowered to change any unwanted inappropriate sexual thoughts or fantasies, to lessen distorted sexual scripts. Fantasy diaries are also employed to record the frequency and content of sexual thoughts, in order to determine if further work is needed outside of the programme, to address deviant sexual arousal.

In common with other accredited sex-offender programmes in prison and probation settings, victim empathy is an area covered by the i-SOTP (and other sources, e.g., Quayle *et al.*, 2006). The i-SOTP draws on group discussions and case studies to highlight the perspectives of the victims, both primary and secondary, which includes looking at the 'ripple effect' of internet offending. Role plays are again used here to consider the point of view of different victims – although care is taken to represent child victims as adults for this purpose (Middleton and Hayes, 2006). The subject of victim empathy has been questioned recently, and early indications are that it has a greatly reduced role in the newly accredited (yet to be piloted at the time of press) Low Intensity Sex Offending Programme. However, the emphasis placed on enhancing empathy skills appears to be relevant to those offenders with poor interpersonal skills (or intimacy deficits pathway).

The i-SOTP draws on strengths approaches, such as Ward and Stewart (2003, in Middleton, 2008). The range of exercises in the i-SOTP addressing the offender's values and goals can also be found in Quayle *et al.* (2006). The i-SOTP concludes these exercises with a graphic representation of the discrepancy between the offender's stated values and how consistent their behaviour has been with the said value, in the form of a wheel representing the different elements of a person's life, or 'goods' (Ward, Polaschek and Beech, 2006). This brings an element of visual recognition that the tabular version in Quayle *et al.* (2006) lacks. Drawing on these values, approach goals are then established as ambitions for enhancing areas of their lives, bringing a holistic element to the programme, conveying a motivational message to the offenders that they are not defined by their offences (Middleton, 2008). These goals play key part in the conclusion of the programme, the New Lives Plan, which provides the offender with a 'blue print' for their non-offending future. Reminders of their goals, their risky situations, thoughts, feelings and behaviours, as well as listing their support networks, the plan should be reviewed and revised where needed on an ongoing basis.

Given that the i-SOTP was designed to be delivered in both group and individual formats, clinicians working one-to-one with offenders can take assurance that the methods described are considered suitable outside of the group work room.

External Measures/Enforcement

Consideration to external controls must be given, especially when working with internet offenders in the community, but also in custody in anticipation of an offender's release on parole or at the end of their custodial sentence. There are a range of externally applied measures that can be utilized in the management and ongoing assessment of risk with sex offenders (of all kinds) in the community.

Sentencing courts can impose a number of orders on convicted sex offenders, in addition to compelling them to sign the Sex Offender Register, held by the Police. Registration obliges those sex offenders to keep the police informed of changes of address (including temporary residences), as well as giving the police power to regularly take the offender's photograph and fingerprints and conduct unscheduled home visits. The Sexual Offences Prevention Order (SOPO) can be imposed with a wide variety of measures, restricting the recipient in terms of geographical locations, who they can associate with, their access to, or use of, the internet and relevant electronic equipment. Disqualification Orders and Foreign Travel Orders can be imposed where there are concerns about the offender attempting victim access behaviours through paid or voluntary work with children, or travelling abroad for the purposes of sexual tourism (Card, 2004).

The Public Protection Units within the police service are responsible for overseeing the Sex Offenders Register and have made use of some technological innovations to assist in the monitoring of those offenders in the community. The Securus software can be programmed onto an offender's computer that sends snapshots of the web pages viewed on that machine directly to the police computers, in order that specific SOPO or licence conditions can be checked. Also, programmes making use of satellite-tracked electronic tags have been piloted in England and Wales (Shute, 2007), and deployed in various States in America and Australia, and have been the subject of political debate in Canada (http://www.salon.com/2006/12/19/offenders_2/, http://www.abc.net.au/news/2011-10-29/satellite-tracking-sex-offenders/3607776, http://www.thestar.com/news/canada/politics/article/1026544--hudak-vows-to-make-sex-offenders-wear-gps-devices).

Circles of Support and Accountability (CoSA) might also be considered as both an internal and external measure, as it provides a core member (high-risk offender) with a circle of trained volunteers who meet up on a weekly basis. This system then provides a source of (non-statutory) prosocial modelling, a social-support network to assist the offender with maintaining their 'New Me' thinking, as well as an additional layer of monitoring and intelligence on the offender's behaviour in the community. (For information on CoSA see http://lucyfaithfull.org/circles_of_support.htm or http://www.quaker.org. uk/files/Circles-Interim-report-Nov-03.pdf).

The inclusion of these external measures was to highlight to the clinician the importance of multi-agency co-operation within the criminal justice and health care systems, in terms of sharing intelligence vital to assessment and management of risk.

MOTIVATIONAL REPORT DISCLOSURE WITH INTERNET OFFENDERS

Working with internet sex offenders is no different from working with any other offender group, insofar as success in treatment will depend on the level of motivation and engagement on the part of the recipient. Willmot attends to this subject with (generic) sex offenders (Chapter 11). He highlights the significance of the Good Lives Model in engaging offenders to recognize their abusive behaviour as the result of applying inappropriate means to achieving legitimate goals. This can then reduce the potentially destructive feelings of shame, which can be a barrier to achieving positive change, which ultimately reduces their risk of recidivism.

Similarly, O'Brien and Webster (2011) stress the necessity of working collaboratively with offenders, stating that confrontational or aggressive methods heighten defensiveness and maintains denial in a group of offenders who often experience poor social functioning styles and are trying to cope with the negative response from society to their behaviour.

CONCLUSION

The term 'internet sex offender' can be seen as a misnomer. While some have suggested that there are subgroups of sexual offenders who have used the internet to acquire child abuse images, there are sufficient grounds for uncertainty as to whether this is the only sexually abusive act they have committed. The research into the differences between 'internet-only' offenders, contact offenders and 'dual offenders' is the latest development in a field of research that can still be considered as in its infancy.

For this reason, the most rational conclusion must be to remain cautious about the potential risks of over- and underestimating the risk such offenders pose of reconviction and causing serious harm. Use all the evidence and assessment tools available to you (accounting for ethical issues and limitations). Be aware that denial of sexual deviance and offending history are both likely, and explore rigorously (but with warmth and empathy) the offender's use of technology as well as their sexual history (online and offline). The most thorough assessment of the risks and needs will then determine the treatment pathway, where more tried-and-tested methods and techniques can be brought to bear or reducing the risks.

RECOMMENDED FURTHER READING

Calder (2004). *Sexual Abuse and the Internet: Tackling the New Frontier* for its interview schedule by COPINE and interview guidance from Quayle and Taylor that lists helpful areas to enquire about when assessing offenders.

Davidson and Gottschalk (eds) (2011). *Internet Child Abuse: Current Research and Policy* is the most up to date text (at the time of writing) that covers the subject in greater detail and broader depth than this chapter can offer.

Two articles from the *Journal of Sexual Aggression* (Glasgow, 2010 and McCarthy 2010) stood out in terms of informing the reader on specific areas around technology and online behaviours that may relate to the risk of reoffending and considering the likelihood of crossover or dual offending.

Quayle, E., Erooga, M. Wright, L., Taylor, M. and Harbinson, D. (2006). *Only Pictures? Therapeutic Work with Internet Sex Offenders,* is an excellent resource for exercises to be completed by offenders, many of which feature in accredited programmes.

REFERENCES

Beech, A. R., Fisher, D. D. and Thornton, D. (2003). 'Risk assessment of Sex Offenders', *Professional Psychology: Research and Practice,* 34(4), 339–352.

Bourke, M. L and Hernandez, A. E. (2009). 'The "Butner Study" Redux: A Report of the Incidence of Hands-On Child Victimisation by Child Pornography Offenders'. *Journal of Family Violence* 24, 183–91.

Briggs, P., Simon, W. T. and Simonsen, S. (2011). 'An Exploratory Study on Internet-Initiated Sexual Offences and the Chat Room Sex Offender: Has the Internet Enabled a New Typology of Sex Offender?', *Sexual Abuse: A Journal of Research and Treatment* 23(4), March, 72–91.

Brown, S. (2005). *Treating Sex Offenders: An Introduction to Sex Offender Treatment Programmes* (Devon: Willan Publishing).

Buschman, J., Wilcox, D., Krapohl, D., Oelrich, M. and Hackett, S. (2010). 'Cybersex Offender Risk Assessment. An Explorative Study', *Journal of Sexual Aggression* 16(2), 197–209.

Card, R. (2004). *Sexual Offences: The New Law* (Bristol: Jordan Publishing Limited).

Calder, M. C. (2004). 'The Internet: Potential, Problems and Pathways to Hands On Sexual Offending', in M. C. Calder (ed.) *Sexual Abuse and the Internet: Tackling the New Frontier* (Russell House Publishing: Lyme Regis), 1–24.

Chapman, T. and Hough, M. (1998) *Evidence Based Practice. A Guide to Effective Practice*. Her Majesties Inspectorate of Probation, Home Office Publications Unit, London.

Craig, L. A. and Beech, A. (2009) 'Best Practice in Conducting Actuarial Risk Assessment with Adult Sexual Offenders'. *Journal of Sexual Aggression* 15(2), 193–211.

Eke, A. W., Seto, M. C. and Williams, J. (2011). 'Examining the Criminal History and Future Offending of Child Pornography Offenders: An Extended Prospective Follow-Up Study', *Law and Human Behavior* 35(6), 466–78.

Elliott, I. A. and Beech, A. R. (2009). 'Understanding Online Pornography Use: Applying Sexual Offence Theory to Internet Offenders', *Aggression and Violent Behaviour* 14, 180–93.

Fisher, D. and Beech, A. (1998). 'Reconstituting Families after Sexual Abuse: The Offenders Perspective'. *Child Abuse Review*, Nov–Dec., 20–35.

Glasgow, D. (2010). 'The Potential of Digital Evidence to Contribute to Risk Assessment of Internet Offenders', *Journal of Sexual Aggression*, 16(1), 87–106.

Glasgow, D., Osborne, A., and Croxen, J. (2003). 'An Assessment Tool for Investigating Paedophile Sexual Interest Using Viewing Time: An Application of Single Case Methodology', *British Journal of Learning Disabilities* 31, 96–102.

Grubin, D. (2010). 'A Trial of Voluntary Polygraph Testing in 10 English Probation Areas', *Sexual Abuse: A Journal of Research and Treatment*, 22(September), 266–78.

Howitt, D. and Sheldon, K. (2007). 'The Role of Cognitive Distortions in Paedophilic Offending: Internet and Contact Offenders Compared', *Psychology, Crime and Law* 13(5), 469–86.

Krone, T. (2004). 'A Typology of Online Child Pornography Offending', *Trends and Issues in Crime and Criminal Justice*. Australian Institute of Criminology, No. 279, July.

Mann, R. E., Carter, A. J. and Thornton, D. (2011). A Bio-Psycho-Social Model of Change for the Treatment of Sexual Offending. Unpublished document.

McCarthy, J. A. (2010). 'Internet Sexual Activity: A Comparison between Contact and Non-Contact Child Pornography Offenders', *Journal of Sexual Aggression* 16(2), 181–95.

Middleton, D. (2008). 'From Research to Practice: The Development of the Internet Sexual Offences Treatment Programme (i-SOTP)', *Irish Probation Journal*, 5(September), 49–65.

Middleton, D., Elliott, I. A., Mandeville-Norden, R. and Beech, A. R. (2006) .'An Investigation into the Applicability of the Ward and Siegert Pathways Model of Child Sexual Abuse with Internet Offenders', *Psychology, Crime and Law* 12, 589–603.

Middleton, D. and Hayes, E. (2006). *Internet Sexual Offences Treatment Programme Theory Manual* (NOMS Interventions Unit, Ministry of Justice, London).

Middleton, D., Mandeville-Norden, R. and Hayes, E. (2009). 'Does Treatment Work with Internet Sex Offenders? Emerging Findings from Internet Sex Offender Treatment Programme (i-SOTP)', *Journal of Sexual Aggression* 15, 5–19.

National Offender Management Service (NOMS) (2009). *SARN Treatment Need Analysis Scoring Guide – April* (Ministry of Justice).

O'Brien, M. and Webster, S. (2011). 'Assessment and Treatment Approaches with Online Sexual Offenders', in J. Davidson and P. Gottschalk (eds) *Internet Child Abuse: Current Research and Policy* (Routledge, Abingdon), 153–85.

Offending Behaviour Programmes Unit (2004). *Structured Assessment of Risk and Need (Sexual Offenders) Manual v. 2*, November (HM Prison Service).

Quayle, E., Erooga, M. Wright, L., Taylor, M. and Harbinson, D. (2006). *Only Pictures? Therapeutic Work with Internet Sex Offenders* (Russell House Publishing, Lyme Regis).

Seto, M. C. and Eke, A. W. (2005). 'The Criminal Histories and Later Offending of Child Pornography Offenders', *Sexual Abuse: A Journal of Research and Treatment*, 17, 201–10.

Seto, M. C., Hanson, R. K. and Babchishin, K. M. (2011). 'Contact Sexual Offending by Men with Online Sexual Offenses', *Sexual Abuse: A Journal of Research and Treatment* 23(1), 124–45.

Shute, S. (2007). 'Satellite Tracking of Offenders: A Study of the Pilots in England and Wales', *Research Summary 4* (Ministry of Justice).

Tate, T. (1993). 'The Child Pornography Industry: International Trade in Child Sexual Abuse', in C. Itzin (ed.) *Pornography: Women, Violence and Civil Liberties* (Oxford : Oxford University Press), 203–16.

Taylor, M. and Quayle, E. (2003). *Child Pornography: An Internet Crime* (Brunner-Routledge, Hove).

Thornton, D. (2010). Scoring Guide for Risk Matrix 2000.10/SVC: November 2010 Version. Unpublished manuscript.

Wakeling, H. C., Howard, P. D. and Barnett, G. D. (2011). 'Comparing the Validity of the RM2000 Scales and OGRS3 for Predicting Recidivism by Internet Sexual Offenders', *Sexual Abuse: A Journal of Research and Treatment* 23(1), March, 146–68.

Ward, T., Polaschek, D. L. L. and Beech, A. R. (2006). *Theories of Sexual Offending* (Chichester : John Wiley and Sons).

ONLINE REFERENCES

http://www.cps.gov.uk/legal/d_to_g/extreme_pornography/index.html#a02, Downloaded 16/02/2012.

http://www.salon.com/2006/12/19/offenders_2/, Downloaded on 16/02/2012.

http://www.abc.net.au/news/2011-10-29/satellite-tracking-sex-offenders/3607776, Downloaded on 16/02/2012.

http://www.thestar.com/news/canada/politics/article/1026544--hudak-vows-to-make-sex-offenders-wear-gps-devices. Downloaded on 16/02/2012.

http://lucyfaithfull.org/circles_of_support.htm. Downloaded on 17/02/2012.

http://www.quaker.org.uk/files/Circles-Interim-report-Nov-03.pdf Downloaded on 17/02/2012.

10 Female Offenders

Phil Coombes

INTRODUCTION

This chapter will look at the female forensic population, which has been shown to be an under-researched area of specialty, compared to other forensic populations. This disparity was identified by the Department of Health where concerns were raised about the services provided for females in forensic settings. A number of studies, particularly *Women's Mental Health: Into the Mainstream this also is a title by the DOH* (Department of Health, 2002), were generated in order to look at the appropriate treatment and detention of females within forensic settings; it was recognized that there was a need for female-specific services, as opposed to slight changes and adaptations to existing evidence-based male services. The chapter will identify the theories that have been discussed in previous chapters and any adaptations that have been made to them for a female population. It will then look at some of the different pathways females may take to come to the attention of forensic services, the role that trauma may present within this population and the impacts of all of these areas upon assessment and treatment interventions. It will look to finish with some practical implications for working with this population.

THEORETICAL OVERVIEW

There are numerous theories concerning female offending, which have developed over the past five decades, starting with biological through to social and psychological. For a fuller review of general female theories see chapter 6 ('Feminist Theories of Imprisonment and Penal Politics) in *Analysing Women's Imprisonment* (Carlen and Worral, 2004). Most feminist criminology involves critiques about how women offenders have been ignored, distorted or stereotyped within traditional criminology, but there is no shortage of separate theories and modifications of existing theories. Historically, criminologists have addressed the 'gender ratio' problem (why women are less likely, and men more likely, to commit crime) and from this, the generalizability problem. The 'generalizability problem' is concerned with whether or not general theories take account of both women's and men's criminality. In essence, the question is whether or not the same theories can be used to explain female and male crime. According to Gelsthorpe and Morris (1994), this idea 'has profound significance for theory construction'. With this in mind, the influential body of work 'doing gender – doing difference' emerged (Messerschmidt, 1986).

In more recent times, theories have moved away from being based on a feminist perspective to a more global theory of offending and females, endeavouring to highlight that it is not purely a female component alone, but there are numerous similarities to, as well as differences from, male offenders. This, however, seems to hit a stumbling block when an attempt is made to define more serious types of female offending. It would appear that explanation of serious crimes by males and females is more problematic, partly because the lower frequencies of offending complicate the task of quantitative analyses. Qualitative studies reveal major gender differences in the context and nature of offending. Traditional theories have not adequately explored such gender differences.

Early Theory

Studies of female offenders highlight the importance of relationships and the fact that criminal involvement often arises through relationships with family members, significant others or friends, also highlighting that abusive families and battering relationships are often strong themes in their lives (Chesney-Lind, 1997; Owen, 1998; Owen and Bloom, 1995; Pollock, 1998). Women offenders who cite drug abuse as self-medication often discuss personal relationships as the cause of their pain (Pollock, 1998). This has significant implications for therapeutic interventions that deal with the impact that these relationships have on women's present and future.

Criminology has treated women's role in crime with a large measure of indifference. Women who do not comply with societal expectations and go on to offend may be seen as those who question established beliefs or practices or who engage in activities associated with men or who commit crimes. These women are doubly damned and doubly deviant (Bottoms, 1996). They are seen as 'mad' not 'bad' (Lloyd, 1995). These behaviours frequently lead to interpretations of being mentally abnormal and unstable.

Female Theory: Current Adaptation

One of the most significant initial advancements was Adler's development of liberation theory in 1975, which allowed a shift from biological to social. It was hypothesized that with this increase in female prominence in society there would be a 'darker side', the premise of heavily increased crime rates among women (Adler, 1975). It would appear that the prediction of such high increases in female crime was overestimated, as statistics show the gender difference in offending is still substantial. Any alteration in criminal statistics with female offending has to be put into context, as rates are still low (minor alterations in offending can have high levels of significance and as such should be investigated further). Looking at the actual make up of female offenders, it is not those who have benefited positively from the feminist liberation movement who have gone on to become offenders, it is more likely to be those who fit lower economic and underprivileged backgrounds.

Agnew and Passas (1997) when looking at Strain theory hypothesized that individual deviance is a result of negative treatment from others, which often results in fear, despair and defeat. This in turn can lead to anger, which they believe is the component most linked to criminal behaviour (see Tables 10.1 and 10.2). They propose that external stressors decrease standard prosocial coping strategies and enforce maladaptive styles due to the negative affect that is created. This negative affect may then be internalized within the female population, and it could be suggested that this is more likely to be evidenced by passive aggressive acts. When looking at the amount of contextual strain people experience, it is shown that women actually have more strain on them. For example, historically there has been higher social pressure to conform and higher investment in creating and maintaining relationships than males and yet committing less crime (Broidy and Agnew, 1997).

From this, Broidy and Agnew proposed that the differences might not only be in the type of strain experienced but also in the emotional response.

Table 10.1 *Sex differences in types of strain*

Females	Males
Concerned with creating and maintaining close bonds and relationships with others – thus lower rates of property and violent crime	Concerned with material success – thus higher rates of property and violent crime
Face negative treatment, such as discrimination, high demands from family and restricted behaviour	Face more conflict with peers and are likely to be the victims of crime
Failure to achieve goals may lead to self-destructive behaviour	Failure to achieve goals may lead to property and violent crime

Source: Broidy and Agnew, 1997.

This led to a number of factors that Broidy and Agnew believed were protective of female criminality:

- Females more likely to lack confidence in this arena
  - As such less likely to initiate criminal acts

- Are more likely to employ avoidance to relieve strain
  - Avoidance often falling into self-defeating nature to self or nurturance of others rather than externalized anger out
- Have strong relational ties as a protective factor
  - With the investment in others comes greater responsibility and increases the difficulty in committing crime which may impact negatively on those we care about
- Be part of smaller less hierarchical groups
  - Within these groups the pressure to be 'top dog' is greatly reduced and with this less need to prove your worth by committing exaggerated offending to gain status in the group.

Factors leading to female crime were proposed:

- Females are also the targets of sexual, emotional and physical abuse, which are considered to be negative stimuli.
  - Possibly leading to feelings of guilt and shame which could lead to anger at the perpetrators of these events or anger at the lack of help preventing this from happening
- Females have this is correct expanded opportunities for financial gain through prostitution and related illicit sexual roles
  - With these roles being criminal in nature, risks in this area for conviction are high and are often linked to further types of criminal behaviour by the nature of those involved within this subgroup.

Table 10.2   *Sex differences in emotional response to strain*

Female	Male
More likely to respond with depression and anger	More likely to respond with anger
Anger is accompanied by fear, guilt and shame	Anger is followed by moral outrage
More likely to blame themselves and worry about the effects of their anger	Quick to blame others and are less concerned about hurting others
Depression and guilt may lead to self-destructive behaviours (e.g., eating disorders)	Moral outrage may lead to property and violent crime

Source: Broidy and Agnew, 1997.

PATHWAYS TO OFFENDING

So far, the study of criminal careers has centred almost exclusively on male offenders. As Gilfus (1992) notes, 'Little attention has been paid to questions such as whether there is such a thing as a female "criminal career" pattern and, if so, how that career begins and what shapes its contours.' The limited offence type research shows that female offenders are less likely to have committed violent offences and more likely to have been convicted of drug and alcohol-related crime. If convicted of violent crime, Phillips and Harm (1998), identified that it is likely to have been against an ex spouse or partner and offenders often report that they have been previously abused by the person they offended against.

Dobash *et al.* (1992) point out that the context of spousal violence is dramatically different for men and women. Compared to men, women are far more likely to kill only after a prolonged period of abuse, when they are in fear for their lives and have exhausted all alternatives.

'Doing gender' research proposes that gender pre-empts criminal involvement or directs it into scripted paths. For example, prostitution draws on and affirms femininity, while violence draws on and affirms masculinity.

Yet there are similarities between the two populations. Like male offenders, female offenders gravitate to those activities that are easily available, are within their skills, provide a satisfactory return, and carry the fewest risks.

Bloom and Steinhart (1993) identified that shame and guilt appeared to play a large component within the female offending population (often linked to limited or discontinued interaction with their children). This element has not been so heavily endorsed by male offenders. This difference is discussed further in this chapter when looking at assessment and intervention.

Chesney, Lind and Bloom (1997) identified that survival of abuse, poverty and substance abuse were the most common pathway to female offending. This is emphasized by Daly (1992) in which he identified five pathways to female offending:

1. The street woman, who was severely abused as a child, lives on the street, and generally ends up in court because she has been supporting her drug habit through selling drugs, prostitution and stealing;
2. The harmed-and-harming woman, who was also abused as a child, but who responded with anger and 'acting out', and who may have become violent through use of alcohol and/or other drugs;
3. The battered woman, who usually reaches court when she has harmed or killed a violent man with whom she is in or has just ended a relationship (unlike the previous two types of women, the battered woman usually does not have a previous criminal record);
4. The drug-connected woman, who 'uses or sells drugs as a result of her relationships with her male intimate, children, or mother ... like the battered women, she does not tend to have much of a criminal record';
5. Other women, who commit economically motivated crimes, either out of greed or poverty.

THE PREVALENCE OF TRAUMA WITHIN THE FEMALE OFFENDING POPULATION AND THE ROLE OF TRAUMA WORK

It was found by Burgess *et al.*, (1997) that offenders commonly have some history of abuse, and Finkelhor and Browne (1985) highlighted that victims of child sexual abuse were at a high level of risk to becoming prostitutes.

Van der Kolk *et al.* (1989) identified that exposure to extreme stress affects people at many levels of functioning, including somatic, emotional, cognitive, behavioural and characterological. Sighting a couple of key areas, that is, substance misuse (see Abueg and Fairbank (1991 and self-mutilation, Herman, Perry, Van der Kolk *et al.* (1989)), Van der Kolk highlights the need not to make simple causal relationships between trauma and these behaviours, and advises not being drawn in to blanket acceptance. However, he also argues that if we ignore past trauma, we may miss the ability to formulate and see past patterns re-emerging, Understanding how women create their lives to lessen the impact of these traumas could help to identify previous risk predictors and potential future risk increasing factors.

Briere and Runtz (1988) identified that traumatized people often have difficulty with affect regulation which can become self-destructive in nature, ranging from self-mutilation, unusual sexual practice and drug and alcohol abuse. Often such behaviours are seen in the female offending population. Exposure to abuse may lead to identification with the aggressor and expression of hate for those who remind them of their own helplessness. This can lead to lowered anxiety, but can also highlight that a move from a power position could weaken a sense of safety and mastery. This would emphasize the need to stay in what they see as a functional role and a safe way to view the world. Van der Kolk and Fisler (1995) goes on to identify that the inability to gain a sense of safety and security can lead to characterlogical deficits or the emergence of self-blame, guilt and shame, which in turn leads to difficulty trusting others, potentially increasing social isolation and a skewed narrative of the world. It would seem apparent that if in assessment post-traumatic stress disorder (PTSD) is identified, then this will have implication for intervention. This affect regulation difficulty can be best explained using Gilbert's Affect Regulation System (see Figure 10.1)

In compassion-focussed therapy it is hypothesized that this affect regulation system is poorly accessible in people with high shame and self-criticism, in whom the 'threat' affect regulation system dominates orientation to their inner and outer worlds. Compassion-focussed therapy is an integrated and multimodal approach that draws from evolutionary, social, developmental and Buddhist psychology and neuroscience.

The attachment styles and trauma histories above are often seen within the female offending population. If these issues are apparent, then it is likely these areas need to be addressed first in order to gain some emotional recognition

Figure 10.1   *Affect regulation systems*

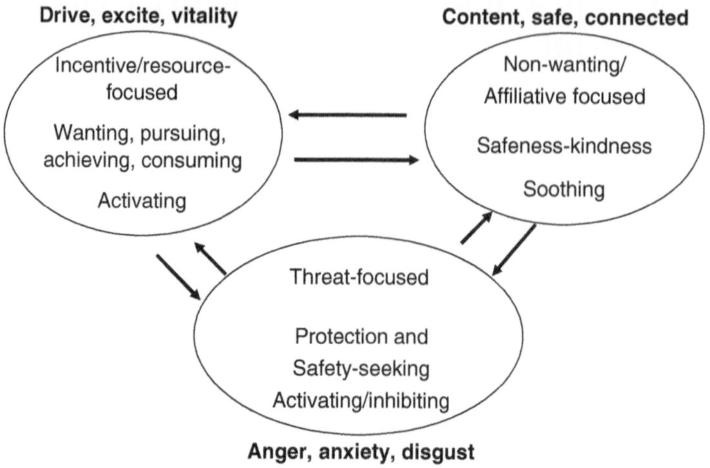

Drive, excite, vitality   **Content, safe, connected**

Incentive/resource-focused

Wanting, pursuing, achieving, consuming

Activating

Non-wanting/Affiliative focused

Safeness-kindness

Soothing

Threat-focused

Protection and Safety-seeking

Activating/inhibiting

Anger, anxiety, disgust

Source: Gilbert (2005a) *Compassion Focussed Therapy*. Reproduced with permission from Constable and Robinson.

and regulation skills prior to approaching offence-related work, by increasing understanding of self and internal structures as well as self and place in the world which can reduce the risk of recidivism.

Kluft (1990) showed that traumatized people often showed a lack of internal locus of control. This lack of internal control is often seen with the offending population and is targeted by a number of offending programmes, When looking at substance misuse in this context, the correlation between substance abuse and PTSD was considerably higher than in the general population (see Keane and Wolf, 1990). It was shown that substance abusers often select types of drugs dependent upon their effects, that is, heroin has effects on muting feelings of rage, cocaine acts as antidepressant and alcohol may act as a short-term medication for sleep disturbance. It is intuitive that if the underlying problem driving people to these maladaptive coping strategies is not addressed, then they are likely to recur, as they have historically been perceived to work by the individual.

There are some offenders who cycle through the system, who are labelled as untreatable or provoke strong responses of anger within psychologists. It may be worth taking time to examine what dynamic is being played out within therapy and to formulate the behaviours exhibited into a combined understanding of each person's role in sustaining this behaviour. Herman (1992) identifies that often those clients who lack the ability to negotiate within treatment are often most at risk of re-enacting this abuse within treatment, as they do not give clear indications of their emotions and thoughts. This could equally be applied to their daily interaction and approaches to situations in the community. With this population it is likely there will be increases in self-injurious behaviours or maladaptive coping styles as they try to make sense of how current stress is being linked to historical events. As such psychologists need to be able to offer valida-tion, support and avoid participating in re-enactments of past behaviours.

ASSESSMENT OF FEMALE OFFENDERS

A thorough and robust assessment is paramount in being able to understand and formulate an offender's presenting behaviours and future treatment needs. This is best achieved if the assessment can be built up over a number of sessions, to work on building a successful therapeutic relationship. Bearing in mind the earlier identification of views of authority figures and the role they play within their lives (Herman, 1992) it can be seen how difficult it may be for female offenders to engage in the assessment and treatment process.

Many will have an established protective persona in place that will allow them to achieve the desired sense of self that they require in order to 'survive' the envi-ronment in which they find themselves. Part of the assessment and intervention should look at how to work collaboratively with the offender in obtaining a joint understanding of previous behaviours and how they may then be played out over the coming months and years. The empowerment to look at this jointly is often a very useful technique to allow psychologist and the offender to challenge cognitive distortions (see chapter 7 ('Survivor of Trauma') in Herman, 1992).

The assessment process should also provide the basis for developing indi-vidual treatment plans, establishing a baseline from which progress in treat-ment can be monitored, and generate data for programme evaluation (Wellisch, Prendergast and Anglin, 1994).

Recent research has suggested that 'gender-informed' measures are likely to be a more valid tool than existing methods when classifying offender need and risk. Evaluation of how we assess the need and risk of women incarcerated in England and Wales is required, with focus on the criminogenic needs of women, the con-text of their lives and their pathways into crime. While an entirely new method of assessment focussed on women may be required, it seems equally possible that a more simple 'reweighting' of existing methods may be sufficient – focussed on both gender-mutual and female-specific needs.

Psychometric assessment should be utilized as part of procedure and not to be viewed in isolation. A full battery of assessments is most useful, as well as obser-vation over initial weeks. This allows the build up of a full baseline of data as well as an understanding of the individual, their risks to others and themselves, problem areas that are apparent and the working out of an individualized treat-ment pathway in collaboration with the offender. Having this as a start point also allows the therapeutic relationship to be generated alongside the process. Having a broad array of standardized assessments allows the psychologist to keep track of the interventions proposed and then allow checks to see if those interventions have reduced risk.

One of the difficulties working with the female population is that some of the standard risk assessments and measures that are used do not have validated norms for the client group. This is becoming less common with more normative data becoming available as the importance of female offending and recidivism is stepped up.

SPECIAL CONSIDERATIONS WHEN INTERVIEWING FEMALE OFFENDERS

A basic principle that should be considered with all forensic populations is to know who the client is and what strengths and limitations they bring to the treatment setting.

Therapist Gender

The ability to offer female offenders the choice of gender they would feel most comfortable working with can be very beneficial. If, for example, you are a male psychologist, a female offender may prefer to discuss a previous rape with a female. However, do not assume this is the case; a female psychologist may be construed as more intimidating. The ability to offer flexibility while ensuring dignity, respect and safety to both parties is paramount. The benefits of being a positive role model with offenders no matter what your gender should always be in mind.

Transference

One of the most useful ways of understanding the role of the psychologist and others within assessment and treatment could be to utilize the transactional analysis model (see Figure 10.2) (Karpman Drama Triangle, Karpman, 1968) Historically, it was used to look at cognitive distortions among sexual offenders both as abusers and victims. However, it is a handy way of observing and questioning our roles in most situations.

The model posits three habitual psychological roles that people often take in a situation:

- The person who is treated as, or accepts the role of, a *victim*
- The person who pressures, coerces or *persecutes* the victim and
- The *rescuer* who intervenes out of an ostensible wish to help the situation or the victim.

It also represents the development of an ideal role as healthy in the middle where both parties are able to access parts of the corners but not to an extent that inhibits healthy dialogue.

Figure 10.2 *Karpman Drama Triangle*

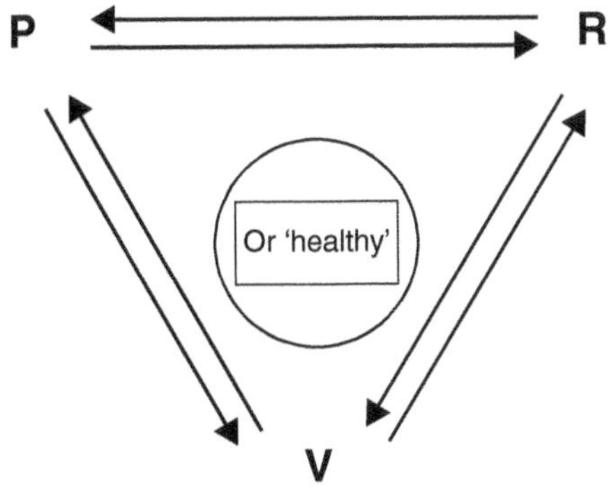

P ←————————→ R

Or 'healthy'

V

Source: Karpman, 1968.

When working with offenders from any group, the power dynamic is always biased towards the psychologist. As such it is very easy to be placed in one of these roles by the person you are working with. All roles are equally perilous and the skill lies in being able to manage these roles by oneself while enabling movement for the offender.

Female offenders may have had historic abuse issues that could increase the propensity to fall to the victim role, thus pushing psychologist either to rescuer or persecutor. If meeting for the first time, it is more likely the role of the persecutor will be assigned due to power imbalance.

If stuck in any of these roles, the ability to allow shift/change for the offender you are working with is important. The benefit of maintaining a neutral stance or healthy role is to allow the offender to move from their default role and experience other roles while the psychologist maintains a healthy functional role within this. The hope is that as the person in front of the psychologist checks out these roles over time, they may come to be able to spend time in the healthy role looking at the dysfunctional aspects of the corners previously occupied. This is also a good way to understand and check the psychologist's own practice when reflecting on session delivery. If you have experienced extreme emotions, it is likely that you will have shifted from the healthy centre towards one of the corners.

Bowlby (1988) identified that in behavioural re-enactments of the trauma, the victim can take on the role of the victim, victimizer or both, and as an assessor and treatment provider it is essential to bear this in mind.

If the offender has a history of targeting, the psychologist needs to be aware of previous instances and how events have occurred. A thorough file review and discussions with those who work with that individual regularly will enable the psychologist to put the strongest and safest measures in place.

Ensure that the offender is safe if they have a history of significant self-harm. Work on how to keep them safe during interventions. Behavioural plans can work well in this regard, identifying trigger factors, types of likely outcomes and best ways to deal with the onset of behaviours. Behavioural contracts can sometimes be useful when working with someone who presents with high risk to self or others; a contract can be drawn up at the start of sessions to ensure both persons safety within session.

As with any population, there is the possibility of assault during session, if challenging beliefs or cognitive distortions are held by the client. As a psychologist, always ensure you inform another person that you are in a session with a client; if working in the community, arrange to phone in before and after sessions to ensure safety. As a psychologist walks into a room with an offender, be aware of how the room is set up, if possible the psychologist should place themselves in a visible position from the door and be aware of any obstructions in their way in case of need for emergency exit. If appropriate, they should be aware of breakaway techniques that can be implemented. It is always paramount that the psychologist feels safe within a session. If not, then termination of the session at a point that is most suitable is appropriate. With some clients groups a psychologist will be issued an alarm; it is the responsibility of the psychologist to check if this is in working order and that they know how to activate this if necessary.

If a psychologist feels unsafe within session, they are unlikely to implement an effective intervention, and as such termination of the session is most appropriate. Following this, evaluation is necessary in order to ensure it is the appropriate intervention and that the identified psychologist is the appropriate individual to undertake this piece of work and the client is suitable and appropriate to work with.

Transparency

Honesty and transparency with all can allow difficult discussions to be had. If a psychologist is honest and transparent, it is likely that they will develop a stronger trusting therapeutic relationship that is likely to have a more beneficial outcome. It is also less likely to encourage collusion or splitting, as offenders know 'where they stand'. It also allows the psychologist to hold a different standpoint to the offender with discussions possible, as they will have been aware of the psychologist's position from the start.

Consistency

The ability to be consistent can allow a degree of certainty and security that the offender may not have felt often before. If they are aware of how the psychologist reacts and are able to replicate this within sessions, then while they may push to achieve reactions within the psychologist, they can feel confident in the knowledge of who the psychologist is and how they approach issues.

FORMULATING AND INTERVENTION WITH FEMALE OFFENDERS

Undertaking formulation with this client group is best done, as mentioned, in a collaborative process that is ever evolving alongside assessment and then latterly intervention. Validation and challenge are beneficial and are often easiest achieved if there is a trusting therapeutic relationship. The development of a shared understanding and language will facilitate the offender's insight into their own past and current behaviours while allowing them to share this concept with the rest of their clinical team. Disclosure of this nature by offenders can cause disagreements within teams regarding belief or non-belief of explanation. This can be particularly anxiety provoking for offenders to share their ideas of the rationale or reasons behind offences they may have committed or identifying potential risks to themselves and others in current or future arenas. However, if an offender is encouraged and validated to share this information, then this challenge can work at developing their own understanding of the roles they play and the roles they put other people in to. With relationships being so key to safety and risk in this population, being able to see these dynamics played out within the team can be helpful. It can be seen that the more the offender takes ownership of their formulation, the more they are able to challenge distorted cognitions both in themselves and others, which will be beneficial when looking at past, current and future risk.

Intervention

Development of interventions has been orientated towards male offenders who comprise a much larger segment of the offender population. Interventions based upon male offending characteristics are rarely appropriate for women (Murphy, 2004), or easily adapted for their use. For example, women who receive additional requirements to probation orders which are designed for delivery through group work may end up completing the work on a one-one basis, rather than within a group as intended, and with resultant questionable effectiveness in terms of reducing reoffending. This can be due to a number of reasons. If these interventions are being undertaken in the community, the availability for offender's childcare may impact upon availability to attend regular group sessions. Alternatively, the adaptations for a female population within group work have not been undertaken and as such the delivery of otherwise standardized interventions for males would not be appropriate and therefore the alterations and delivery are more achievable on an individual basis. It is worthy of note that as has been highlighted earlier in this chapter, the support that females offer each other and the relationships that can be built can lead to very supportive and effective group interventions.

In Carlen and Worrall's (2004, p. 152) *Analysing Women's Imprisonment* they cite Eaton (1993): 'women offenders need to feel that they are people of worth and be sustained in reciprocal rather than subordinate or exploitative relationships'. This concept should be built in to develop appropriate interventions within this population where previous abuse is often prevalent and the need for reciprocal roles is paramount for potential change in behaviours.

Most interventions continue to merely follow the 'what works' literature which highlight that, in essence, current interventions with female offenders are those designed for male offenders with a few alterations, potentially, to the scenarios which are used. This seems to miss some of the fundamental areas that have been highlighted that interventions should 'take into account real differences between men and women in their learning and relationship styles and life circumstances'.

King and Brosnan (1998) identified that women at times find it difficult to address issues via group work due to the difficulty they may encounter from discussing personal traumatic histories that may be high in affect. Unless this is addressed, women may be unable or unwilling to engage constructively in programmes in a genuine effort to avoid repeated exposure to traumatic emotion/reliving of the trauma narrative.

It has been highlighted that the path to offending is markedly different between genders, as is the content and context of offending. As such, the necessity of gender-specific treatments appears evident. Herman (1992), whose work is predominantly framed around trauma and recovery, has highlighted the benefits of a multiphasic approach to treatment which would seem to fit well within this population, where the propensity of negative attachments and relationships are often prevalent both in the initial pathway to offending and subsequently the possible difficulty in developing and maintaining therapeutic relationships to assist potential change.

Beckman (1994) recommends in the criteria for a gender-specific treatment programme that the following should have been assessed and a formulation should look at these areas and allow them to develop:

- It is delivered in a setting compatible with females' interactional styles, such as their need for and responsiveness to social relationships.
- It takes into account gender roles and female socialization.
- It does not allow sexual harassment.
- It supports active, interdependent roles for women and girls.
- It addresses females' unique treatment issues, such as trauma, parenting skills, coping mechanisms, and self-worth.
- It encourages the development of a sense of self and self-esteem.
- It nurtures the establishment of trusting, growth-fostering relationships.
- It develops physical health.
- Developing awareness and address of substance misuse.

- Developing and addressing understanding of sexuality.
- Awareness of mental health.
- Knowledge of pregnancy and parenting skills.
- Help with decision-making skills.
- Understanding of trauma from physical, emotional, and sexual abuse – treatment and prevention.
- Focussing on cultural awareness and sensitivity.
- Being knowledgeable of spirituality needs.

Koons *et al.* (1997, p. 513) note 'that a sizable number of promising programme models approached the treatment of women offenders using a comprehensive and holistic strategy for meeting their needs'. Wellisch, Prendergast and Anglin (1994) identify a correlation between longer therapeutic programmes and positive therapeutic results.

Awareness of these areas should assist in effective treatment. Often, the need for safe attachment allows the development of appropriate self-regulatory behaviours (Putnam, 1988). The development of self-regulation and trust are often a perfect first step of treatment. It is frequently seen that the offender will try to recreate their historic relationship dynamic within treatment, putting the psychologist in the role of victim rescuer of or victimizer depending upon the offender's needs.

To encourage mindfulness and compassion as a focus of intervention can be very effective within this population. If the individual is allowed and supported to experience and tolerate the distressing emotion or thought, then they are often able to survive without needing to resort to maladaptive strategies. Reduced affect often leads to the ability to attend to the problem and implement alternative strategies of a prosocial nature.

CONCLUSION

This chapter is a very brief overview of what is a complex and under-researched population. The need to develop offender programmes which are specific to a female client group, highlighting awareness of the complexity and different need in this population, is paramount. While the female offending population is smaller than its male counterpart, it is no less worthy of investment and understanding. Over the past twenty years, many advancements have been made in theory of female offending, however, there are still some under-reported areas, for example, trauma and its impact upon offending behaviours, which is still rarely taken in to consideration when delivering interventions. This population is challenging in nature with high levels of displayed affect and skewed attachment styles; however, it can be a highly rewarding population to work with.

RECOMMENDED FURTHER READING

Carlen, P. and Worrall, A. (2004). *Analysing Women's Imprisonment* (William Publishing). This provides a good general overview of theory related to female offending as well as treatment.

Broidy, L. and Agnew, R. (1997). 'Gender and Crime: A General Strain Theory Perspective', *Journal of Research in Crime and Delinquency* 34(3), 275–306. This a good paper for a review of the better theories about female crime.

Herman, J. (1992). *Trauma and Recovery* (New York: HarperCollins). This book assists in understanding the role of phased interventions when working with victims of abuse and their subsequent presentations

Gilbert, P. (2005). *The Compassionate Mind* (London: Constable and Robinson Ltd.). An excellent resource for understanding the biology of the brain as well as then linking that to multiple treatment models.

REFERENCES

Abueg, F. and Fairbank, J. (1991). 'Behavioural Treatment of the PTSD Substance Abuser', in P. A. Saigh (ed.) *Post-Traumatic Stress Disorder: A Behavioural Approach to Assessment and Treatment* (New York: Pergamon Press).

Adler, F. (1975). *Sisters in Crime* (New York: McGraw-Hill).

Broidy, L. and Agnew, R. (1997). 'Gender and Crime: A General Strain Theory Perspective', *The Journal of Research in Crime and Delinquency* 34, 275–306.

Agnew, R. and Passas, N. (1997). *The Future of Anomie* (Boston: Northeastern University Press).

Arnold R. (1989). 'Processes of Criminalization from Girlhood to Womanhood', in M Zinn, B Dill (ed.) *Women of Color in American Society* (Philadelphia: Temple University Press).

Beckman, L. (1994). 'Treatment Needs of Women with Alcohol Problems', *Alcohol, Health and Research World* 18(3), 206–11.

Bloom, B. and Steinhart, D. (1993). *Why Punish the Children? A Reappraisal of the Children of Incarcerated Mothers in America* (San Francisco, CA: National Council on Crime and Delinquency).

Bowlby, J. (1988). *A Secure Base* (New York: Basic Book).

Bottoms, A. E. (1996). 'The Philosophy of Punishment and Sentencing', in C. M. V. Clarkson and R. Morgans (eds) *The Politics of Sentencing Reform* (Oxford: Clarendon Press).

Briere, J. and Runtz, M. (1988). 'Post-Sexual Abuse Trauma', in G. E. Wyatt and G. Powell (eds) *The Lasting Effects of Child Sexual Abuse* (Newbury Park, CA: Sage).

Brody, L. R. (1985). 'Gender Differences in Emotional Development: A Review of Theories and Research', *Journal of Personality* 14, 102–49.

Broidy, L. andAgnew, R. (1997). 'Gender and Crime: A General Strain Theory Perspective', *Journal of Research in Crime and Delinquency* 34(3), 275–306.

Burgess, A, Baker, T, Greening, D, Hartman, C, Burgess, A, Douglas, *et al.* (1997). 'Stalking Behaviours within Domestic Violence', *Journal of Family Violence* 12(4), 389–403.

Carlen, P. (1983). *Women's Imprisonment: A Study in Social Control* (London: Routledge).

Carlen, P. and Worrall, A. (2004). *Analysing Women's Imprisonment* (Cullompton, Devon: William Publishing).

Chesney-Lind, M. (1997). *The Female Offender: Girls, Women, and Crime* (Thousand Oaks, CA: Sage).

Chesney-Lind, M. (1989). 'Girls, Crime and Women's Place: Towards a Feminist Model of Female Delinquency', *Crime and Delinquency* 35(1), pp. 10–31.

Chesney-Lind, M. and Bloom, B. (1997). 'Feminist Criminology: Thinking about Women and Crime', in B. MacLean and D. Milovanovic (eds) *Thinking Critically about Crime* (Vancouver, Canada: Collective Press), 45–55.

Chesney-Lind, M. and Pasko, L. (2004). *The Female Offender* (Thousand Oaks, CA: Sage).

Daly, K. and Chesney-Lind, M. (1988). 'Feminism and Criminology', *Justice Quarterly* 5(4), 497–538.

Daly, K. (1992). 'Women's Pathways to Felony Court: Feminist Theories of Lawbreaking and Problems of Representation', *Review of Law and Women's Studies* 2, 11–52.

Department of Health (2002). *Women's Mental Health: Into the Mainstream* (London, Department of Health, October).

Durkheim, E. (1893). *The Division of Labor in Society*, W. D. Halls (tr.) (1984) (New York: Free Press).

Dobash R., Dobash, R. E., Wilson, M., Daly, M. (1992). 'The Myth of Sexual Symmetry in Marital Violence', *Social. Problems*, 39, 71–91.

Eaton, M. (1986). *Justice for Women* (Milton Keynes: Open University Press).

Finkelhor, D. and Browne, A. (1985). 'The Traumatic Impact of Child Sexual Abuse: A Conceptualization', *American Journal of Orthopsychiatry* 55(4), 530–41.

Gelsthorpe, L. and Morris, A. (eds) (1994) *Feminist Perspectives in Criminology* (Milton Keynes: Open University Press).

Gilbert, P. (ed.) (2005a). *Compassion: Conceptualisations, Research and Use in Psychotherapy* (London: Routledge).

Gilfus, M. (1992). 'From Victims to Survivors to Offenders: Women's Routes of Entry into Street Crime', *Women and Criminal Justice*, 4(1), 63–89.

Herman, J. (1992). *Trauma and Recovery* (New York: HarperCollins).

Herman, J. L., Perry, J. C., Van der Kolk, B *et al.* (1989). 'Childhood Trauma in Borderline Personality Disorder', *American Journal of Psychiatry* 146(4), 490–5 (April 1989).

Karpman, S. (1968). 'Fairy Tales and Script Drama Analysis', *Transactional Analysis Bulletin* 7(26), 39–43.

Keane, T. M. and Wolf, J. (1990). 'Co-Morbidity in Post Traumatic Stress Disorder: Analysis of Community and Clinical Studies', *Journal of Applied Social Psychology* 20, 1776–88.

King and Brosnan, M. (1998). 'Psychological Group Programmes for Female Prisoners at HMP Holloway', *Prison Research and Development Bulletin* 6, 14–15.

Klein, D. and Kress, J. (1979). 'Any Woman's Blues', in F. Adler and R. J. Simon (eds) *The Criminology of Deviant Women* (Boston: Houghton Mifflin), 82–90.

Koons, B., Burrow, J., Morash, M. and Bynum, T. (1997). 'Expert and Offender Perceptions of Program Elements Linked to Successful Outcomes for Incarcerated Women', *Crime and Delinquency*, 43(4), 512–32.

Kluft, R. P. (ed.) (1990). *Incest-Related Syndromes of Adult Psychopathology* (Washington, DC: American Psychiatric Press).

Kruttschnitt C. (1994). 'Gender and Interpersonal Violence', in J. Roth and A. Reiss (eds) *Understanding and Preventing Violence: Social Influences* (Washington, DC: National Academic Scientist), 295–378.

Leonard, E. B. (1982). *Women, Crime and Society: A Critique of Criminology Theory* (New York: Longman).

Lombroso, C. (1911). *Crime: Its Causes and Remedies* (New York: Little, Brown).

Lloyd, E. (1995). *Prisoners Children: Research, Policy and Practice* (London: Save the Children).

Mann, C. R. (1984). *Female Crime and Delinquency* (University, AL: The University of Alabama Press).

McCarthy, B. and Hagan, J. (1992). 'Mean Streets: The Theoretical Significance of Situational Delinquency and Homeless Youths', *American Journal of Sociology* 98, 597–627.

Merton, R. K. (1957). *Social Theory and Social Structure.* 2nd edn (New York: The Free Press).

Messerschmidt J. (1986). *Capitalism, Patriarchy, and Crime: Toward a Socialist Feminist Criminology* (Totowa, NJ: Rowman and Littlefield).

Morash, M. and Chesney-Lind, M. (1991). 'A Reformulation and Partial Test of the Power Control Theory of Delinquency', *Justice Quarterly*, 8, 347–77.

Murphy, K. (2004). The Female Offender: Existing Gaps and Underlying Issues of Female Focussed Interventions. Probation and community corrections officers' association conference.

Naffine, (1981). 'Theorizing about Female Crime', in S. Mukherjee and J. A. Scutt (eds) *Women and Crime* (North Sydney: Allen and Unwin), 70–91.

Owen, B. (1998). *'In the Mix': Struggle and Survival in a Women's Prison* (Albany: State University of New York Press).

Owen, B., and Bloom, B. (1995). *Profiling the Needs of California's Female Prisoners: A Needs Assessment* (Washington, D.C.: National Institute of Corrections).

Phillips, S. and Harm, N. (1998). 'Women Prisoners: A Contextual Framework', in J. Harden and M. Hill (eds) *Breaking the Rules: Women in Prison and Feminist Therapy* (New York: Haworth Press), 1–9.

Pollak, O. (1950). *The Criminality of Women* (Philadelphia: University of Pennsylvania Press).

Pollock, J. (1999). *Criminal Women* (Cincinnati, OH: Anderson).

Putnam, F. W. (ed.) (1988). *Diagnosis and Treatment of Multiple Personality Disorder* (New York: Guilford Press).

Rossi A. (1984). 'Gender and Parenthood', *American Sociological Review* 49, 1–19.

Steffensmeier, D. J. (1983). 'Organization Properties and Sex-Segregation in the Underworld: Building a Sociological Theory of Sex Differences in Crime', *Social Forces*, 61(4), 1010–32.

Steffensmeier, D. J. *and* Steffensmeier, R. H. (1980). 'Trends in Female Delinquency: An Examination of Arrest, Juvenile Court, Self-Report, and Field Data', *Criminology* 18, 62–85.

Steffensmeier, D. J. and Allan, E. (1996). 'Gender and Crime: Toward a Gendered Theory of Female Offending', *Annual Review of Sociology* 22, 459–87.

Steinmetz, S. and Lucca, J. (1988). 'Husband Beating', in R. Hassselt, A. Morrison, S. Bellack and M. Hersen (eds) *Handbook of Family Violence* (New York: Plenum), 233–46.

Van der Kolk, B. A., and Fisler, R. (1995). 'Dissociation and the Fragmentary Nature of Traumatic Memories: Overview and Exploratory Study', *Journal of Traumatic Stress* 8, 505–25.

Van der Kolk, B. A. Van der Hart, O. and Pierre, J. (1989). ' the Breakdown of Adaptation in Psychological Trauma', *American Journal of Psychiatry* 146, 1530–40.

Wellisch, J., Prendergast, M. and Anglin, D. (1994). 'Drug-Abusing Women Offenders: Results of a National Survey', National Institute of Justice: Research in Brief (Washington, DC: Government Printing Office).

11 Sexual Offenders

Phil Willmot

INTRODUCTION

Sexual offenders are likely to be among the most complex and challenging clients that forensic psychologists have to work with. While developing a respectful, compassionate and boundaried approach is important with any forensic group, such an approach is often more difficult but more essential with sexual offenders.

It is important for forensic practice to be grounded in theoretical understanding of sexual offending, and this chapter begins with a theoretical overview of the subject. It deals with theoretical understandings of adult male sex offenders and particularly those whose offending involves physical contact with their victims. Different considerations apply to female and juvenile offenders (see Chapter 8) and those involved in internet pornography (see Chapter 9). However the subsequent practical sections of this chapter arguably apply equally to all sexual offenders. It then goes on to consider the relationship between psychologist and sexual offender, a little considered aspect of this type of work, but an important one. The final section of this chapter will discuss particular considerations when assessing, formulating and disclosing reports to sexual offenders.

THEORETICAL OVERVIEW OF SEX OFFENDING

There are a number of different theories to account for sexual offending. For a review and critique of these models, readers should refer to Ward and Sorbello (2003).

The first model to inform clinicians was Finkelhor's (1984) *Four Preconditions Model* of child sexual abuse, which proposed four steps or preconditions on the path towards child sexual abuse. These were: (1) motivation to offend, which involved either sexual arousal to, or emotional congruence with, children and a blockage in the adult's ability to meet their sexual needs with an adult partner; (2)

overcoming internal inhibitions to offend, which involved factors such as stress, substance abuse or distorted thinking which justified or minimized the effect of offending; (3) overcoming external inhibitions, by creating an opportunity for abuse to take place; and (4) overcoming the victim's resistance.

Hall and Hirschman's (1992) *Quadripartite Model* also proposed four preconditions for sexual offending against adults or children. These conditions were: (1) deviant sexual preference; (2) distorted beliefs about offending and about the victim; (3) lack of emotional control; and (4) problematic personality traits resulting from early adverse experiences.

Marshall and Barbaree's (1990) *Integrated Theory* of sexual offending focussed more on the developmental pathway leading to sexual offending behaviour. It proposed that men who went on to offend sexually typically underwent a range of developmental experiences which led to insecure patterns of attachment, low self-worth, poor emotion regulation and poor interpersonal coping skills. These patterns were reinforced, particularly in adolescence, by dysfunctional patterns of social and sexual interaction and cultural influences including the media, pornography and social norms.

Ward and Siegert's (2002) *Pathway's Model* provides a more complex and comprehensive model, based on elements of the other theories, and is arguably the most influential and widely used current model of sexual offending behaviour. It proposes that biological factors, childhood experiences and cultural influences lead to vulnerabilities in a number of areas. The pathways model proposes four distinct and interacting psychological mechanisms relating to sexual offending, with each mechanism involving a specific pathway towards sexual offending, each with its own psychological and behavioural profiles. While each pathway is associated with specific mechanisms and problems, the mechanisms also interact to lead to sexual offending. Ward and Siegert proposed that every sexual offence will involve components of all four domains of dysfunction, but that one would be primary. They described the different pathways as follows:

Intimacy deficits. Individuals who offend on this pathway tend to offend only at specific times, for example when a preferred partner is not available or in response to rejection or loneliness.

Distorted sexual scripts. Individuals who offend on this pathway have distorted scripts and so tend to equate sex with intimacy, possibly as a result of experiences of early sexual abuse.

Emotional dysregulation. Individuals who offend on this pathway have problems with identifying, labelling or regulating emotions. This may lead, particularly when sexually aroused, to disinhibited or impulsive sexual behaviour in an attempt to relieve intense and distressing emotions.

Antisocial cognitions. Individuals who offend on this pathway have pro-criminal, as well as patriarchal and misogynistic, attitudes and beliefs. Sexual offending may be opportunist and disinhibited by substance misuse.

Multiple dysfunctional mechanisms. The final pathway involves individuals with deviant sexual scripts and deviant sexual arousal as well as dysfunction in other domains. These offenders are often described as pure or 'fixated' paedophilic offenders.

The different models have a number of features in common. In particular there are a number of factors in common to most or all of these models, which can be summarized as:

- Dysfunctional schemas and distorted beliefs
- Attachment and interpersonal problems
- Deviant sexual arousal and distorted sexual scripts
- Difficulties in regulating emotional states

Dysfunctional Core Schemas and Distorted Beliefs

Many cognitive theories of psychology involve the concept of schemas. One of the most developed of these is Young's (1990, Young, Klosko and Weishaar, 2003) concept of early maladaptive schemas, which are self-defeating, core themes or patterns of core beliefs that develop in childhood and are repeated throughout life. Such early maladaptive schemas are ubiquitous in the general population, though Bernstein, Arntz and de Vos (2007) have proposed a general schema-based model of offending.

Mann and Beech (2003) distinguished two types of schemas that were relevant in sexual offenders; *category schemas* that involve hostile or sexual beliefs about women or children, and *belief schemas* that contain assumptions about the self and how the world and other people should be. These belief schemas are similar to Young's concept of early maladaptive schemas.

Examples of category schemas include:

- Seeing children as sexual beings, willing and able to engage in sexual activity with adults
- Women as being deceitful or untrustworthy

Examples of belief schemas include:

- Seeing oneself as worthless or unable to control the world or one's own behaviour.
- Entitlement, seeing one's own needs as more important than others.
- A need to control others.
- Seeing the world as dangerous, others as rejecting and abusive.
- Overvaluing sex as a source of happiness.

According to Mann and Beech, dysfunctional schemas interact with life events to produce hostile thoughts. In the context of other vulnerability factors such as

intimacy deficits, impulsivity, poor self-management and deviant sexual interests, these thoughts increase the risk of sexual offending behaviour.

According to Marshall and Barbaree's (1990) model of sexually abusive behaviour, developmental adversity, poor parenting, inconsistent or harsh discipline and
abuse lead to such dysfunctional schemas in sexual offenders, though this pattern
is by no means unique to sexual offenders (Young, Klosko and Weishaar, 2003).

A number of researchers have found evidence for particular category schemas.
For example Ward and Keenan (1999) identified five implicit theories that account
for many of the cognitive distortions presented by sex offenders. These are:

- Seeing children as sexual beings, willing and able to engage in sexual activity
  with adults.
- Entitlement, seeing their own needs as more important than others.
- Believing that sex with children is not harmful to them.
- Seeing the world as dangerous and others as rejecting and abusive.
- Seeing the world as uncontrollable; offences are also beyond the offender's
  control.

Malamuth *et al.* (1991) found that among acquaintance rapists, childhood experiences of parental conflict had led to the development of aggressive adversarial
schemas about intimate relationships between men and women. Malamuth
and Brown (1994) found evidence for a suspiciousness schema among sexually
aggressive men.

Mann and Hollin (2007) identified a number of categories of schemas from
the treatment records of convicted rapists; these included a sense of grievance,
particularly towards women, seeing self as a victim, a need to be in control
over others, entitlement and disrespect for certain women, such as prostitutes.
Among sexual offenders against children they found evidence for the grievance
and need for control schemas, though Mann and Hollin suggested that dysfunctional schemas appeared to be more salient for rapists than for child molesters.

Attachment and Interpersonal Problems

Childhood patterns of insecure attachment are common among sexual offenders. Ward, Hudson and Marshall (1996) reported that 67 per cent of non-violent
offenders, 97 per cent of violent offenders, 70 per cent of rapists and 82 per cent
of child abusers were found to have an insecure attachment style and reported
attachment difficulties in their adult relationships. Smallbone and Dadds (1998)
compared the attachment styles of sexual offenders, property offenders and
non-offenders and found that sexual offenders reported significantly less secure
maternal, paternal and adult attachment than the non-offenders and less secure
maternal attachment than the property offenders. Intra-familial child abusers
reported more problematic relationships while stranger rapists were found to
have particularly problematic relationships with their fathers, reporting them to

have been unsympathetic, uncaring, abusive and violent. Smallbone and Dadds (2000) examined the relationship between childhood attachment and coercive sexual behaviour in a sample of male students. They found that insecure childhood attachment, particularly insecure paternal attachment, was predictive of aggressive and sexually coercive behaviour in adulthood. This appears to be consistent with a social learning model of behaviour in which boys copy a range of paternal behaviours, including patterns of behaviour with women and children, abusive attitudes and emotion regulation strategies.

Ward *et al.* (1995) developed Marshall's insight into the importance of insecure attachment and integrated it with Bartholomew's (1990) model of attachment styles.

Individuals with a secure attachment styles (positive view of self/ positive view of others) feel worthy of intimacy and have an expectation that others are generally warm and accepting. Their interpersonal strategies and internal working models generally result in high levels of intimacy in close adult relationships.

Individuals with an anxious/ambivalent attachment style (negative view of self/ positive view of others) constantly seek the approval of valued others, resulting in a preoccupied, dependent relationship style. They blame themselves when relationships go wrong, leading to reduced self-esteem and increased approval-seeking behaviour. Because they tend to be preoccupied with relationships they are likely to be often in emotional relationships. Ward *et al.* (1995) suggest that, since such individuals lack self-confidence and see themselves as unworthy of love, they tend to seek the approval of others. Having a partner whom they can control and who admires them, such as a child, will make these individuals feel secure. If such individuals did form a sexualized relationship with a child, then they would be concerned with the victim's pleasure and would be unlikely to use aggressive coercion.

Individuals with a fearful avoidant attachment style (negative view of self/ negative view of others) see themselves as unlovable and others as uncaring and unreliable. Although they want social contact and intimacy, they are mistrustful of others and fear rejection, so they tend to seek long-term relationships but keep their partners at a distance and will feel most comfortable with partners who are themselves distant. They are unlikely to be actively hostile but may express their aggression indirectly. Ward *et al.* (1995) suggest that the fear of intimacy and avoidance of closeness in relationships leads fearful avoidant individuals to seek impersonal sexual contact with others and where such individuals offend sexually, their offending might be expected to involve a minimum of personal contact, to be unconcerned about their victims' feelings. Since they are not generally hostile, any use of coercion would be likely to be instrumental rather than expressive or sadistic.

Individuals with a dismissive avoidant attachment style (positive view of self/negative view of others) maintain their positive self-image by dismissing or belittling the importance of other people, whom they perceive as rejecting.

These individuals are dismissive of the value of close relationships and place great value on independence. They may be seen as aloof and can be actively hostile in their interpersonal style. When such individuals offend sexually, they are more likely to use excessive or sadistic levels of force. Ward *et al.* (1995) suggest that sadistic offenders would generally have a dismissive avoidant attachment style.

Ward, Hudson and Marshall (1996) found some support for this model. They found that sexual offenders generally had insecure attachment styles but that there were a variety of styles within the different groups of offences. Offenders against children were more likely to have either an anxious-ambivalent or a fearful-avoidant attachment style, while rapists were more likely to have a dismissive avoidant attachment style.

Other authors have noted aspects of the interpersonal relationship styles of sexual offenders that appear to reflect insecure attachment styles. For instance, Ward, McCormack and Hudson (1997) found that many sexual offenders have difficulty with self-disclosure, expression of affection, self-satisfaction, giving and receiving support, empathy, conflict resolution and oversensitivity to rejection. Segal and Marshall (1995) found men who sexually abuse children to be less competent in their interactions with women, and they rated themselves as anxious and under-assertive during this task. Overholser and Beck (1986) found that men who sexually abused children reported high levels of fear of negative evaluation by others, though these problems were less noticeable among rapists.

Deviant Sexual Interests and Attitudes

Deviant sexual interests are likely to develop from exposure to deviant material or behaviour in childhood or adolescence, for example to pornography or sexual abuse. These interests are likely to be reinforced by the classical conditioning effects of masturbation to deviant sexual fantasies (Laws and Marshall, 1990).

For some offenders, deviant sexual preference is fixated, while for others, deviant interest appears to be more mood-specific. Proulx, McKibben and Lusignan (1996) found that deviant fantasy is often linked to negative mood states such as boredom or humiliation. Cortoni and Marshall (2001) found that sexual offenders use sex as a coping strategy far more than non-sexual offenders. This may because they have problems of emotion regulation and inadequate coping strategies for problem solving, conflict resolution or distress tolerance. For such individuals sexual fantasy and masturbation can become reliable methods of self-soothing.

Emotional Dysregulation

Subjective distress and negative mood states have been found to be frequent precursors of sexual offending and offence-related sexual fantasy. Hanson and Harris (2000) identified acute changes in mood as one of the proximal dynamic factors that distinguished recidivist from non-recidivist sexual offenders. Intense, usually negative emotions such as anxiety, depression, boredom and anger have been described as a frequent precursor of sexual offending (Pithers *et al.*, 1988). Anger is frequently implicated in rape and physically violent sexual offending; Pithers *et al.* (1988) reported that 88 per cent of rapists and 32 per cent of sexual offenders against children identified generalized global anger as a precursor to sexual offending. There is also evidence that anger disinhibits sexual arousal for rape; Yates, Barbaree and Marshall (1984) found subjects who had been angered by female collaborator showed more arousal to rape depictions.

Marshall and Marshall (2000) proposed that sexual offenders frequently learnt to use masturbation as a coping strategy in childhood and displayed earlier onset of masturbation and at a higher frequency during adolescence. Negative emotions have also been found to be a common trigger for deviant sexual fantasies. Proulx, McKibben and Lusignan (1996) found that negative mood and conflict coincided with deviant sexual fantasy in both rapists and sexual offenders against children (anger, loneliness and humiliation in rapists, loneliness and humiliation in sexual offenders against children). Looman (1995) reported that sexual offenders against children were more likely to fantasize about a child than an adult if they were depressed, had rowed with their partner or felt rejected or lonely, but were more likely to fantasize about a woman if they were happy. Both Looman and Proulx, McKibben and Lusignan suggested that sexual offenders used deviant sexual fantasies in order to reduce their distress and cope with unwanted emotions.

Proeve and Howells (2006) have drawn attention to the importance of shame among sexual offenders, particularly sexual offenders against children. Ward, McCormack and Hudson (1997) found that sexual offenders against children were more likely than rapists to have preoccupied or fearful attachment styles, both of which involve negative appraisals of oneself. Proeve and Howells argued these negative self-appraisals made people with these attachment styles particularly vulnerable to what Gilbert (1988) defined as 'internal shame', that is, shame derived from negative self-evaluations. They also described sexual offending as 'a quintessential shame-eliciting behaviour' (p. 128) and described the various ways in which sexual offending contributes to external shame as well; it involved breaking fundamental sexual and social taboos, its perpetrators were often treated as social outcasts with low social status. Shame is therefore both an important antecedent of sexual offending and a significant consequence, making it likely that it will, in some cases lead to a recurring cycle of deepening shame and more serious offending.

Although much attention has focussed on the role of negative mood states in sexual offending, Ward and Hudson (2000) have identified a role for positive emotions in sexual offending, for example, where the offender seeks to develop an 'affectionate' relationship with a child against whom they offend sexually, their associated emotional state may be positive. Moreover, they argued that all offenders will experience positive emotions associated with increased sexual arousal during their offence cycle.

There is evidence that sexual offenders against children in particular consistently adopt emotion-focussed coping strategies (Looman *et al.*, 2004) and that many sexual offenders engage in avoidance-focussed coping, including the use of sex (Cortoni and Marshall, 2001).

In summary, a broad range of factors are involved in the development of sexual offending behaviour in adult men. In particular, their dysfunctional core beliefs and problems with emotion regulation and attachment will also have a significant impact on the engagement of such offenders in assessment and treatment. In addition, the fact of being identified and labelled as a *sex offender*, with all the implications that this emotive term carries in our culture means that these offenders are likely to feel unsafe, vulnerable and deeply ashamed. This may manifest itself overtly as avoidance, shame or self-harm, or offenders may try to hide it by denying or justifying their offending, or going 'on the offensive' against anyone who threatens to get close to them. The rest of this chapter is largely concerned with how the forensic psychologist understands and manages these different challenging responses.

SPECIAL CONSIDERATIONS WHEN INTERVIEWING SEX OFFENDERS

Know Yourself

Sexual offending is widely regarded as one of the most abhorrent and emotive forms of offending, and those who commit such offences often provoke revulsion and anger. A significant proportion of the adult population has experienced some form of sexual victimization at some time in their life and there is no reason to suppose that this will be any less among forensic psychologists. Survivors of sexual abuse respond in many different ways and a history of sexual victimization should not necessarily preclude someone from working with sexual offenders. Nevertheless, forensic psychologists working with sexual offenders should reflect on their ability to engage in a therapeutic, respectful and boundaried relationship and, if possible, discuss this in supervision. Other life events, such as becoming a parent, knowing someone who is sexually assaulted or starting or finishing an intimate relationship, may also impact on the psychologist's ability to work with sexual offenders.

Be Prepared

Sexual offenders, like other offender groups, have various reasons to minimize and distort accounts of their offending behaviour, including shame, fear of the reactions of professionals or their own family and friends, or fear of the legal consequences of fully disclosing the extent of their offending. As Maruna and Mann (2006) have pointed out, denial is a normal human behaviour and one that implies some understanding that that the behaviour being denied was inappropriate and shameful.

Because of the likelihood of denial or minimization, it is important for the psychologist to have as much information about the offender and their offences before starting the assessment process, so that distortions and omissions can be highlighted and challenged. Failure by the psychologist to point out discrepancies and distortions from the beginning can risk giving the offender the impression that the psychologist accepts their account, reinforcing the distortion and making future challenging more difficult. At the same time, particularly in the early stages of working with an offender, the psychologist should avoid appearing too confrontational or challenging, which may damage the therapeutic relationship. Moreover, if the denial or minimization is driven by feelings of shame, a confrontational approach at this early stage is likely to make the offender even more determined to maintain his denial. It is not necessary, particularly in the assessment phase, to successfully challenge every denial and minimization; in general it will be sufficient simply to point out that the offender's account differs from other accounts or that there may be other interpretations of events.

Assessment of sexual offending will generally involve asking extremely personal questions about, for example masturbatory fantasies or sexual behaviour, which can be embarrassing for the psychologist as well as for the offender. Particularly for inexperienced practitioners, it can be useful to rehearse beforehand questions about such topics, and to be sensitive about the appropriate time to ask them.

It is useful to have a framework for interviewing offenders. A common example is the BAREPCS framework (Table 11.1), which provides key headings that should be explored when discussing the antecedents, behaviour and consequences of an offence.

Get the Relationship Right

The importance of a warm, empathic and collaborative therapeutic relationship is a foundation of most forms of psychological therapy. However, it is only relatively recently that its importance has been recognized in forensic settings, and particularly with sexual offenders. This is all the more surprising given that most forms of sexual offending involve dysfunctional and abusive interpersonal relationships, and that for many sexual offenders this occurs in the context of a lifelong pattern of similar relationships. Therapist features that facilitate therapeutic change in sexual offenders include empathy and warmth, encouragement and reward for progress, balanced with directiveness towards key goals (Marshall *et al.*, 2003).

Table 11.1 *The BAREPCS interviewing framework*

Behaviour
Lifestyle before the offence, sequence of events before, during, after offence.
Was there any offence paralleling behaviour or behavioural tryouts in the
lead up?

Attitudes
Ways of thinking about people and activities that underpin the offence process,
e.g., sexualized or demeaning attitudes towards women or children, which may
be consistent or may only emerge in states of heightened arousal. Attitudes about
the world, life, relationships, crime. What is important to the offender and what
doesn't really matter?

Relationships
Significant intimate and attachment relationships and friendships, in particular
any changes or significant events to these in the build-up to the offence, e.g.,
beginnings or endings of relationships, conflict, separations, rejection or jealousy.

Emotions and states
States could include, e.g., 'high', detached or dissociated, numb, tired, withdrawn
into a fantasy world or manic. Thoughts associated with the emotions and states
are recorded under cognitions.

Physical state
E.g., heart rate, breathing rate, physical arousal or physical illness.

Cognition
Cognitive distortions and self-talk. Schemas that are active during the offence
process. Thoughts about self, others, particularly victims.

Sexual interest
Any sexual components of the processes, e.g., whether the offender had an
erection or was experiencing impotence, sexual fantasies, thoughts or plans.

Be Aware of Counter-Transference

Probably more than any other client group, sexual offenders can evoke strong
counter-transference reactions, even among experienced clinicians. The nature
of their offending and the justifications and distortions offenders use when
describing their offending, as well as the high rates of personality disorder and
interpersonal difficulties can often trigger strong feelings of disgust, rage or
fear among clinicians. Moreover, the developmental histories of many sexual
offenders leaves them sensitized to any sign of rejection by others, and this
is generally only made worse once they acquire the label of 'sex offender'. It
can be difficult at times to suppress feelings of anger or frustration when an
offender blames his victim or makes himself out to be the victim. Blanchard

(1998) offers a useful framework for managing the practitioner-offender relationship. He argues that such countertransference reactions provide useful information about the client's pattern of interpersonal relationships and that the clinician needs to be honest with themselves, their colleagues and supervisor about these reactions and take responsibility for managing them rather than blaming the client.

Use Language and Labels Sensitively

Practitioners should think carefully about the way they describe their clients as their choice of language communicates powerfully to the client (Yantzi, 1998). Few labels in our society are more stigmatizing that that of 'sex offender', or its subgroups; 'rapist', 'child molester' or paedophile'. The use of such terms by clinicians can easily be interpreted by offenders as conveying hostility or abuse, which would seriously undermine any therapeutic relationship. These terms are also flawed because they define the person purely in terms of their past behaviour, and so, by definition, the person will always be a 'rapist' or a 'child molester'. It is preferable to use alternative terms that define the person in terms of their current situation (client, group member) and as distinct from their offending (person who has committed sexual offences).

Avoid Aggressive Confrontation, or Collusion

In the past, some authors (e.g., Salter, 1988; Wyre, 1989) have advocated the aggressive confrontation of sexual offenders on the basis that sexual offenders are generally deceitful and defensive when discussing their offending. However, such an approach has been found to increase resistance and reduce the effectiveness of treatment (Beech and Hamilton-Giachritsis, 2005; Drapeau, 2005).

At the same time, those working with sexual offenders should avoid being unconditionally supportive of the offender, and inadvertently colluding with their denial or minimization. Such distorted thinking should be challenged in a firm but in a supportive and respectful manner. For example:

> *You said there that you believed he wanted sex with you because he didn't say or do anything to stop you. Can you think of any other reasons why a young child might not say anything when an adult tells them to do something?*

Remember that Assessment is Always a Two-Way Process

As the psychologist is assessing the offender, he or she is also being assessed. In any institution or service, the time spent in initial assessment will be the time when offenders form impressions and expectations about psychologists and other professionals, as well as about relationships, their environment and their own ability to engage in a process and to affect their own behaviour. For many sexual offenders previous experience of institutions and their own sense of shame at their offending will shape their expectations of how they will be treated. It is therefore all the more important that their first impressions of staff and relationships in a new institution are positive.

ASSESSMENT OF SEX OFFENDERS

Special Considerations when Formulating Cases with Sexual Offenders

It is often useful to begin by developing a shared understanding of the offender's core beliefs and self-concept. Young's schema-focussed approach (Young, Klosko and Weishaar, 2003) is one that can be easily grasped and applied by most offenders. Schema theory provides a simple model that links core childhood needs (for example, for nurturance, protection, safety, love) with a developmental history that failed to provide one or more of these needs and patterns of schema-related thinking and behaviour. It does this in a way that is readily grasped by most people and which provides a framework for understanding themselves and their behaviour using simple, non-judgemental language. It also, often for the first time, provides offenders with a readymade vocabulary to describe painful and distressing aspects of their lives and their personality that they have previously been unable to express, and to do so in a way that allows them to externalize their thoughts, emotions and behaviours and make them easier to consider.

Where possible, assessment should involve multiple perspectives, including that of the offender. Disagreement within teams is probably inevitable when assessing sexual offenders, who may tend to behave in different and sometimes extreme ways with teams, particularly where different team members adopt different roles. Lifelong patterns of insecure attachment, abusive and transient relationships and trauma are common among this group and it should be no surprise that they can experience intense anxiety, discomfort and negative transference reactions when faced with new relationships with people in authority, people who want to get close to them, health professionals or other groups that may have previously been associated with trauma. Nor should it be a surprise that people who are perceived as caring or protecting should trigger equally intense positive or negative transference reactions.

Differences of opinion will inevitably occur within the team when faced with such different behaviours. Such disagreements should be seen as a natural and healthy. Teams should be able to discuss such differences of opinion and synthesize them into a formulation that is shared by the whole team and the offender. The inevitability of such disagreements among teams working with patients with personality disorders highlights the need for regular and protected forums for team formulation and supervision.

MOTIVATIONAL REPORT DISCLOSURE WITH SEX OFFENDERS

Sexual offenders may lack intrinsic motivations to engage in assessment or treatment. Often they arrive in treatment having been compelled by the courts, Parole Board or Mental Health Review Tribunal. They may also have rationalized their sexual offending as 'not their fault' and so not see the need to change anything. The clinician needs to understand this.

It has been argued that sexual offenders seek the same goals as other people (Marshall, Anderson and Fernandez, 1999) but choose inappropriate means of achieving those goals because the lack the necessary skills, attitudes or beliefs to achieve them in prosocial ways and so offend sexually to achieve them. The Good Lives Model (Ward, 2002) has helped to reframe sexual offending behaviour as the way in which offenders seek the satisfaction of normative needs (e.g., for intimacy, sex or control) in inappropriate ways. When understood in this way, the goal of treatment is to provide offenders with the skills, attitudes, thoughts and perceptions necessary to meet their needs in prosocial ways. The goal of assessment with sexual offenders should be to help the offender frame their offending in this way, to identify the needs that are being met inappropriately through offending and to set goals that will allow them to lead prosocial and satisfying lives.

The assessment process should also generate hope in the offender about their prospects of successfully achieving these goals. Frank (1989) has suggested that enhancing hope is an important factor in promoting treatment gains for all types of therapy and client groups. Snyder (2000) identified three components to hope in this context: the establishment of goals, the development of pathways to achieve those goals and the person's belief that they can achieve their goals. The assessment process should contribute to all three of these components by helping the offender to identify realistic and achievable goals which will help to reduce their risk and promote a satisfying life, start to break these goals down into achievable sub goals and identify the strengths and skills that they already have which will help them to achieve their goals.

Allowing the offender to reframe offending behaviour as the selection of inappropriate strategies to achieve appropriate and legitimate goals also helps the offender to see themselves as separate from their offending. This shifts their feelings of shame ('I am a bad person') to guilt ('I have done a bad thing'). Tangney and Dearing (2002) have shown that feelings of shame inhibit therapeutic change ('I am a bad person, therefore I cannot change') but guilt motivates change ('I have done a bad thing but I can stop').

Goal setting should be a collaborative process. This does not mean doing what the client wants but helping them to agree on goals that are realistic and achievable. Collaboration with offenders means being open with them about the aims, goals and content of therapy. It means being willing to discuss objections the offender may have about the content of therapy without being defensive and being prepared to be flexible where this appropriate.

Shingler and Mann (2006) have argued that collaboration is particularly important in the risk assessment process and suggested a number of guidelines for risk assessment with sexual offenders. These include introducing and explaining clearly the risk assessment process and its rationale, dealing openly with any initial suspicion or doubts the offender may have, presenting the results of assessments openly and clearly, seeking feedback from the offender as the risk assessment proceeds and incorporating their opinions into the report where possible, and avoiding pejorative or labelling terms.

CONCLUSION

Working with sex offenders is perhaps one of the most demanding and challenging aspects of the forensic practitioners role, both because of the complex nature of the offending and the emotion that sexual offending can engender. However, despite the many demands of working with this client group there are also many rewards. It is worth noting that between 75 and 100 per cent of professionals delivering therapeutic services with sexual offenders describe this as the most rewarding and satisfying element of their career (Edmunds, 1997; Kadambi and Truscott, 2003).

RECOMMENDED FURTHER READING

Beech, A. R., Craig, L. A and Browne, K. D. (2009). *Assessment and Treatment of Sex Offenders* (Chichester: John Wiley and Sons Ltd.). A thorough and accessible introduction to the field.

Ward, T., Polaschek, D. and Beech, A. R. (2006). *Theories of Sexual Offending* (ChichesteraJohn Wiley and Sons Ltd.). A comprehensive review and critique of different theories of sexual offending.

Blanchard, G. T. (2012). *The Difficult Connection: The Therapeutic Relationship in Sex Offender Treatment*, 2nd edn (Brandon VT: Safer Society Press). A short and very readable guide to building and maintaining a therapeutic relationship with sex offenders.

REFERENCES

Bartholomew, K. (1990). 'Avoidance of Intimacy: An Attachment Perspective', *Journal of Social and Personal Relationships* 7, 147–78.

Beech, A. R. and Hamilton-Giachritsis, C. E. (2005). 'Relationship between Therapeutic Climate and Treatment Outcome in Group-Based Sexual Offender Treatment Programs', *Sexual Abuse: A Journal of Research and Treatment* 17, 127–40.

Bernstein, D. P., Arntz, A. and de Vos, M. (2007). 'Schema Focused Therapy in Forensic Settings: Theoretical Model and Recommendations for Best Clinical Practice', *International Journal of Forensic Mental Health* 6, 169–83.

Blanchard, G. (1998). *The Difficult Connection: The Therapeutic Relationship in Sex Offender Treatment* (Brandon, VT: Safer Society Press).

Cortoni, F. A. and Marshall, W. L. (2001). 'Sex as a Coping Strategy and its Relationship to Juvenile Sexual History and Intimacy in Sexual Offenders', *Sexual Abuse: A Journal of Research and Treatment* 13, 27–43.

Drapeau, M. (2005). 'Research on the Processes Involved in Treating Sexual Offenders', *Sexual Abuse: A Journal of Research and Treatment* 17, 117–25.

Edmunds, B. S. (1997). 'The Personal Impact of Working with Sex Offenders', in B. S. Edmunds (ed.) *Impact: Working with Sexual Abusers* (Vermont: Safer Society Press), 11–26.

Finkelhor, D. (1984). *Child Sexual Abuse: New Theory and Research* (New York: Free Press).

Frank, J. D. (1989). 'Non-Specific Aspects of Treatment: The View of the Psychotherapist', in M. Shepherd and N. Sartorius (Eds) *Non-Specific Aspects of Treatment* (Toronto: Hans Huber), 95–114.

Gilbert, P. (1988). 'Shame and Humiliation in the Treatment of Complex Cases', in N. Tarrier, A. Wells and G. Haddock (eds) *Treating Complex Cases: The Cognitive Behavioural Therapy Approach* (London: Wiley), 241–71.

Hall, G. C. N. and Hirschman, J. R. (1992). 'Sexual Aggression against Children: A Conceptual Perspective of Etiology', *Criminal Justice and Behavior*, 19, 8–23.

Hanson, K. and Harris, A. J. R. (2000). 'Where Should We Intervene? Dynamic Predictors of Sex Offence Recidivism', *Criminal Justice and Behaviour* 27, 6–35.

Kadambi, M. and Truscott, D (2006). 'Concept Mapping Professionals' Perceptions of Reward and Motive in Providing Sex Offender Treatment', *Journal of Offender Rehabilitation* 42, 37–58.

Laws, D. R. and Marshall, W. L. (1990). 'A Conditioning Theory of the Etiology and Maintenance of Deviant Sexual Preferences and Behavior', in W. L. Marshall, D. R. Laws and H. E Barbaree (eds) *Handbook of Sexual Assault: Issues, Theories and Treatment of the Offender* (New York: Plenum Press), 209–29.

Looman, J. (1995). 'Sexual Fantasies of Child Molesters', *Canadian Journal of Behavioural Science* 27, 321–32.

Looman, J., Abracen, J., DiFazio, R. and Maillet, G. (2004). 'Alcohol and Drug Abuse Among Sexual and Nonsexual Offenders: Relationship to Intimacy Deficits and Coping Strategy', *Sexual Abuse: A Journal of Research and Treatment* 16, 177–89.

Malamuth, N. M. and Brown, L. M. (1994). 'Sexually Aggressive Men's Perceptions of Women's Communications: Testing Three Explanations', *Journal of Personality and Social Psychology* 67, 699–712.

Malamuth, N. M., Sockloskie, R. J., Koss, M. P. and Tanaka, J. S. (1991). 'Characteristics of Aggressors against Women: Testing a Model Using a National Sample of College Students', *Journal of Consulting and Clinical Psychology* 59, 670–81.

Mann, R. E. and Beech, A. R. (2003). 'Cognitive Distortions, Schemas and Implicit Theories', in T. Ward, D. R. Laws and S. M. Hudson (eds) *Sexual Deviance: Issues and Controversies* (Thousand Oaks: Sage), 135–53.

Mann, R. E. and Hollin, C. R. (2007). 'Sexual Offenders' Explanations for Their Offending', *Journal of Sexual Aggression* 13, 3–9.

Marshall, W. L. Anderson, D. and Fernandez, Y. M. (1999). *Cognitive Behavioural Treatment of Sexual Offenders* (Chichester: Wiley).

Marshall, W. L. and Barbaree, H. E. (1990). 'An Integrated Theory of Sexual Offending', in W. L. Marshall, D. R. Laws and H. E. Barbaree (eds) *Handbook of Sexual Assault* (New York: Plenum Press), 257–75.

Marshall, W. L. and Marshall, L. E. (2000). 'The Origins of Sexual Offending', *Trauma, Violence and Abuse* 1, 250–63.

Marshall, W. L., Serran, G. A., Fernandez, Y. M., Mulloy, R., Mann, R. E. and Thornton, D. (2003). 'Therapist Characteristics in the Treatment of Sexual Offenders: Tentative Data on their Relationship with Indices of Behaviour Change', *Journal of Sexual Aggression* 9, 25–30.

Maruna, S. and Mann, R. E. (2006). 'A Fundamental Attribution Error? Rethinking Cognitive Distortions', *Legal and Criminological Psychology* 11, 155–77.

Overholser, J. C. and Beck, S. (1986). 'Multimethod Assessment of Rapists, Child Molesters, and Three Control Groups on Behavioral and Psychological Measures', *Journal of Consulting and Clinical Psychology*, 54, 682–7.

Pithers, W. D., Kashima, K. M., Cumming, G. F., Beal, L. S. and Buell, M. B. (1988). 'Relapse Prevention of Sexual Aggression', *Annals of the New York Academy of Sciences* 528, 244–60.

Proeve, M. and Howells, K. (2006). 'Shame and Guilt in Child Molesters', in W. L. Marshall, Y. M. Fernandez, L. E. Marshall and G. A. Serran (eds) *Sexual Offender Treatment: Controversial Issues* (Chichester: Wiley), 125–39.

Proulx, J., McKibben, A. and Lusignan, R. (1996). 'Relationships between Affective Components and Sexual Behaviours in Sexual Aggressors', *Journal of Sexual Abuse* 8, 279–89.

Salter, A. C. (1988). *Treating Child Sex Offenders and Victims: A Practical Guide* (Newbury Park, CA: Sage).

Segal, Z. V. and Marshall, W. L. (1995). 'Heterosexual Social Skills, in a Population of Rapists and Child Molesters', *Journal of Consulting and Clinical Psychology* 53, 55–63.

Shingler, J. and Mann, R. E. (2006). 'Collaboration in Clinical Work with Sexual Offenders: Treatment and Risk Assessment', in W. Marshall, Y. Fernandez, L. Marshall and G Serran (eds) *Sexual Offender Treatment: Controversial Issues* (Chichester: Wiley), 225–40.

Smallbone, S. W., and Dadds, M. R. (1998). Childhood Attachment and Adult Attachment in Incarcerated Adult Male Sex Offenders', *Journal of Interpersonal Violence* 13, 555–73.

Smallbone, S. W. Dadds, M. R. (2000). 'Attachment and Coercive Sexual Behavior', *Journal of Sexual Abuse* 12, 3–16.

Snyder, C. R. (2000). *Handbook of Hope: Theory, Measures and Applications* (New York: Academic Press).

Tangney, J. P. and Dearing, R. L. (2002). *Shame and Guilt* (New York: Guilford).

Ward, T. (2002). 'Good Lives and the Rehabilitation of Offenders: Promises and Problems', *Aggression and Violent Behavior* 7, 513–28.

Ward, T. and Hudson, S. M. (2000). 'A Self-Regulation Model of Relapse Prevention', in D. R. Laws, S. M. Hudson and T. Ward (eds) *Remaking Relapse Prevention with Sex Offenders: A Sourcebook* (Thousand Oaks: Sage), 79–101.

Ward, T., Hudson, S. M., and Marshall, W. L. (1996). 'Attachment Style in Sex Offenders: A Preliminary Study'. *The Journal of Sex Research* 33, 17–26.

Ward, T., Hudson, S. M., Marshall, W. L. and Siegert, R. (1995). 'Attachment Style and Intimacy Deficits in Sexual Offenders: A Theoretical Framework', *Journal of Sexual Abuse* 7, 317–35.

Ward, T. and Keenan, T. (1999). 'Child Molesters' Implicit Theories', *Journal of Interpersonal Violence* 14, 821–38.

Ward, T., McCormack, J. and Hudson, S. M. (1997). 'Sexual Offenders' Perceptions of Their Intimate Relationships', *Journal of Sexual Abuse* 9, 57–74.

Ward, T. and Siegert, R. J. (2002). 'Toward a Comprehensive Theory of Child Sexual Abuse: A Theory Knitting Perspective', *Psychology, Crime and Law*, 8, 319–51.

Ward, T. and Sorbello, L. (2003). 'Explaining Child Sexual Abuse: Integration and Elaboration', in T. Ward, D. R. Laws and S. M. Hudson (eds) *Sexual Deviance: Issues and Controversies* (Thousand Oaks: Sage), 3–20.

Wyre, R. (1989). 'Working with the Paedophile', in M. Farrell (ed.) *Understanding the Paedophile* (London: ISTD/The Portman Clinic), 17–23.

Yantzi, M. (1998). *Sexual Offending and Restoration* (Scottsdale, PA: Herald Press).

Yates, E. Barbaree, H. E. and Marshall, W. L. (1984). 'Anger and Deviant Sexual Arousal', *Behaviour Therapy* 15, 287–94.

Young, J. E. (1990). *Cognitive Therapy for Personality Disorders* (Sarasota FL: Professional Resources Press).

Young, J. E., Klosko, J. S. and Weishaar, M. E. (2003). *Schema Therapy: A Practitioner's Guide* (New York: Guilford).

12 Gangs

Paul Summers

INTRODUCTION

Gang behaviour and related offending has become a cornerstone of media coverage of crime in recent years. Recent high-profile instances of 'knife crime' in major UK cities, in which predominantly young, predominantly black, predominantly male, victims have been stabbed (and occasionally killed) have only served to promote the portrayal of gang offending as a twenty-first-century phenomenon, at least in the UK. This exposure – combined with statements such as those given by the Metropolitan Police Service when it asserted that more than half of the fifty-five deaths of young people (aged thirteen to nineteen) on the streets of London in 2007 and 2008 were due to gang affiliations (Toy, 2008) – has placed considerable pressure on the government to reduce the risk of harm to both the public and those susceptible to joining gangs themselves. The widespread riots and civil unrest that occurred throughout England in August 2011 (for which gang membership was proposed as a contributing factor) have further cemented this call for an appropriate, timely and effective response.

The purpose of this chapter is two-fold: The majority will be devoted to providing an overview of the problematic nature of gangs, the predictors and likely duration of membership and the multiplicity of reasons that may be offered for why the sharing of a common vision or lifestyle can lead to a descent into offending. Although, for reasons of brevity, this chapter will be geared towards examining gangs operating solely in the UK, the findings or theoretical viewpoints from researchers in America will also be included – largely due to the predominance of studies undertaken in comparison with any other nation. Community and prison gangs will be addressed simultaneously since gangs can easily traverse geographical boundaries; from streets to prison wings and vice versa. The final section of the chapter will put forward a number of recommendations that practitioners in the UK may wish to consider when working with self-identifying gang members or those suspected of involvement in gang activity, based on previous or current behaviour, with the view to addressing risk. From the outset, it should be acknowledged that this final section is based on conjecture rather than empirical evidence.

THEORETICAL OVERVIEW

The aforementioned sudden and significant media interest in gangs belies their extensive history. In reality, gangs have existed for centuries. Indeed, one of the earliest records of gang activity in the US dates back to the end of the Revolution (Sante, 1991). The violence-prone 'scuttlers' of Victorian Manchester are another example of how gang violence is anything but a modern phenomenon (Davies, 2008). Despite this, gang membership has increased steadily in many countries in the last century. Factors such as the rise of immigration and population levels, the availability of vehicles and lethal weapons and the gradual involvement of some street gangs in illegal drug markets have all been put forward as explanations for the increasing levels of membership (Thornberry et al., 2003).

Over the years, and in addition to the suggestions noted above, a variety of criminological and psychological explanations have also been proposed for why people join community gangs. One of the oldest examples of the former was that economic destabilization, combined with social disorganization, leads to a breakdown in institutions such as school and family life (Thrasher, 1927). This, in turn, leads youngsters to seek excitement elsewhere. Gangs come into existence, it was argued, when they become formal, more organized and engage in conflict after attaching themselves to specific territories. Shaw and Mackay (1969) built on this initial theory and proposed that the environment was a major factor in deciding whether a person joins a gang. Individuals growing up in poor, inner-city areas are exposed to a level of delinquency not found in middle-class areas. As a result of this contact, gang membership is recognized as an attractive alternative to conventional norms, providing youths in inner-city areas with a social structure they are unable to obtain elsewhere. Sutherland (1960), however, disagreed and proposed – in his theory of Differential Association – that criminal behaviour is learnt by associating with individuals who favour law violation and abide by delinquent norms. This would account for why criminal behaviour occurs across all social classes. Sutherland has been criticized, however, for not explaining how these attitudes develop, only that they can be attributed to interacting with delinquent personal groups (Akers and Sellers, 2009).

Most psychological explanations have, to date, shown a tendency to be directed towards elucidating delinquency in general, rather than gang behaviour in particular (Davis, 1993). The developmental approach suggests that delinquency in youth can be traced back to childhood maldevelopment when interacting with the environment. This may include being detached from one or both parents or adopting unhealthy role models. There is also the proposal that juveniles operating at a lower level of moral development compared to their peers are more likely to progress into delinquency (Brandt and Zlotnick, 1988). At the time of writing, there is no consensus on whether sociological or psychological theories best explain youth delinquency and, as a corollary, why gangs form. As Davis (1993, p. 91) states, however, it is debatable whether one is more important than the other and that 'theoretical schemes employing multiple-factor explanations across disciplines, including biological and physical factors, will likely account for greater unexplained variance rather than relying solely upon sociological or psychological factors in isolation'.

Attempts to account for how gangs form and behave are, however, impacted by another, more fundamental issue. Inserting the word 'gang' into a PC Thesaurus provides two clusters of options – the ranking of which is interesting if not altogether revealing. The first cluster of alternative terms refers to a 'bunch of hooligans' or a 'mob'. The second cluster offers a far more positive spin: 'Team' and 'squad' are both listed; terms that imply cooperation, unity and mutual benefit. These contrasting definitions neatly encapsulate one of the most significant and immediate problems arising from any serious consideration of gangs and their behaviour, regardless of the context: what actually constitutes a gang? One way of responding to this question is to scrutinize how gangs and groups differ.

Groups form when a number of individuals come together and, through self-perception and interaction, encourage the formation of shared goals, internal norms, roles and affective relations (Fraser and Burchell, 2001). Gangs form in a similar fashion. Members may share the same goals: the need for friends, recognition, respect, acceptance, social support and a sense of belonging. Material attractions may also feature (money along with less tangible – but equally valued – possessions such as 'territory') (Direct Gov., 2011). Gangs may also have appropriate standards for behaving. Just as someone who refuses to abide by the social norms operating when waiting to board a bus (by refusing to queue, pushing or generally aggravating those in front of him) risks disapproval from those around him, so a gang member risks rejection by his peers when his actions fail to correspond to the conduct expected by the majority. Indeed, it is interesting to note that gang members who commit crime represent an anomaly among offenders in general; in that they are often portrayed as having characteristics that may otherwise be regarded as socially acceptable, albeit erroneously displayed or directed. Loyalty, for example, is often praised by social commentators as being overwhelmingly positive and enters many aspects of social life; from loyalty to one's family to a particular sporting team. It is also an overwhelmingly central element of the gang member's make up. New or prospective members are often required to demonstrate their commitment through an act of aggression to a rival group (Short and Strodtbeck, 1974). Finally, some gangs have also been found to have established leaders (Sharp, Aldridge and

Medina, 2006) and become dependent on each other. Using this definition, a gang does not appear dissimilar from a group in many respects.

The problems involved in delineating the nature of gangs and/or gang-related behaviour has led to wide variation in the definitions being offered by politicians, policy makers and academics (Ebensen *et al.*, 2001; Ebsensen and Weerman, 2005; Spergel, 1995). Even the definition from the Eurogang Network – a group of leading European and American researchers in the field of violent youth groups – as 'any durable, street-orientated youth group whose own identity includes involvement in illegal activity' (Klein, Weerman And Thornberry, 2006, p. 418) is disputable, since it presupposes that gangs are always composed of young men and/or women and that distinguishing youth from maturity in terms of age is entirely straightforward.

The situation is similarly equivocal when questions surrounding the definition of prison (as opposed to community) gangs are raised. Again, academics disagree over the size and flexibility of their structure and indicators of their existence (Camp and Camp, 1985; Fong and Buentello, 1991). Gang membership – and the accompanying research – can also depend, to an extent, on members' self-identification. This, in turn, raises the risk of discrepancy between what self-identifying gang members perceive a gang to be and how academics, policymakers and the media define the term. Contrary to the portrayal by the media, gangs are predominantly heterogeneous in nature, differing greatly in terms of beliefs, hierarchy and organization.

The term 'gang' (it would seem) is an unhelpful way to describe this social phenomenon. As Ebensen *et al.* (2001, p. 106) state, 'even the "experts" cannot agree on what constitutes a gang or gang behaviour, and many experts find fault with nearly every definition'. This is despite the fact that most definitions pay attention to the number of members, their age range, the fact that they share an identity, view themselves (and are recognized by others) as belonging to a gang, have a degree of permanence and organization and are involved in an elevated level of criminality (Esbensen *et al.*, 2001; Spergel, 1995).

Whether the above criteria can lead researchers to an exact and all-encompassing definition of gangs is debatable. Equally, the belief that such a universal definition even exists is perhaps unrealistic. The need to reflect on and appreciate how definitional issues have the potential not only to influence policy but also impede investigations into gang membership and behaviour, however, is essential. The existence of gangs in other nations has been acknowledged (and therefore investigated) for some time. The reluctance to acknowledge the issue in the UK can be attributed to what has been labelled the 'Eurogang Paradox': when European authorities base their beliefs about gang activity according to the American stereotype (drive-by shootings, gun crime) which, according to researchers, is actually rare (Klein *et al.*, 2001). Readers are also asked to look beyond the academic nature of this discussion and consider how this definitional issue may obstruct professional practice.

CURRENT PREVALENCE OF GANGS

In April 2009, it was reported that 2800 organized criminal gangs currently operated in the UK (*Times Online*, 2009). This figure, if accurate, was approximately three times the number previously acknowledged by officials – thereby demonstrating the extent to which estimations vary. Approximately two-thirds of these gangs were believed to be involved in some form of criminal activity, often characterized by the use of violence. A number almost as high were believed to be involved in supplying illicit substances. In the UK (as in the US), gang membership tends to be concentrated in major cities (Shropshire and McFarquhar, 2002), although their existence in more rural areas appears to be growing (*Telegraph*, 2007).

Theoretically, it should be expected that levels of gang activity in UK prisons are significantly less when compared with community levels. Members denied their freedom are, consequently, deprived of the opportunity to directly engage in gang-related behaviour that impacts on their community, at least for the duration of their sentences. This is not to say that their influence is always completely eradicated, since some lines of communication have been found to persist (e.g., mobile phones are sometimes recovered from prisoners who have been using them to communicate to fellow gang members in the community (BBC, 2008) or intimidate victims/witnesses). Nor can it be assumed that gang affiliations are 'left at the gate' when a prisoner's sentence begins. It is, of course, possible that members view custodial sentences as recruiting opportunities, a chance to publicize and potentially increase the status of their gang or to intimidate rival gang members who find themselves similarly incarcerated.

Prison gangs in the US have received more attention in literature than their UK counterparts. This is perhaps understandable when the largest survey of their existence found that 60 per cent of Federal and State prisons contain some element of gang presence and that 2 per cent of the entire prison population were composed of gang members. (Camp and Camp, 1985). In contrast to the relative plethora of studies emanating from the US, however, research into the prevalence of gang membership in UK prisons is sparse. In a key study, Wood and Adler (2001) interviewed 374 staff members at sixteen establishments in England. They found that officers in their sample reported that gang activity appeared to be most prevalent in medium-security establishments holding male prisoners and Young Offender Institutions. In contrast, staff in both male low and high-security prisons reported the least activity. Gangs also tended to form by race and be influenced by regional affiliations. Wood (2006) went on to investigate prisoner (as opposed to staff) opinions on the matter a few years later – a valuable enquiry when it is remembered that those engaged in criminal activity may have very different views as to the nature and attraction of gang membership compared to the opinions of those entrusted with their care. Interviews with 360 prisoners across nine establishments in England and

Wales revealed that gang-related incidents – particularly those based on drug possession or regional origins – were perceived as occurring more frequently in male as opposed to female prisons. Offenders serving custodial sentences for the first time reported less gang-related activity than prisoners who had previously served time, perhaps due to a lack of awareness of likely indicators. Interestingly, Wood's investigation also revealed the rather concerning perception of prisoners that groups of offenders (gangs?) have more control over events in an establishment than members of staff.

In spite of these figures, the prevalence of gang activity in both the community and penal institutions is difficult to effectively calculate or confirm, due not only to the aforementioned problems surrounding their definition but also to the secrecy that pervades their existence and/or actions (Wood, 2006). This is problematic for a number of reasons. First, the possibility of under- or overestimating the prevalence of gang activity, be it in communities or custodial environments, has direct implications for resource allocation and public concern (Esbensen *et al.*, 2001). It is also important to remember that crime estimates are compiled using recorded statistics, victim surveys and self-report studies. None of these methods can be completely objective since they depend on the estimator's conceptual definitions (such as what constitutes 'crime', 'gang membership', 'gang activity'), the validity of the statistical techniques used and the way in which findings are interpreted. Statistics are also vulnerable to being impacted by political priorities, current law and public tolerance. These factors, coupled with sensationalistic media reporting, make estimating the true extent of gang membership appear more complicated.

WHO JOINS A GANG AND WHY?

The theoretical suggestions discussed at the beginning of this chapter were expressed in a very general manner. However, it is interesting to note which factors have been shown to increase the risk of gang involvement. As far as age is concerned, the vast majority of individuals entering gangs in the UK and US are between twelve- and eighteen-years old (Rizzo, 2003; Spergel, 1995). Research also indicates that the ethnic composition of a gang is linked proportionally to their presence in the community (Bullock and Tilley, 2002). Thus, according to this view, gangs are far more likely to feature white members in areas predominantly occupied by white communities and black members in largely black communities. Ethnically diverse neighbourhoods, at least in the UK, also appear to give rise to ethnically diverse gangs (Sharp, Aldridge and Medina, 2006). Although there seems to be a consensus among researchers that the majority of gang members are male (Bennet and Holloway, 2004; Rizzo, 2003), some studies have speculated that women have a minority presence (Esbensen and Winfree, 1998; Sharp, Aldridge and Medina, 2006) or that there are significant differences in the attitudes towards and involvement in violent crime between male and female gang members (Deschenes and Esbensen, 1999). As Esbensen (2000, p. 3) concedes, this goes against the view presented in early literature that women associated with gangs are 'socially inept, promiscuous, maladjusted and suffer from low self-esteem'.

Aside from demographics, researchers have drawn attention to a number of other factors that appear to have some bearing on whether someone joins a gang. Perhaps unsurprisingly, it has been found that young people are more susceptible to joining gangs in communities with high levels of juvenile delinquency/offending (Hall, Thornberry and Lizotte, 2006). Deficits in parental supervision/discipline along with the presence of significant peer pressure have also been identified as risk factors (Alleyne and Wood, 2011; Thornberry *et al.*, 2003). According to findings from the Seattle Social Development Project (SDDP) – a longitudinal self-report study conducted in the US and supported by the Office of Juvenile Justice and Delinquency Prevention – antisocial influences in peers, families and/or the neighbourhood, poor performance at school and early initiation between the ages of ten to twelve were all predictive of a child joining and remaining in a gang between the ages of thirteen to eighteen (Hill *et al.*, 1999). There are, then, a large number of risk factors that may increase an individual's likelihood of joining a gang. According to findings from the SDDP, it is the number of factors rather their nature that probably has the biggest influence. Indeed, it was highlighted that those children experiencing seven or more of the risk factor identified in the study were thirteen times more likely to join a gang (Hill, Lui and Hawkins, 2001).

There appears to be conflicting viewpoints on how long membership of gangs can last for. According to some researchers, involvement in gangs can continue into early adulthood and beyond (Bullock and Tilley, 2002). Interestingly, however, the aforementioned SDDP identified that the majority of gang members (just under 70 per cent) stayed within a gang for one year or less. Moreover, less than 1 per cent was a member for five years.

RESPONSE

Various elements of the gang phenomenon have now been highlighted. The question now arises as to whether the presence of such gangs, in the community or prison, demands a response. If so, a second question presents itself: What can forensic psychologists do, if anything, to reduce the risk posed by and/or support the rehabilitation of suspected or self-identifying gang members, regardless of the extent to which their index offence is related to membership?

The answer to the first question appears relatively straightforward. First, the safety of members of the public, particularly those who are subject to direct persecution and/or violence, must be protected from harm. Equally, in the prison setting, the well-being of all staff and prisoners (including rival gang members) must be protected. Second, it is apparent that the vast majority of prisons in the UK are, at the very least, approaching full capacity (*Guardian*, 2011). In December 2011, the prison population was estimated at 86,131, just 4349 places below the maximum number of offenders that can be accommodated (Justice. gov.uk, 2011). As far as gang members are concerned, this may have a number of consequences. It is likely that unrealistic pressures on establishments to house offenders may lead to more recommendations that gang members should serve community rather than custodial sentences for their offences. This may lead to an increase rather than reduction of gang-related violence and the gradual erosion of public confidence in the criminal justice system's ability or willingness to respond appropriately to gang-related crime. Alternatively, a reduction in availability over the prison estate may lead to rival gang members being transferred to different establishments, encroaching on the need to be close to their families and increasing the risk that these offenders will seek support from less-than-reputable sources. As a corollary, it may be suggested that being part of gang impedes an individual from cultivating a prosocial identity and successfully reintegrating into his local community.

On a community level, the government has sought to assuage public concern by organizing gang practitioner forums, hiring gang specialists and providing support for a number of gang interventions (Hallsworth and Young, 2008). To date, this response has been criticized for being 'devoid of any comprehensive survey of gang structure or action (Densley, 2011, p. 13). In the UK, 'Getting to the Point' – a government initiative to reduce knife crime – recommended that police should be handed the authority to ban youths from particular trouble spots. It also suggested that there should be an anti-violence curriculum in which all students are encouraged to recognize and learn to reject the temptations that gang membership offers. There also needs to be more communication between schools and parents in which the former highlight suspected gang involvement to the latter. In 2008, the Association of Chief Police Officers recommended that some schools should be given a full-time police presence. A network across government agencies to track particular offenders was also recommended. According to Densley, however, 'ministers are developing popular policy on gangs without first developing proficiency with the issues' (Densley, 2011, p. 13).

There is, however, the possibility of a community gang having presence in an establishment (should enough members be held in custody there) and a prison gang progressing into the community as members complete the sentences or are released on licence. The probability of the former can be lessened, though not totally eradicated, through the appropriate diversification of members to alternate prisons. The probability of the latter occurring can also be lowered through the use of effective relocation and monitoring by offender managers and improved interagency communication.

PRACTITIONERS' INVOLVEMENT

Psychologists – certainly those working in the UK – have had little opportunity to apply direct interventions to gang offenders. In fact, their awareness of membership may arise in the context of providing other interventions, such as those that focus on reducing substance misuse or through reading files and records on specific prisoners. Aside from this, the forensic practitioner must also contend with a number of additional obstacles that may serve to impede his or her practice and research into gang activity:

The definitional issues surrounding gangs have already been covered. Psychologists are in no better position than other members of staff to define what constitutes a gang. Additionally, however, there are questions over the sensitivity of staff to the existence of gang activity and what universal signs, if any, denote it. Although many gang members in the US declare their allegiances by wearing particular clothing, adopting elaborate hand signals or specific tattoos, gang membership in the UK is generally less pronounced. It may be pertinent to question whether staff reports are reliable (and if they rest on stereotypes informed by the media) and whether records of observed behaviour are accurate, comprehensive and germane to the issue of gang membership. A code of secrecy can also frame gang activity. For reasons of self-preservation or group cohesiveness, revealing specific details of a gang or its actions can lead to condemnation and reprisal. Practitioners must also consider the possibility that governors/senior management staff may be disinclined to reveal the true extent of gang activity in their establishments for fear that it projects a sense of instability, mismanagement and incompetence. These issues combine to make the search for an effective, economical and durable response to gang membership increasingly difficult. Having said this, it is possible to make a number of tentative recommendations for practice.

FORMING A THERAPEUTIC ALLIANCE

The importance of building and maintaining a positive therapeutic relationship with a (suspected) gang member – regardless of their index offence – is no different from working with other offenders. As detailed elsewhere in this book, practitioners should aim to develop rapport though the use of listening, observation, accurate reflection and validation. It must be possible for feedback, both verbal and non-verbal, to be comprehended by the interviewee. This will depend greatly on a practitioner's ability to be responsive to various factors such as the interviewee's level of education, learning style, reading/writing ability, capacity to retain information, motivation to engage and their willingness to disclose life experiences.

If it were to be assumed that a self-identifying gang member wished to denounce their affiliations and distance themselves from troublesome peers, an appropriate model for the practitioner to employ would be Prochaska and DiClemente's Cycle of Change (1982). This encouragingly simple model – also cited in Chapter 13 – can be adopted by anyone wishing to change their behaviour and/or reduce certain habits. In the forensic arena, its application is usually reserved for working with problematic substance users during individual or group interventions with a trained practitioner. There are, of course, no set times for moving between the different stages of the model. The duration an individual spends in any one particular stage will depend on a number of factors, including the level of internal motivation he or she is experiencing, the goals that have been set and the resources available to support change. The simplicity of the model in contrast to the challenge of successfully changing elements of a lifestyle is striking, particularly if the target behaviour has been established as part of a person's life for a considerable period of time. Nevertheless, it may be useful to consider the applicability of this model to a self-identifying gang member who is interested in changing his behaviour. Used correctly, the cycle may help a gang member to understand the negative aspects of their association. With careful guidance (through the use of Socratic questioning), a practitioner may be able to encourage the individual to reflect on how the benefits of changing may be greater than not changing at all.

The use of motivational 'tools' such as the Cycle of Change may be useful for those working with self-identifying gang members. Problems arise, however, when an individual does not wish to confirm or discuss his suspected membership. Interviewing suspected as opposed to self-identifying gang members can be an immensely difficult task, particularly as the person may deny all knowledge of the particular gang in an effort to protect other members as well as himself. Clearly, the identification of peers may have deleterious consequences for the identifier, either within custody or in the community, since such an action is highly likely to violate the shared behavioural norms that exist for that gang.

UNDERSTAND HOW GANG MEMBERSHIP MAY IMPACT ON THE ASSESSMENT PROCESS

Practitioners must be sensitive to the fact that self-report measures are likely to suffer from a degree of socially desirable responding. This is especially true if the suspected gang member is keen to distance himself from affiliations that may impact on his ability to serve his sentence peacefully or to preserve the secrecy that surrounds his or her gang. As such, members' affiliations may not be immediately obvious or pronounced. Practitioners must also contend with the possibility that gang members may be reluctant to divulge information during interview, thereby leaving the former with an imprecise account of that person's life history and their involvement in criminal activity. Despite being a downside of the assessment process, the practitioner can attempt to minimize this tendency by emphasizing the benefits of being as accurate as possible, particularly if the prisoner wishes to denounce his affiliations. Practitioners may also be advised to consult the files relating to specific offenders in order to ascertain if their interviewee's responses match up with official records (e.g., index offence, previous convictions, known affiliations, pre-sentence reports).

MAKE REPORTS (AND REPORT DISCLOSURE) MOTIVATIONAL

When writing reports on those suspected of gang activity (regardless of the reason for completing the report), practitioners must be mindful when making references to their peer group in the community. Indeed, it is probable that the offender views these people as an integral part of their identity. Recommending that the individual in question removes himself from their company may risk, at least temporarily, alienating that person from the positive aspects of rehabilitation and damage the therapeutic relationship the practitioner has strived to build. The emphasis, therefore, must be on raising the motivation of the gang member to adopt an alternative lifestyle by highlighting the positives of interacting with new associates. Reports must be sensitive to that possibility that the subject may have limited reading ability and/or low levels of educational achievement, which may not be due to their involvement with gang activities. As such, the report should be written and presented in a way that makes it accessible for the client and allows them to understand the recommendations made by the practitioner. Care should be taken to ensure that the report is disclosed in a non-threatening environment that will allow the subject to ask questions and clarify comments made in the report. Given that other members of the same or opposing gangs may be serving custodial sentences in the same wing of an establishment, it is essential that the report be disclosed in a confidential manner. Care should also be taken in responding to issues arising from the disclosure, particularly if the client is due to return to the wing immediately afterwards. It would then be prudent to inform wing officers of the meeting and the need to be vigilant to the client's short-term behaviour.

REVIEW/ENHANCE STAFF KNOWLEDGE ON GANG BEHAVIOUR

At the time of writing, there are no accredited training packages specifically tailored to promote the issue of gang membership and inform/educate existing members of staff on how to respond to offenders with gang affiliations in UK prisons. Given that Psychology or Programmes department personnel in HM

Prison Service regularly provide educational sessions to other members of staff in establishments, it may be profitable for similar sessions to be implemented that focus on the issue in hand. It is also important that discipline members of staff (such as prison officers) are encouraged to develop skills that facilitate gang members in discussing and potentially renouncing their affiliations. This is particularly the case for designated personal officers who, in addition to getting to know the offenders that are allocated to them, are given the responsibility of collaborating with these individuals on activities such as sentence planning. These members of staff are likely to be the first and most accessible point of contact for prisoners. Regardless of how gang membership is defined, staff awareness as to the indicators of probable – as opposed to guaranteed – gang behaviour should be improved. Specifically, members of staff must become familiar with the identity of prominent gangs in their community and how affiliations with these gangs may impact on the behaviour of members when in custody. Indicators of membership, if known, must be communicated at all levels.

CONCLUSION

The chapter has sought to highlight the nature of gangs: what they are, how they form, the many attractions surrounding membership and how the collective behaviour of members can sometimes (though not always) lead to criminal acts. The problems inherent in uncovering a universal definition for this form of collective behaviour have also been exposed along with the implications for research and practice until commentators enforce stricter guidelines on its definition.

At the time of writing, there is no agreed way of responding to gang membership, either in prisons or the community. There is also little direct involvement from forensic practitioners. It is likely that this situation will need to change in the future. Positively, many of the skills learnt and cultivated by psychologists working with forensic populations have the potential to be useful when working with gang members, suspected or otherwise.

RECOMMENDED FURTHER READING

Practitioners keen to expand their knowledge of this offender type are encouraged to consult the following sources:

Alleyne, E. and Wood, J. L. (2011). 'Gang Involvement: Social and Environmental Factors', *Crime and Delinquency* 57(6), 1–22. The authors are leading researchers in this area and the information is very current.

Ebensen, F-A., Winfree, L. T. Jr., He, N. and Taylor, T. J. (2001). 'Youth Gangs and Definitional Issues: When is a Gang a Gang and Why Does it Matter?' *Crime and Delinquency* 47, 105–30. This paper provides a comprehensive review of the problematic definitional issues surrounding gangs

Pyrooz, D. C., Decker, S. H. and Fleisher, M. (2011). 'From the Street to the Prison, from the Prison to the Street: Understanding and Responding to Prison Gangs', *Journal of Aggression, Conflict and Peace Research*, 3(1), 12–24. This is a very recent paper that provides an interesting additional perspective on gang behaviour in prisons

REFERENCES

Alleyne, E. and Wood, J. L. (2011). 'Gang Involvement: Social and Environmental Factors', *Crime and Delinquency* 57(6), 1–22.

Akers R. L. and Sellers, C. S. (2009). *Criminological Theories: Introduction and Evaluation*, 5th edn (Oxford: Oxford University Press).

Bennett, T. and Holloway, K. (2004). 'Gang Membership, Drugs and Crime in the UK', *British Journal of Criminology* 44, 305–23.

Brandt, D. E. and Zlotnick, J. L. (1988). *The Psychology and Treatment of the Youthful Offender* (Springfield, Il: Charles C. Thomas).

British Broadcasting Corporation (BBC) (2008). 'Huyton Convict Ran Drugs and Guns Gang from Prison Cell', Retrieved 1 December 2011, from the BBC News website: http://www.bbc.co.uk/news/uk-england-merseyside-11971312.

Bullock, K. and Tilley, N. (2002). 'Shootings, Gangs and Violent Incidents in Manchester: Developing a Crime Reduction Strategy', Crime Reduction Research Series Paper 12, London: Home Office.

Camp, G. M. and Camp, C. (1985). *Prison Gangs: Their Extent, Nature and Impact on Prisons* (US Department of Justice, Washington, DC: US Government Printing Office).

Davies, A. (2008). *The Gangs of Manchester: The Story of the Scuttlers, Britain's First Youth Cult* (Wrea Green: Milo).

Davis, J. (1993). 'Psychological vs Sociological Explanations for Delinquent Conduct and Gang Formation', *Journal of Contemporary Criminal Justice*, 9(2), 81–93.

Densley, J. A. (2011). 'Ganging up on Gangs: Why the Gang Intervention Industry Needs an Intervention', *British Journal of Forensic Practice* 13(1), 12–21.

Deschenes, E. P. and Esbensen, F-A. (1999). 'Violence and Gangs: Gender Differences in Perception and Behaviour', *Journal of Quantitative Criminology* 15, 53–96.

Direct Gov. (2011). 'Gangs and Gang Crime: The Facts', Retrieved 1 December 2011, from the Direct Gov website: http://www.direct.gov.uk/en/Parents/Yourchildshealthandsafety/WorriedAbout/DG_171314

Esbensen, F-A. (2000). 'Preventing Adolescent Gang Involvement', *Juvenile Justice Bulletin*. Office of Juvenile Justice and Delinquency Prevention. US Department of Justice.

Ebsensen and Weerman (2005). 'Youth Gangs and Troublesome Youth Groups in the United States and the Netherlands – A Cross-National Comparison', *European Journal of Criminology* 2(1), 5–37.

Esbensen, F-A., and Winfree, L. T. (1998). 'Race and Gender Differences between Gang and Nongang Youths: Results from a Multisite Survey', *Justice Quarterly* 15(3), 505–26.

Ebensen, F-A., Winfree, L. T. Jr., He, N. and Taylor, T. J. (2001). 'Youth Gangs and Definitional Issues: When is a Gang a Gang and Why Does it Matter?', *Crime and Delinquency* 47, 105–30.

Fong, R. S. and Buentello, S. (1991). 'The Detection of Prison Gang Development: An Empirical Assessment', *Federal Probation* 1, 66–9.

Fraser, C. and Burchell, B. (2001). *Introducing Social Psychology* (Oxford: Blackwell).

Guardian. The. (2011). 'Prison Population Hits Record High in England and Wales',. Retrieved 19 January 2011, from *The Guardian* website: http://www.guardian.co.uk/society/2011/aug/19/prison-population-record-high.

Hall, G. P., Thornberry, T. P. and Lizotte, A. J. (2006). 'The Gang Facilitation Effect and Neighbourhood Risk: Do Gangs Have a Stronger Influence on Delinquency in Disadvantaged Areas?', in J. F. Short and L. A. Hughes (eds) *Studying Youth Gangs* (Oxford, UK: Altamira Press), 47–61.

Hallsworth, S. and Young, T. (2008). 'Gang Talk and Gang Talkers: A Critique', *Crime Media Culture* 4, 175–95.

Hill, K. G., Howell, J., Hawkins, J. D. and Battin-Pearson, S. R. (1999). 'Childhood Risk Factors for Adolescent Gang Membership: Results from the Seattle Social Development Project', *Journal of Research in Crime and Delinquency* 36(3), 300–22.

Hill, K. G., Lui, C. and Hawkins, J. D. (2001). 'Early Precursors of Gang Membership: A Study of Seattle Youth', *Juvenile Justice Bulletin December 2001*. US Department of Justice.

Justice.gov.uk. (2011). 'Population Bulletin – Monthly December 2011', Retrieved 19 January 2011, from the Justice.gov.uk website: http://www.justice.gov.uk/publications/statistics-and-data/prisons-and-probation/prison-population-figures/index.htm.

Klein, M. W., Kerner, H-J., Maxson, C. L. and Weitkamp, E. G. M. (eds) (2001). *The Eurogang Paradox: Street Gangs and Youth Groups in the US and Europe* (Dordrecht, Kluwer Academic Press).

Klein, M. W., Weerman F. M. and Thornberry, T. P. (2006). 'Street Gang Violence in Europe', *European Journal of Criminology* 3(4), 413–37.

Prochaska, J. O. and DiClemente, C. C. (1982). 'Transtheoretical Therapy: Toward a More Integrative Model of Change', *Psychotherapy: Theory, Research and Practice* 19(3), 276–88.

Rizzo, M. (2003). 'Why Do Children Join Gangs?' *Journal of Gang Research* 11, 65–74.

Sante, L. (1991). *Low Life: Lures and Snares of Old New York* (New York, NY: Vintage Books).

Shaw, C. R and Mackay, H. D. (1969). *Juvenile Delinquency and Urban Areas* (Chicago: The University of Chicago Press).

Sharp, C., Aldridge, J. and Medina, J. (2006). *Delinquent Youth Groups and Offending Behaviour: Findings from the 2004 Offending, Crime and Justice Survey* (Home Office Online Report 14/06. London: Home Office).

Short, J. F. and Strodtbeck, F. L. (1974). *Group Process and Gang Delinquency* (Chicago: University of Chicago Press).

Shropshire, S., and McFarquhar, M. (2002). *Developing Multi-Agency Strategies to Address the Street Gang Culture and Reduce Gun Violence among Young People* (Briefing No.4) (Manchester, UK: Steve Shropshire and Michael McFarquhar Consultancy Group).

Spergel, I. A. (1995). *The Youth Gang Problem: A Community Approach* (New York: Oxford University Press, Inc).

Sutherland (1960). *Principles of Criminology* (Chigago: Lippincott).

Telegraph, The. (2007). 'Foreign Gangs Moving to Rural Areas', Retrieved 1 December 2011, from *The Telegraph* website: www.telegraph.co.uk/news/uknews/1565049/Foreign-gangs-moving-to-rural-areas.html.

Thrasher, F. (1927). *The Gang: A Study of 1313 Gangs in Chicago* (Chicago. University of Chicago Press).

Thornberry, T. P., Krohm, M. D., Lizotte, A. J., Smith, C. and Tobin, K. (2003). *Gangs and Delinquency in Developmental Perspective* (Cambridge: Cambridge University Press).

Times Online (2009). '2800 Crime Gangs Ravage UK Streets', Retrieved 1 December 2011, from *The Times Online* website: www.thetimes.co.uk/tto/news/uk/crime/article1876139.

Toy, J. (2008). 'Die Another Day: A Practitioner's Review with Recommendations for Preventing Gang and Weapon Violence in London in 2008', (London. MPS Research and Analysis Unit).

Wood, J. and Adler, J. (2001). 'Gang Activity in English Prisons: The Staff Perspective', *Psychology, Crime and Law*. 7, 167–92.

Wood, J. (2006). 'Gang Activity in English Prisons: The Prisoners' Perspective', *Psychology, Crime and Law* 12(6), 605–17.

13 Victims of Crime

Sarah Barnes

INTRODUCTION

It might seem rather unusual for a book such as this to include a chapter on working with victims. It is an interesting observation that historically, therapeutic work with offenders and victims has generally been treated as two separate domains. In fact, some would consider working with both client groups to present a conflict of interests and perhaps as a consequence, work with victims is not often considered within the role of the forensic psychologist. But what happens when the offender you are working with is also a victim? Research suggests that, at least in relation to sex offenders, this is likely to be so in up to half of cases (e.g., Dhawan and Marshall, 1996; Marshall, Serran and Cortoni, 2000). In addition to sexual offenders, Hanson and Slater's (1988) meta-analysis revealed that an average of 28 per cent of all offenders (nearly 25,000 people based on current prison populations) have suffered sexual abuse as a child (Hanson and Slater, 1988). Unfortunately, with the exception of childhood sexual abuse in sexual offenders, research investigating offenders as victims remains sparse, with little consideration of other forms of victimization such as physical assault, robbery or theft, particularly in adulthood. It is therefore a sad state of affairs that the evolution of accredited intervention programmes for offenders has comprehensively neglected the victim needs of offender clients. Therefore, this chapter focusses primarily on the psychology of victimization with consideration of how victim issues may affect offenders.

WORKING WITH VICTIMS OF CRIME

When working with victims of crime, it is important to consider the person before they became a victim as well as their reactions to victimization in the days, weeks, months and even years following the crime; not only the person at the time when the crime was committed. Before applying theories and research into the effects of victimization, it is important for the reader to understand that victims are not a homogenous group. A victim of a seemingly minor crime may experience a very negative response to the crime and be traumatized for many years following the event, whereas a victim of a serious crime may cope very well in the aftermath, and not require any additional support in getting back to normality. Also, it is important that professionals never blame the victim for any part of the crime, even when the victim's actions may have directly led to them being victimized, such as leaving a window open through which burglars have entered a property. Portioning such blame can lead to a process known as secondary victimization, in which the victim experiences negative emotions and stigmatization following the crime due to the reactions of others (Brown, 1991), which can delay recovery, or increase the severity of response, following a crime (Campbell and Raja, 1999; Campbell *et al.*, 1999).

THEORETICAL OVERVIEW

There are numerous models of victimization and recovery in the literature. Casarez-Levison (1992) reviewed a number of such models and proposed a simple theory that incorporated the main features of the various other theories. She suggests that victims of crimes should be considered in four separate states: before the crime, during the crime, the initial coping and short-term adjustment following the crime and finally when victims accept the crime as being a past experience in their life. The model that she put forward can be seen in Figure 13.1, with the individual stages described in detail below.

PREVICTIMIZATION: LIFE BEFORE THE CRIME

Before considering how to work with a victim and setting goals to be achieved, it is important to gain an understanding of who the person was before the crime. Prior to being victimized, the victim had a life, a past, hobbies, commitments and so forth. Many of these are likely to remain throughout the periods of recovery and reorganization. Therefore an understanding of the victim's current commitments, such as family and financial pressures, will be beneficial, as these will often need to be maintained in the confusion following the crime. The victim may require additional support in order to fulfil these commitments. Additionally, it is important to understand certain things about the

Figure 13.1 *The process of victimization and recovery*

Previctimisation ➡ Victimisation ➡ Transition ➡ Reorganisation

Source: Casarez-Levison, 1992.

victim's past, including any prior experiences of crime, as previous responses and adjustments following earlier traumas have been found to be good predictors of how the client will respond in the present instance (Brunet *et al.*, 2001). Knowledge of any previous or current mental illness or substance misuse may be beneficial as the crime may trigger a relapse (Brunet *et al.*, 2001).

VICTIMIZATION: THE CRIME AND THE IMMEDIATE AFTERMATH

This stage begins either at the time of the crime, for example, following a street robbery, or when the victim discovers the crime, for example, coming home from work to find that they have been burgled. The stage is characterized by the thoughts and feelings of the victim as they attempt to make sense of what has happened. The length of this stage will vary from victim to victim but typically lasts for a few days. The most commonly reported emotions experienced in the aftermath of a crime are confusion, helplessness, anger and fear (Casarez-Levison, 1992). The victim may also have experienced physical, emotional and/or mental injuries with which they now have to cope. This stage includes the more practical aspects following the crime, such as informing the police, contacting an insurance company and securing points of entry that have been broken during the crime. When making a decision on what to do following a crime, the decision-making process does not always seem like a logical or rational one. A victim may decide not to report the crime to the police because they feel foolish or embarrassed, they may believe that there is little chance of the offender being caught and that they are wasting police time or have had negative experiences with the police previously, they may think that people will not believe them or may not want to go to court, the offender might be known to the victim or the victim may just want to forget that the crime happened. It is important that although encouragement to report a crime may be appropriate, the decision to report a crime is ultimately the victim's, and they should not be pushed into doing something they do not wish to do.

Crime often invokes attributions of blame, with others blaming the victim resulting in secondary victimization, or the victim blaming themselves or their actions leading up to the crime. Self-blame following crime can have both positive and negative outcomes. Where the consequences of the crime are relatively low (e.g., in burglary), self-blame can help the victim feel as if they have control of a situation and enables the crime to be processed as there are things that can be done to prevent the crime from happening again, leading to better psychological adjustment (Thompson *et al.*, 1993). However, in crimes with serious and often long-term consequence (e.g., rape) it has been found that self-blame attributed to one's character (e.g., agreeing with statements such as 'I'm a bad person', 'I got what I deserved' and 'I'm weak', items taken from the

Sexual Victimization Attributions Measure, Breitenbecher, 2006) is positively correlated with psychological distress (Breitenbecher, 2006; Koss, Figueredo and Prince, 2002) but not behavioural self-blame (one's behaviour). Other studies, however, have demonstrated that both behavioural and characterological self-blame are associated with increased psychological distress (Frazier, 2000; Hill and Zautra, 1989). This suggests that while blaming oneself for the crime can, in some instances, assist the victim to process what has happened, it can also increase psychological distress. Therefore, emphasizing facts about the crime that the victim could not have foreseen or avoided (e.g., if where the crime occurred was on a regular route home or if the victim was intoxicated at the time of the crime) may be beneficial.

TRANSITION: COPING AND ADJUSTMENT FOLLOWING THE CRIME

Following the initial response to the crime, in the following weeks, months and even years, the victim then must learn to adjust and cope with the long-term effects of the crime. This stage involves the victim going through a process of learning to accept what has happened to them and moving on with their lives. This meaning-making process is often thought to be part of a grieving process of loss as result of the crime, as well as be an important part of coping (Davis, Nolen-Hoeksema and Larson, 1998). Davis, Nolen-Hoeksema and Larson (1998) argue that people are motivated to find meaning in negative life events to conform to beliefs that one's life should be comprehensible, reasonable and just. When placed in a situation that contradicts these beliefs, the conflict can cause psychological distress and a resolution through meaning making is required to recover from the experience.

It is during this transition period when the individual is likely to require the most assistance and support from friends, family and professionals. This may include providing both emotional and practical support. This is also the stage when the victim is at the greatest risk of relying on maladaptive coping strategies such as the abuse of substances, social isolation and withdrawal (Casarez-Levison, 1992). It is important when working with victims to be mindful that, on face value, the individual may appear to be coping well in the circumstances that they have found themselves in. However, there may be chaos and confusion behind the apparently robust front; particularly if the victim feels that they need to remain resilient for other people (e.g., children, spouse or elderly parents). Furthermore, the victim may not be aware of the negative effects of the crime in other aspects of their lives. While bearing this in mind, it is also imperative that one does not assume that a victim, even a victim of a serious crime, is traumatized and requires help and support when they may not and may be coping very well on their own (Nelson, Wangsgaard, Yorgason, Higgins-Kessler and Carter-Vassol, 2002); this is known as trauma bias. Furthermore, the victim may not yet be ready to accept help, be in denial or are not currently ready to address their victimization issues. Casarez-Levison (1992) suggests that it is essential that this stage is fully completed in order for the victim to progress to the final stage; if not the victim is likely to turn to maladaptive coping strategies or burn out from exhaustion.

REORGANIZATION: THE FUTURE

The final stage of the Victimization and Recovery Model focusses on the transition of the individual from a victim to a survivor of crime. It involves the client rebuilding their lives so that the crime is an aspect of their past. However, reorganization does not necessarily mean retuning to normality as was prior to victimization, and it is important that the survivor also understands that they may never return to being exactly the person they were before they were victimized (Norris, Kaniasty and Thompson, 1997). For example, an adult victim of rape may have appeared to have completed the process of victimization and recovery. However, they may continue to be uncomfortable with being alone or, understandably, have issues trusting people for many years following the reorganization period. Reorganization involves the survivor successfully engaging in personal and romantic relationships, as well as returning to, and maintaining, employment and engaging in social and recreational activities where applicable.

SPECIAL CONSIDERATIONS WHEN WORKING WITH VICTIMS

When working with a victim of any crime, the most important thing to remember is that all victims are different and they may not react in the way that you might expect. In the first few meetings it is vital that an understanding is gained about the victim's life before the crime. If they already have a number of stressors in their lives, a crime, even a relatively minor crime, may tip the victim from just about coping to not coping at all. Also, a victim of a serious crime may have the resources to cope very well either alone or with the support network that they already have available to them, and therefore may require little input from a therapeutic professional. The main point to remember is to remain flexible in the approach employed when working with victims.

In order to provide a suitable service for the individual, it is necessary to gain a good understanding of their needs as well as their personal history and characteristics. The following provides a reader with issues a professional may want to be mindful of while working with a victim. It is not a comprehensive checklist, but designed to be a guide to inform professionals (list adapted from Hill, 2009).

Historical Factors

When working with many different client groups, an understanding of a person's past can be very useful in explaining current behaviours; this is no different for victims. Knowledge of previous victimization in both childhood and adulthood may help both the professional and the victim understand the way the victim feels now and how they may feel in the future. Previous victimization experiences may also allow the victim to evaluate previously employed coping strategies and learn more adaptive strategies from the ones they may have used previously when required. Knowledge of any history of mental disorder or substance misuse may be invaluable, particularly if the victim is able to identify triggers that may lead to a deterioration in mental health or cause a relapse in substance use. Knowledge of a previous diagnosis of post traumatic stress disorder (PTSD), including severity, may be useful as sufferers of PTSD are more susceptible to reoccurrences of the disorder (Kilpatrick and Resnick, 1993) and it provides information about a person's recovery following a serious mental illness. Finally, it may be important to learn of any coping strategies the victim has used in the past. They may not be aware of the coping strategies that they naturally employ and therefore it may be useful speaking to friends and family of the client for a more objective opinion, confidentiality allowing.

Current Characteristics

As mentioned previously, knowledge of a victim's current situation can often provide clues as to the response they may have to the crime. It is important to have an understanding of personality characteristics (historical factors will be important here too), as well as their current living situation, including financial and family obligations, work arrangements and other daily life stressors. As noted above, knowledge of coping strategies that the victim has employed previously, or approaches they are currently using, particularly if they are, or have previously used substance misuse or self-harm as means of coping with stress can be used as an indicator of how they might cope with present or future experiences of crime. While considering the victim's personal and historical factors, it is vital that professionals do not assume how the client will react this time or to second guess what it is that they want or need. Suggestions can be made of things that may be beneficial to the victim or their family; however it is important to listen to what the victim wants and feel that they need – even if you or others disagree.

Crime-Related Factors

Specific aspects that have happened during and in the aftermath of the crime are highly likely to affect how the victim reacts and recovers from the crime. Such factors may include the severity of the crime, including the use of violence or the use of a weapon. It may also include whether the victim feels that they are to blame for the crime or the responses of others, including professionals, to the crime, which may lead to secondary victimization. Other points to contemplate may be whether the victim knows the perpetrator(s), whether the offender is caught and prosecuted or whether the crime is a single event or the person has been victimized a number of times. These elements of the crime may all affect the impact that it has on the victim. Consider how such events are perceived from the point of view of the victim; empathy is an important skill for professionals to have when working with victims of crime.

Additional Factors

In addition to all of the above information it may also be pertinent to be mindful of additional issues that are present in the victim's life. Such things may include mental and physical disabilities, both prior, and as a result of the victimization, as well as the victim's cognitive abilities and communications skills – including if English is not the victim's first language or if the victim is deaf. The victim's self-efficacy to cope with the situation and their self-esteem, again both prior and post crime, are also likely to be relevant and require consideration to assist the victim's transition through the model of recovery. It is very important to consider the victim's support network and, where necessary, keep the support network informed of your work and progress made; bearing in mind issues surrounding confidentiality. Furthermore, it is vital for professionals to understand that a victim may not be ready to address their issues immediately or may deny that they have any problems. Therefore the victim, or their family, may appreciate information about where they can get help when the time comes that they are ready to move forward with their recovery.

The idea of this overview is to provide professionals working with victims of crime of factors that may or may not be present in the victim that they are working with but are important to bear in mind. It is hoped that it is clear that a one-size-fits-all approach is not appropriate when working with victims of crimes and that services must be adapted to fit the needs and requirements of each individual victim in order to have the greatest chance of success in allowing the victim to progress through Casarez-Levison's (1992) Model of Victimization and Recovery.

ASSESSMENT: WHEN IS PROFESSIONAL INVOLVEMENT MOST EFFECTIVE?

One problem often faced by professionals, as well as victims and their friends and families, is when is professional involvement most effective? As clients will often experience periods of standing still or even regression in their recovery following a crime, professional input may not always be welcomed or beneficial. Prochaska, DiClemente and Norcross (1992) have developed a model illustrating stages of recovery that was first developed for professionals working with people suffering from substance misuse; however it is highly applicable to victims of crime. People are usually in one stage, but can be in all stages at the same time, and can move both forward and backwards through the model. It is important to assess where a victim may be in the model, as encouraging a victim to change or pushing them to engage in intensive therapy is likely to overwhelm them and cause more and unnecessary distress. The stages of the model can be seen in Figure 13.2 and are described in detail below.

THE STAGES OF CHANGE MODEL

Pre-Contemplation

People in this stage have no intention of changing their current behaviours, often being unaware that their behaviour is problematic, or denying the extent or severity of their problems. Such people often only come to the light of professionals because they have been pushed or referred to by others. Victims in this stage may deny that the crime has affected them, or even deny that a crime was ever committed; however, friends and family may report changes in the victim's mood, behaviours or physical and mental health. Victims may underestimate the benefits of change and overestimate the drawbacks. When working with a victim in this stage, it is best to try to gently encourage the victim to compare who they were before the crime and who they are now, with help from the family where appropriate. It is important to remember, however, that the victim may not want your help, or to change their potentially problematic behaviours. At this time it may be more appropriate to leave literature and information with the victim so that they can access services when they are ready to address their

Figure 13.2 *The transtheoretical model of change*

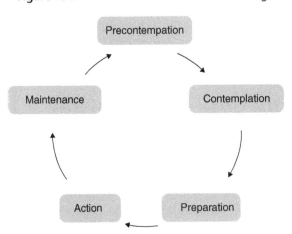

Source: Prochaska, DiClemente and Norcross, 1992.

issues. Do not attempt to force people to change, even if professionals and/or the family believe that it is in the victim's best interest as people in this stage are more likely to experience more distress, progress slower, achieve less or withdraw from therapeutic services (Smith, Subich and Kalodner, 1995).

Contemplation

People in this stage are aware that their behaviour is problematic and are considering changing their behaviour, but are not actively doing anything to change. They may be debating the benefits of change against the effort and energy that would be required to change. Victims may be reluctant to change because of a fear of failure or being perceived as a person who cannot cope. Clients may have anxieties surrounding seeking professional advice, or may believe that talking about the crime may make the situation worse. While working with victims in this stage, it is important to reassure the victim and inform them of the benefits of change. However, it is important to be honest about the difficulties that the victim is likely to experience in their journey, including obstacles that they may encounter and emphasizing that setbacks are not failures.

Preparation

People in this stage are aware of their issues, recognize a need to change and are seriously considering addressing their problems in the near future. They may have made small changes to their lives already, such as changing habits, or else may have attempted to make large-scale changes recently but have been unable to sustain the changes in the long term. This stage is usually very short with victims often easily encouraged to move into the next stage, either by themselves, or with the help of others.

Action

People who are in this stage are actively attempting to modify their behaviour. This stage is often accompanied by a specific goal that the victim particularly wants to achieve. This may be returning to work, continuing with a recreational activity or maybe building up the confidence to report the crime to the police. It is important that professionals do not focus solely on this stage but recognize the endeavour the victim is likely to have gone through to get to this stage, but also to provide them with the tools to maintain the changes they make during this stage in the next, and final stage of the model.

Maintenance

People who are in the final stage of the model are sustaining the skills that they have learnt in the Action stage to allow them to recover adaptively in the long term. Once the Maintenance stage has been reached, it is important that the victim understands that the modified behaviour will require constant evaluation and adjustment to prevent relapse to other stages. At this stage it is important that the victim is aware of any triggers that they might have which makes them susceptible to relapse and to encourage them to monitor their thoughts, emotions and behaviours for signs of relapse.

WORKING WITH OFFENDERS WITH A HISTORY OF VICTIMIZATION

Experiencing crime can have severe and enduring effects on various aspects of victim's life. It therefore seems reasonable that an offender with a history of victimization should be considered in the same manner as victims without an offending history. Remember while working with a victim that they may have a criminal history that they do not wish to disclose to professionals. Much of the research into the effects of victimization in offenders has focussed on severe abuse experienced in the offender's childhood, mainly physical and sexual abuse.

It has been found that perpetrators of both violent and sexual crimes are more likely to have experienced violent and sexual abuse than other offenders and the general population (Lambie, Seymour and Adams, 2002; Widom, 1989). For example, between 5 and 75 per cent of child sexual offenders have a history of sexual abuse (Hanson and Slator, 1988), whereas rapists and violent offenders are more likely to have experienced physical abuse or neglect in childhood (Crassati, McClurg and Browne, 2002; Simons, Wurtele and Durham, 2008; Widom, 1989). This has led to the suggestion that there is a cycle of offending, both in sexual and violent offenders (Glasser *et al.*, 2001; Widom, 1989).

Unfortunately, although there is an ever-growing literature on the effects of childhood sexual abuse on later offending behaviour, particularly sexual offending, research into other offending populations (e.g., people convicted of theft, fraud, robbery or assault) and types of victimization other than childhood abuse remains sparse. This is surprising when it is known that many offenders are victimized while incarcerated. For example, official statistics show that over 14,300 assaults on prisoners were officially reported in England and Wales prisons in the year 2010 alone, of which 10 per cent were classified as 'serious assaults' which include sexual assault (Ministry of Justice, 2011). However, these figures are likely to be conservative, as many assaults go unreported and data about other types of crime (e.g., theft) are unavailable.

If a large number of violent and sexual offenders have experienced victimization both while in custody and prior to incarceration, it appears rational to expect opportunities to address issues related to victimization to be available to offenders. However, in practice this does not seem to happen, with treatment programmes in forensic institutions focussing on directly lowering recidivism and protection of the public and not addressing an offender's victim issues. Furthermore, the government's compensation scheme which awards compensation to victims of violent crime (Criminal Injuries Compensation Authority) may reduce an award payment (potentially to £0) if the victim is known to have previous criminal convictions. This seems unjust, if a victim is assaulted in an unprovoked attack and has the amount of compensation reduced for a previous conviction that has no influence on the current crime and for which they have served their sentence.

Walker (2006) and Ward and Moreton (2008) have argued for this to be addressed in offenders. They apply the term 'moral repair' which allows for victimization issues to be addressed in order to allow successful reintegration into the community and reduce recidivism rates. It should be noted that this does not mean attributing the blame for the offence to anyone but the offender, who, Walker argues, remains responsible and accountable for his or her crimes. Instead, Ward and Moreton argue for professionals to acknowledge and address the impacts of the offender's experiences of crimes, allowing them to repair the psychological harm that they have suffered as a result of their abuse, enabling them to be in a healthier state of mind when the offender addresses their own offending.

Ethical issues, including that offenders with a history of childhood victimization are able to blame others for the crimes that they have committed, surround arguments in favour of moral repair in offenders. However, this is not what is argued by Walker (2006), Ward and Moreton (2008) or the present author. We would suggest that all victims have a right to address the issues that such victimization has left them with, despite what they have developed into as adults. Ward and Moreton also argue that addressing an offender's victimization issues is likely to have a positive impact on the success of a reduction in offending treatment programme; however further empirical research is required to clarify this hypothesis.

CASE STUDY

A CASE FORMULATION EXAMPLE: MR SLATER (FICTIONAL)

Andrew Slater is a fifty-one-year-old man currently serving a seven-year sentence for a serious indecent assault on a child under the age of thirteen. He has a long history of sexual offences against children, receiving his first conviction at the age of eighteen. His offences include both contact and non-contact offences, including buggery and the production and distribution of images over the internet. All of Mr Slater's offences have been committed against young boys aged seven–thirteen. He also has a number of convictions for burglary and petty theft.

Mr Slater is of average intelligence with no known history of mental illness, although has had a long battle with alcoholism. Mr Slater reports that he began drinking around the age of eleven and by the age of seventeen was consuming a litre of vodka a day. He successfully engaged in an alcohol detox programme in 2003 and has been alcohol-free since. There is no known history of further substance misuse.

Mr Slater is the third of four children. He reports that his father was very strict and physically assaulted Mr Slater and his siblings as punishment. Mr Slater's reports suggest that his father also suffered from alcoholism and was most violent after he had been drinking. Mr Slater's mother had a diagnosis of schizophrenia and he remembers her being admitted into a psychiatric hospital for several periods during his childhood. Mr Slater's mother died of breast cancer when he was twenty-one. Mr Slater currently has no contact with any of his family, who disowned him following his first conviction for a sexual offence. This is with the exception of his older sister with whom he has sporadic contact. Mr Slater has two children, a boy aged twenty-six and a girl aged twenty-four; he currently has no contact with either of his children or their mother, although he has expressed a wish to contact his children in the future.

Previous professionals' reports suggest that Mr Slater is a quiet and socially anxious man who interacts minimally with other offenders on the wing, spending prolonged periods of socialization time in his cell. Prior to successfully completing his alcohol detoxification programme, Mr Slater engaged minimally with psychological services, and rarely made or maintained eye contact when speaking to people in authority; he continues to display issues in these areas. He has previously refused to work with women or senior men; however, this seems to have subsided in recent years. He now engages with his female probation officer, although occasionally Mr Slater refuses to see her without stated reason. Mr Slater successfully completed a Sex Offender Treatment Programme at the second attempt after withdrawing a few weeks in the first time. He also began a Better Lives Programme during his last sentence but withdrew within the first six weeks.

During a previous prison sentence, Mr Slater disclosed to a member of prison staff that, from the age of eight, until he was twelve, he had been in a sexual 'relationship' with a man called Peter, to whom his parents were renting a room. Mr Slater reports that this involved frequent anal penetration. Mr Slater reported at the time, and continues to report, that he and Peter were in a relationship and that the abuse was pleasurable. It is believed that Mr Slater found comfort and affection in his abuser that his mother and father failed to provide. Mr Slater has previously admitted that he has masturbated while thinking about his abuse. Mr Slater finds it difficult to view his own offending as abuse due to his experience. He rationalizes his offending as his victims enjoying it, as many did not disclose and some returned numerous times to Mr Slater's house and were abused over a period of time.

Considering what you know about offenders, how would you apply your knowledge of victims when working with Mr Slater? What issues do you think Mr Slater needs to address?

Things to consider:

- Where might Mr Slater be in the Stages of Change model, and what can we do to encourage him to move forward?
- What special considerations do we need to be mindful of?
- Can we force Mr Slater to see his abuse as a crime rather than a relationship? Will encouraging him to do so be beneficial for (a) Mr Slater or (b) your working relationship?
- Could addressing Mr Slater's victimization issues help him to address his own offending behaviours?

CONCLUSION

The aim of this chapter is to emphasize the point that victims are not a single group and require professionals involved in their treatment to adapt their therapeutic style to the specific needs of the victim. It is also hoped that after reading this, professionals will not second guess what is best for the victim or how the victim is feeling in the aftermath of the crime. Professionals are required to consider various historical and current factors in the victim's life, as well as the impact of the crime, while constantly re-evaluating the needs of the victim as well as where they are in the Stages of Change Model (Prochaska, DiClemente and Norcross, 1992).

Alongside working directly with victims, many professionals working in forensic institutions are likely to work with offenders who have been victims of crime. It is important for these professionals to consider the impact that previous victimization may have on both the offender themselves and their offending behaviour. It may also be crucial for professionals to address issues surrounding an offender's victimization if they are to have any success in reducing reoffending, however this requires further investigation.

Despite the large number of people who are victims of crime each year, research into the impacts of crime- and research-based therapeutic interventions remain sparse. There is a need for longitudinal studies into the long-term effects of crime, as well as, possible predictive and protective factors about who gets victimized.

RECOMMENDED FURTHER READING

Hill, J. K. (2009). 'Working with Victims of Crime: A Manual Applying Research to Clinical Practice', 2nd edn (Department of Justice, Government of Canada). Available from *http://canada.justice.gc.ca/eng/pi/pcvi-cpcv/pub/res-rech/hill.pdf*. This is a very thorough paper outlining relevant theory relating to victims and how this can be applied to practice. This paper was highly influential in the writing of this chapter.

Ward, T. and Moreton, G. (2008). 'Moral Repair with Offenders: Ethical Issues Arising from Victimization Experiences', *Sexual Abuse* 20(3), 305–322. An excellent paper examining the implications of victimization in offenders. The paper discusses the potential implications of victimization on offending behaviour and how issues surrounding victimization should be addressed in offenders as a potential to reduce reoffending.

REFERENCES

Breitenbecher, K. H. (2006). 'The Relationships among Self-Blame, Psychological Distress, and Sexual Victimization', *Journal of Interpersonal Violence* 21(5), 597–611.

Brown, S. (1991). *Counseling Victims of Violence* (American Association for Counseling and Development: VA).

Brunet, A., Boyer, R., Weiss, D. S. and Marmar, C. R. (2001). 'The Effects of Initial Trauma Exposure on the Symptomatic Response to a Subsequent Trauma', *Canadian Journal of Behavioural Science* 33(2), 97–102.

Campbell, R. and Raja, S. (1999). 'Secondary Victimization of Rape Victims: Insights from Mental Health Professionals Who Treat Survivors of Violence', *Violence and Victims* 14(3), 261–75.

Campbell, R., Sefl, T., Barnes, H. E., Ahrens, C. E., Wasco, S. M. and Zaragoza-Diesfeld, Y. (1999). 'Community Services for Rape Survivors: Enhancing Psychological Well-Being or Increasing Trauma?', *Journal of Consulting and Clinical Psychology* 67(6), 847–58.

Casarez-Levison, R. (1992). 'An Empirical Investigation of Coping Strategies Used by Victims of Crime: Victimization Redefined', in E. Viano (ed.) *Critical Issues in Victimology: International Perspectives* (New York: Springer Publishing Co), 46–57.

Crassati, J., McClurg, G. and Browne, K. (2002). 'Characteristics of Perpetrators of Child Sexual Abuse Who Have Been Sexually Victimzed as Children', *Sexual Abuse: A Journal of Research and Treatment* 14, 225–39.

Davis, C. G., Nolen-Hoeksema, S. and Larson, J. (1998). 'Making Sense of Loss and Benefiting from the Experience: Two Construals of Meaning', *Journal of Personality and Social Psychology*, 75(2), 561–74.

Dhawan, S. and Marshall, W. L. (1996). 'Sexual Abuse Histories of Sexual Offenders', *Sexual Abuse: A Journal of Research and Treatment* 8(1), 7–15.

Frazier, P. A. (2000). 'The Role of Attributions and Perceived Control in Recovery from Rape', *Journal of Personal and Interpersonal Loss* 5, 203–25.

Glasser, M., Kolvin, I., Campbell, D., Glasser, A., Leitch, I. and Farelly, S. (2001). 'Cycle of Child Sexual Abuse: Links between Being a Victim and Becoming a Perpetrator', *The British Journal of Psychiatry* 179, 482–94.

Hanson, K. R. and Slater, S. (1988). 'Sexual Victimization in the History of Sexual Abusers: A Review', *Sexual Abuse: A Journal of Research and Treatment* 1(4), 485–99.

Hill, J. K. (2009). 'Working with Victims of Crime: A Manual Applying Research to Clinical Practice' 2nd edn (Ottawa: Department for Justice, Canada).

Hill, J. L. and Zautra, A. J. (1989). 'Self-Blame Attributions and Unique Vulnerability as Predictors of Post-Rape Demoralization', *Journal of Social and Clinical Psychology* 8, 368–75.

Kilpatrick, D. G. and Resnick, H. S. (1993). 'Posttraumatic Stress Disorder Associated with Exposure to Criminal Vicitmization in Clinical and Community Populations', in R. T. Jonathon, M. D. Davidson and E. B. Foa (eds) *Posttraumatic Stress Disorder: DSM-IV and Beyond* (Washington: American Psychiatric Press), 113–44.

Koss, M. P., Figueredo, A. J. and Prince, R. J. (2002). 'Cognitive Mediation of Rape's Mental, Physical, and Social Health Impact: Tests of Four Models in Cross-Sectional Data', *Journal of Consulting and Clinical Psychology* 70(4), 926–41.

Lambie, I., Seymour, F., Lee, A. and Adams, P. (2002). 'Resiliency in the Victim-Offender Cycle in Male Sexual Abuse', *Sexual Abuse: A Journal of Research and Treatment* 14(1), 31–48.

Marshall, W. L., Serran, G. A. and Cortoni, F. A. (2000). 'Childhood Attachments, Sexual Abuse, and Their Relationship to Adult Coping in Child Molesters', *Sexual Abuse: A Journal of Research and Treatment* 12, 17–26.

Ministry of Justice (2011). 'Safety in Custody 2010: England and Wales', Ministry of Justice Statistic Bulletin.

Nelson, B. S., Wangsgaard, S., Yorgason, J., Higgins Kessler, M. and Carter-Vassol, E. L. (2002). 'Single- and Dual-Trauma Couples: Clinical Observations of Relational Characteristics and Dynamics', *American Journal of Orthopsychiatry* 72, 58–69.

Norris, F. H., Kaniasty, K. and Thompson, M. P. (1997). 'The Psychological Consequences of Crime: Findings from a Longitudinal Population-Based Studies', in R. C. Davis, A. J. Lurigo and W. G. Skogan (eds) *Victims of Crime*, 2nd edn (Thousand Oaks, CA: Sage Publications), 146–66.

Prochaska, J. O., DiClemente, C. C. and Norcross (1992). 'In Search of How People Change: Applications to Addictive Behvaiors', *Americal Psychologist* 47(9), 1102–14.

Simons, D., Wurtele, S. K. and Durham, R. L. (2008). 'Developmental Experiences of Child Sexual Abuser and Rapists', *Child Abuse and Neglect* 32, 549–60.

Smith, K. J., Subich, L. M.and Kalodner, C. (1995). 'The Trantheorectical Model's Stages and Processes of Change and Their Relation to Premature Termination', *Journal of Counselling Psychology* 42(1), 34–9.

Thompson, S. C., Sobolew-Shubin, A., Galbraith, M., Schwankovsky, L. and Cruzen, D. (1993). 'Maintaining Perceptions of Control: Finding Perceived Control in Low-Control Circumstances', *Journal of Personality and Social Psychology* 64, 293–304.

Walker, M. U. (2006). *Moral Repair: Reconstructing Moral Relations After Wrong Doings*, (New York: Cambridge University Press).

Widom, C. S. (1989). 'The Cycle of Violence', *Science* 244, 160–6.

The Resilient Practitioner

Joanna Clarke

INTRODUCTION

Some occupations are unique with respect to which members risk exposure to traumatic events. Paton and Violanti (1996) describe these as 'critical occupations', a term coined to encapsulate the critical role played by such individuals in protecting communities, as well as the fact that 'in the course of acting in this capacity, these professionals can encounter traumatic events which may, under certain circumstances, exert critical impact on their psychological well-being' (Paton and Violanti, 1996, p. vii). Although the term was originally applied to professions such as Emergency Services and Disaster Response teams, more recently it has been recognized that some jobs involve considerably more *chronic* exposure to potential psychological risk, and although different from the demands of emergency work, should also be included under the umbrella term 'critical occupation'.

Working in forensic environments is one clear example. Working with clients who are, by definition, antisocial and also potentially hostile and/or mentally ill and/or personality disordered are just some aspects of the work that warrant the application of the Critical Occupations title. For example, accounts of violence and abuse perpetrated on others, offenders' own histories of abuse and neglect, statements by children of abuse inflicted by family members or strangers and physical and emotional consequences of self-injury can be almost daily encounters for most practitioners. Add to this environments that are not always conducive to therapeutic intervention, may themselves contribute to the demand when they are tense with the threat of violence, and rarely allow for the expression of distress by staff, and it is a wonder how forensic professionals survive at all. But the reality is that not only do a majority of people survive, many thrive in environments that can present enormous psychological challenges.

The preceding chapters of this book have focussed specifically on some of the skills required to become an effective practitioner, and to consider the application of those skills in the context of working with particular forensic populations. As we will see later in this chapter, competence in these areas is key to resilient practice. The purpose of this chapter however, is to focus exclusively on some of steps that both individuals and organizations can take to enhance the resilience of those working in critical occupations. To achieve this, three key areas are addressed:

- Risk and resilience in high-risk occupations and the relationship between these concepts.
- The application of a model developed to enhance both individual and organizational resilience.
- Personal strategies designed to enhance resilience.

Much of the work presented here is based on the author's experience and research in the areas of working therapeutically with perpetrators of sexual abuse, and with prison and probation staff managing incarcerated and community-based offenders. It draws heavily on work undertaken in high-security prisons, which resulted in a strategy designed to address the complimentary responsibilities of individuals and organizations to maintain good psychological health.

SETTING THE SCENE

Anyone who has travelled by a commercial airline will be familiar with the safety talk presented prior to every flight taking off. First-time flyers usually listen avidly, experienced flyers perhaps less so, but the importance and relevance of the message remains the same; you might just need to know the location of the emergency exits, the operation of the safety belt, how to put on a life jacket and to adopt the brace position. And then there is a reminder about what to do with your oxygen mask should the cabin pressure drop suddenly. Every airline in every country and in every language will tell you 'please apply your own oxygen mask before assisting others'. There is a very good reason for this. Without your own oxygen mask securely in place you will be unable to help anyone else, probably owing to loss of consciousness. This is a very powerful metaphor for self-care in forensic practice. Often driven by a desire to help and support others, it is not unusual to find workers neglecting their own needs, in the (mistaken) belief they are less important than the clients' needs. The argument is made here that in fact the opposite is the case. Without detailed attention to one's own well-being, professional effectiveness can be compromised. Many professional codes of conduct specify the importance of fitness to practice, but they usually refer to more obvious violations such as sobriety and diagnosable mental ill health. The issues covered in this chapter are about day-to-day well-being and about how to actively engage with strategies that are evidenced (in most cases) to enhance resilience and therefore performance.

RISK IN CRITICAL OCCUPATIONS

Critical occupations are considered high risk because, as the definition implies, compared with other jobs, there is a greater risk of exposure to events that may be traumatic. However, to only consider risk of exposure would be to oversimplify a complex situation. Added to this, the word 'risk' has become so overused in modern vocabulary as to have almost lost its significance. The terms risk management, risk assessment, risk reduction and risk aversion, to give just a few examples, are terms so regularly incorporated into everyday language, that people seldom seem to question anymore, 'risk of what?' However, it is argued that without explication, any efforts to manage the risk associated with critical occupations are at best ad hoc and at worst potentially damaging.

In this context, there are a number of areas where the concept of risk requires specific consideration. The first, and the one on which the premise of critical occupations is based, is risk of exposure to events that are potentially traumatic. DSM IV (American Psychiatric Association, 1994) defines a traumatic event as one that is outside of the range of usual human experience and that would be markedly distressing to almost anyone. Examples given of such events include threat to life or physical integrity, seeing another person who has recently been or is being seriously injured or killed or sudden destruction of one's home. From the examples given previously, for some forensic practitioners these risks can be part of the daily work routine. Indeed, studies comparing emergency responders with social services personnel found the latter group reported higher levels of traumatic symptoms despite similar levels of exposure to traumatic stimuli (Paton, Cacioppe and Smith, 1992; Paton and du Preez, 1993).

However, if the event itself caused traumatic symptoms, the shelf-life of members of critical occupations would be dramatically short. Therefore other risks also need to be considered. Paton and Violanti (1996) refer to the 'potential' for an event to be traumatic, suggesting that a second area of risk is that of traumatic *responding* by an individual worker. As will be discussed later in the chapter, just because risk of exposure is high, it does not follow that distress is inevitable. The level of risk of such a response is embedded not just in events, but also in complex psychological and demographic individual differences. Age, gender, length of service, previous trauma history and family history are all examples of factors associated with risk of stressful responding (e.g., Burke, 2007; Clarke, 2004; Clarke and Roger, 2007; Ellerby, 1998; McFarlane, 1987).

Third, organizational practices evidenced to affect risk also require attention. Research undertaken with emergency professions has concluded that organizational variables represent stronger predictors of post-trauma outcomes than the incidents themselves (Dunning, 2003; Gist and Woodall, 2000; Hart, Wearing and Headey, 1995; Paton, 2006; Paton, Violanti and Dunning 2000; Paton, Violanti and Smith, 2003). For example, positive organizational practices, such as adoption of autonomous response systems, consultative leadership styles, training to develop adaptive capacity and tolerance of procedural flexibility can all enhance the likelihood of positive outcomes (Dunning, 2003; Gist and Woodall, 2000; Hart, Wearing and Headey, 1994; Paton, 1994). Conversely, organizations characterized by high levels of bureaucracy, internal conflicts regarding responsibility, persistent use of established procedures (even in novel situations) and a strong motivation to protect the organization from blame or criticism, have all been found to increase the risk of poor post-trauma outcome (Alexander and Wells, 1991; Gist and Woodall, 2000; Paton, 1997).

Finally, the extent to which risk levels might be compounded by events removed from the work context, but significant to the individual, also needs to be understood if risk potential is to be comprehensively managed. For example, in a study of over 200 prison and community-based sex offender treatment providers in the UK, respondents who had experienced a non-work related adverse event in the previous six months, also reported significantly higher levels of dissatisfaction with their organizations (Clarke, 2004). Such events included illness, relationship breakdown, house moves and so on. Although similar research failed to find an impact of traumatic life events twelve to twenty-four months after the event (Creamer, Burgess and Pattison, 1990), recent occurrence does appear to impact negatively on well-being, at least in the short-term. An approach to managing risk incorporating these areas can underpin the development of a comprehensive strategy to enhance well-being for staff in critical occupations.

RESILIENCE IN CRITICAL OCCUPATIONS

Until recently, research into the psychological impact of traumatic events, whether in an occupational or personal context, had focussed almost exclusively on the potential for deleterious outcome. In a review of the literature concerned with the impact on treatment providers of working therapeutically with sex offenders (Clarke, 2004), not one study prior to 2000 considered positive aspects of the work. Perhaps because of the invidious nature of sexual violence against children and adults, and the consequent exposure of therapists to detailed accounts of sexual abuse, there has been a pervasive acceptance of detrimental effects. This has been reflected in the nature of the psychometric instruments and surveys employed to assess impact. Measures of burnout (e.g., Maslach Burnout Inventory, Maslach and Jackson 1986), vicarious trauma (Traumatic Stress Institute Belief Scale – Revision L, Pearlman, 1996) and secondary traumatic stress and compassion fatigue (Compassion Fatigue Self-Test, Figley, 1995) prevail. Consequently it should be expected that symptoms indicative of trauma, including intrusive imagery, avoidance, cognitive disturbance, mood changes and disruption of core beliefs, have been identified. In a similar review of the trauma literature, Stamm (1995, p. 5), concluded, 'the great controversy about helping-induced trauma is not, can it happen, but what shall we call it?'

It is somewhat surprising then that, consistently across studies, from the UK to North America and Canada, prevalence of symptoms, and perhaps therefore the risk of stressful responding, has been moderately low, ranging between 20 per cent and 25 per cent (Ellerby, 1998; Farrenkopf, 1992; Jackson *et al.*, 1997; Rich, 1997; Turner, 1992). The reliability of these figures is also brought into question by the retrospective, snapshot research methodology by which they were derived. Failure to incorporate longitudinal components into impact research means no reliable conclusions can be drawn about why some people are affected and not others, how long symptoms persist, what the long-term prognosis is or whether or not deleterious outcome is caused directly by work-related exposure to trauma. Given these deficits in the research, these percentages are likely to be even lower.

The cost of the focus on measurement of psychological harm has also meant that another consistently occurring statistic has, until recently, been overlooked; that which reflects that anywhere between 75 per cent and 96 per cent of treatment providers experience their work as immensely satisfying and rewarding (Edmunds, 1997; Ellerby, 1998, Kadambi, 2000; Kadambi and Truscott, 2006; Myers, 1995; Rich, 1997; Turner; 1992). In the critical occupations literature generally, there is a growing body of evidence that positive outcomes are not only possible, they often outweigh the negatives (Gist and Woodall, 2000; North *et al.*, 2002; Paton, Violanti and Smith, 2003; Tedeschi and Calhoun, 2003).

So why might this be? The term most often associated with positive outcome in the face of adversity is resilience, the apparent ability to 'bounce back' following exposure to critical events. Also referred to as hardiness (e.g., Kobasa, 1979; Maddi, 2001), stress-related growth (e.g., Park, Cahoun and Murch, 1996) and invulnerability (Haggerty *et al.*, 1994), to name a few, Rutter (2007) refers to it as 'the phenomenon that some individuals have a relatively good outcome despite suffering risk experiences that would be expected to bring about serious sequelae. In other words, it implies relative resistance to environmental risk experiences, or the overcoming of stress or adversity' (p. 205). At this relatively early stage in resilience research there is still lively debate about whether resilience is a personality trait, measurable and relatively stable over time (see, for example, Jacelon, 1997), or a skill, acquired as a result of exposure to adversity (see, for example, Rutter, 2007 or Gillespie, Chaboyer and Wallis, 2007). Whichever perspective is adopted, and it is unlikely to be an either/or resolution, the popularity of the concept of resilience and its seeming potential to offer a basis for interventions to those at risk has resulted in a flurry of research activity over the past twenty years. Unfortunately it is beyond the scope of this chapter to incorporate a survey of this literature, but readers are directed to reviews and commentaries by Atkinson, Martin and Rankin (2009), Manyena (2006) and Rutter (2007). However, whether inherent or learnt, ensuring a staff that is characterized by resilience, either through selection or training, makes intuitive sense, for individuals and organizations.

In the context of critical occupations, Paton *et al.* (2008) expand definitions of individual resilience to include not just the impact of past events but also the management of future ones, both for the person and the organization. They thus define resilience as the capacity of organizations and staff to 'draw upon their own individual, collective, and institutional resources and competencies to cope with, adapt to, and develop from the demands, challenges, and changes encountered during and after a critical incident' (p. 2). These authors argue that understanding and managing resilience is underpinned by the assumption that beneficial and constructive outcomes occur when individuals and groups can use their psychological and physical resources and competencies in ways that allow them to render challenging events coherent, manageable and meaningful.

Perhaps one the greatest challenges to researchers and practitioners is identifying the relevant significance of the multitude of individual, environmental and organizational factors that facilitate and enable constructive outcomes, and it is to this area that attention is now turned.

A MODEL OF RESILIENT OUTCOME

A number of models exists that attempt to make sense of factors that are at least theoretically implicated in adaptive and hence resilient outcome from trauma. Examples include the Stress Shield Model (Paton *et al.*, 2008), derived from operational research in the critical occupations arena, and more generic occupational health models, such as that proposed by Hart and Cooper (2001). For the purposes of this chapter, the Model of Dynamic Adaptation (MDA) (Clarke, 2004, 2008; Clarke and Roger, 2002) derived directly from research in forensic settings, is the model of choice (see Figure 14.1). So named in an attempt to encapsulate the fluid risk status of an individual at any given time, the MDA is based on the principles emanating from the risk prediction field (Grove and Meehl, 1996). Accordingly, factors considered to contribute to risk are grouped by their static, stable or dynamic nature (e.g., Hanson and Bussiere, 1998; Thornton, 2001) and are considered in the context of their contribution to positive or negative outcome.

Static Factors are those from an individual's history that are either fixed or unchanging, or change in a highly predictable way. Age and gender are examples of these. Stable Factors are those that are potentially changeable but relatively stable. Under normal circumstances they would change only slowly, usually as a result of intervention or experience. Personality variables such as emotional sensitivity, coping styles and ability to take perspective are examples. Dynamic factors are those that can change rapidly, unpredictably and may well

Figure 14.1 *The model of dynamic adaptation*

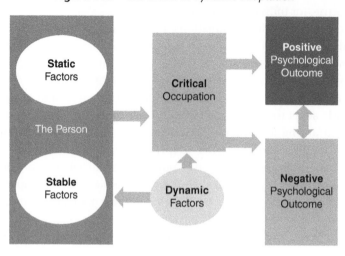

Source: Clarke, 2004, 2008.

be outside the sphere of influence of the individual. Examples might include winning the lottery, a spouse losing a job, a new colleague joining the team or having an accident.

The Critical Occupation category incorporates all those variables relevant to the workplace and the work people do. It includes risk of exposure to critical incidents, team cohesiveness, the physical environment in which the work takes place, policies and procedures, organizational support practices, supervisory relationships and so on.

The two outcome boxes refer to positive or negative psychological consequences, but are not mutually exclusive. As the figures from the sex offender treatment provider literature suggest, both rewarding and deleterious outcomes are possible simultaneously. The aim of any strategy to enhance well-being should be to tip the balance in favour of positive outcome for a majority of workers for a majority of the time.

The MDA is intended as a functional model for application to any critical occupation. However, identification of static, stable and dynamic variables, as well as rewards and cost of the work, needs to be specific to the occupation under consideration. Ideally, organizations will conduct their own longitudinal research, working with new, experienced and former practitioners, to establish the relative importance of the multitude of potential variables. The very nature of critical occupations though, means that some variables are likely to be common to all.

For example, within the static domain, age, gender, length of time in the role, family status and previous history of trauma repeatedly emerge as significant to well-being (e.g., Clarke, 2004; Clarke and Roger, 2007; Ellerby, 1998; McFarlane, 1987; Murphy, 1991). Within the stable category, dispositional optimism, emotional response style, coping strategies, perspective taking skills and empathy have all been identified as significant (e.g., Clarke, 2004; Clarke and Roger, 2007; Moran and Massam, 1997; Myers, 1995; Roger, Guarino and Olason, 2000). Dynamic factors, although little researched, include exposure to an event perceived to be traumatic within the previous six months, and quality of social support network post-event (Clarke, 2004; Pearlman and Saakvitne, 1995; Rich, 1997). Job and organizational characteristics include training, on-the-job support, preparedness and cultural issues (blame vs. learning) (Alexander and Wells, 1991; Eisenberger *et al.*, 2002; Gist and Woodall, 2000; Paton, 1997).

It is important to note that the extent to which a particular variable might influence either positive or negative outcome has not been elaborated upon here, and would need to be established in the context of other variables and the role to which it was being applied. For example, when applying the model to staff working with personality-disordered offenders, Fox (2010) found age, detached coping style and perception of organizational culture to be the three factors most predictive of a resilient outcome. Further, in a review of the literature on humour and coping in emergency work, Moran and Mossam (1997) concluded there is scope for some but not all humour to act as a positive coping strategy. Other variables may well be double-edged swords. For example, high levels of emotional inhibition have been demonstrated to be detrimental to psychological and physical health (Roger, 2002). However, emotional expressiveness needs to take account of time and place. It is unlikely to be conducive to high performance or well-being in the face managing of a critical incident.

Understanding the rewards of working in a particular critical profession is also essential if well-being is to be enhanced. In a concept-mapping exercise with sex offender treatment providers, Kadambi and Truscott (2006) identified seven key areas in which providers found reward and meaning in their work. These were labelled protection of the public, socially meaningful curiosity, enjoyment of counselling, professional benefits, connection to colleagues, offender wellness and change and offending specific change. Knowing such specifics affords organizations the opportunity to maximize workers' development in these domains.

ENHANCING RESILIENCE

One of the advantages of adopting a model to understand the factors implicated in adaptive or dysfunctional outcome is that it allows for two critical actions. First, intervention points become apparent, whereby strategies designed specifically to address the given issue can be implemented. Second, the complementary responsibilities of both the individual and organization for sustaining and enhancing well-being can be identified. The purpose of this book is to provide the practitioner with concrete and workable pointers for enhancing practice. For this reason, after a brief overview of the intervention points on the MDA,

Figure 14.2   *The model of dynamic adaptation with potential intervention points*

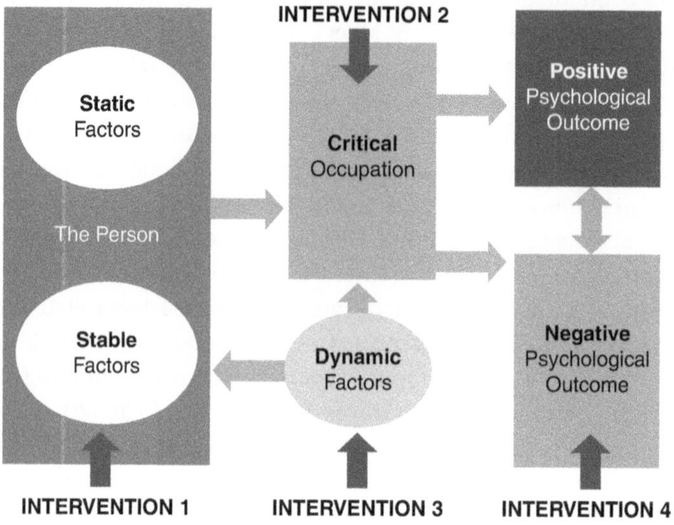

Source: Clarke, 2004, 2008.

the remainder of the chapter will focus on strategies for adoption by individuals, as opposed organizations, to enable and enhance resilient practice.

The points of intervention on the MDA (see Figure 14.2) may be considered primary, secondary and tertiary in nature (Department of Health, 2007). Primary intervention aims to promote good psychological health and requires action on its determinants to prevent dysfunctional outcomes (preventative); secondary intervention involves the early detection of dysfunctional outcome, followed by appropriate intervention (preventative); and tertiary intervention aims to reduce the impact of the dysfunctional outcome and promote quality of life through active rehabilitation (reactive).

Intervention 1 is concerned with the individual. It covers issues of selection, training and preparation of the individual to undertake a critical role. In addition to skills and competencies to do the job, self-care skills also need to be considered (psychological self-maintenance). The aim here is not necessarily to deselect staff who have yet to acquire the requisite skills, competencies or values to stay psychologically well and perform highly, but to generate a profile that enables the individual and organization to work together to achieve such a position if potential is shown to do the job. Point 1 is thus considered a primary intervention.

Intervention 2 concerns the job itself, and relates to the workplace, the work force and the work people do. Here, consideration needs to be given to the environment, organizational policies and procedures, on-the-job support, frequency of exposure to traumatic events, recognition of distress and so on. Essentially in a primary intervention, elements of secondary intervention would be applicable, if, for example, detrimental organizational practices were identified.

Opportunities to intervene at point 3 are minimal. However, recognition and understanding of the impact that dynamic factors can have on well-being enables appropriate responses at both the individual and organizational level. Disclosure by a worker of difficult family circumstances, for example, can enable a manager to initiate different support options; understanding the impact on the team of a new manager can allow apposite preparation and so on. Intervention here would be an example of secondary prevention.

Intervention 4 concerns action to be taken in the event of deleterious outcome, whether the result of a critical incident, other events related to organizational practices or individual circumstances. Generally tertiary in nature, responses might include referral to a mental health professional, adjustment of work demands, retraining and so on.

Many of these interventions require organizational action, but there is a range of (often evidence-based) interventions that can be practiced by the individual (see Clarke, 2011). What follows is description of a selection of these. Readers are encouraged, however, to keep an active search for their own effective well-being strategies.

Intervention Point 1: The Individual

While organizations have a responsibility to recruit the right people into the right job, individuals entering a critical profession are advised to consider their motivation for doing so. Working with offenders may initially seem exciting and somehow clandestine, but the reality can be very different. It is easy to overlook the impact of working in harsh, unforgiving and sometimes anti-therapeutic environments, or the reality of working with clients who are, by definition, antisocial and potentially dangerous. For example, those who enter forensic professions with a drive to rescue or save the world should be cautioned by the words of a participant in Farrenkopf's (1992) research into the impact of working therapeutically with sex offenders. She reminisced about entering to work to save the world but was soon grateful to save a few. Ultimately she was just relieved to have saved herself!

A realistic and informed approach to the work is advised, with a thorough and honest exploration of motivations and meaning. Johnston and Paton (2003) identify meaning as a central element of environmental resilience, a composite of cognitive components that cultivate a sense of empowerment. Brief and Nord (1990) describe a sense of meaning as a level of congruence between a task and the values, attitudes and behaviours of the worker. Given the level of challenges that can be encountered in critical occupations, a role without meaning, or where one's values are at odds with the requirements of the job, can result in may of the negative consequences identified in early research.

In addition to appreciating personal motivations, an understanding of individual coping and emotional management style is helpful. For example, levels of empathy and sensitivity are typically high in people motivated to help others, but are recognized to increase risk of stressful responding to critical events. When accompanied by high levels of detached coping (Roger and Hudson, 1995) however, deleterious outcome can be moderated (Clarke, 2004). Rumination, the tendency to become preoccupied with emotionally upsetting events (Roger, 2002), has been empirically linked to both emotional and physical poor health (Roger and Najarian, 1998). In one of the few pieces of longitudinal research into the impact of working therapeutically with sex offenders (Clarke, 2004), rumination and emotional inhibition were found to significantly increase over a twelve-month period among twenty-eight new therapists. Although based on only small numbers, such an empirical finding is perhaps unsurprising. Critical occupations provide plenty of material to ruminate about and in environments where expressions of distress are likely to be censured. Friedman and Higson-Smith (2003) describe this as disenfranchised distress, distress experienced but not allowed. For this reason, knowing and monitoring changes in emotional response style and coping is a substantial part of knowing when and for how long to apply one's oxygen mask. For a more comprehensive review of coping and emotion management, see Roger (2002).

Intervention Points 2 and 3: Critical Occupation and Dynamic Factors

These two areas are combined as one intrinsically linked with the other. Dynamic factors may have professional or personal relevance, but in either case have the potential to influence positive or negative outcome as a consequence of the work environment. Three strategies are described to enhance resilience related to on-the job performance; energy management (Loehr and Schwartz, 2003), supervision (Carroll, 2009; 2010) and mindfulness (Glomb *et al.*, 2011).

The concept of energy management is a useful one when applied to forensic settings. The very features that include forensic practice as a critical occupation (in terms of both the risk of and actual exposure to potentially traumatic events, situations or material) can be very depleting of energy. Loehr and Schwartz (2003) define four key domains in which the expenditure and renewal of energy should be carefully managed: physical, emotional, mental and spiritual. Physical energy is described as the source of energy, and is measured in terms of quantity, while emotional energy is measured in terms of quality. Mental energy is related strongly to competence and is described as the focus of energy, and spiritual energy, defined as the force of energy, is related highly to meaning. The authors propose that it is the effective management of energy in these domains, rather than time management, that lead to improved performance and increased happiness. While it is beyond the scope of this chapter to provide a thorough evaluation of the theory, the fundamental principle is that when energy is expended in any of the four domains, a commensurate amount of renewal is required in order to maximize performance and well-being. The consequences of an imbalance between over-expenditure and under-renewal of energy in any of the domains looks remarkably similar to the negative symptoms associated with working in critical occupations. Understanding the importance of energy renewal means the risk of complete energy depletion is reduced. Not regularly renewing energy and continuing to practice is the equivalent of continuing to help others in conditions of low cabin pressure without your own oxygen mask in place. It is a situation to be avoided.

Supervision is a requirement in many professions, largely as a method of ensuring the development of competence. Carroll (2009) defines it as a process that allows the practitioner to move from 'dependent novice to autonomous practitioner' (p. 40). The importance of this to resilient practice comes in a number of guises. First, competence is another key component of environmental resilience. Johnston and Paton (2003) liken competence to self-efficacy or a belief in one's ability to do the job at hand. Self-efficacy in turn is considered to be a cornerstone to successful adaptation to adversity. Facing complex and emotionally charged situations with difficult offenders can be overwhelming when you do not know what to do or how to react. Competence, developed over time through the acquisition of relevant skills and the process of supervision, can most certainly lessen the negative impact.

Second, supervision enables reflective practice, or learning from experience, developing what Gilmer and Markus describe as 'the capability to reflect critically and systematically on the work-self interface … fostering a personal awareness and resilience' (2003, p. 23). How this process happens is a chapter in itself, but it is likely, in part, to be a result of the perspectives that the supervisory process can bring. Carroll (2010) asserts 'supervision is strong on helping supervisees look again at their work and see it from other perspectives' (p. 28). The ability to take perspective has been statistically significantly linked with lower levels of organizational dissatisfaction (Clarke, 2004) and is also closely aligned to detachment, a coping style demonstrated to be predictive of adaptive outcome (Roger and Hudson, 1995). Supervision also offers a third-party perspective in the form of feedback from the supervisor, someone who by definition is less attached to the issues than the supervisee.

Third, supervision is a forum where personal reactions to professional work can be explored (Carroll, 2007), allowing for the expression of emotion and thus reducing the risk of disenfranchised distress (although this does not appear to have been empirically tested). The effectiveness of supervision appears to be largely dependent on the quality of the supervisor/supervisee relationship (Kilminster and Jolly, 2000), thus the extent to which emotional issues are a focus in supervision is likely to be a direct reflection of the quality of this relationship. However, a skilled supervisor should ensure that such opportunities are provided, and even if the emotion is not explicitly expressed, the process of verbalizing an experience can in itself be beneficial.

The final strategy to be discussed here for use at Intervention point 2 and 3 is mindfulness. Rooted in Buddhist philosophy, mindfulness has entered mainstream Western consciousness with considerable impact over the last three decades. Glomb *et al.* (2011) define it as 'a state of consciousness characterized by receptive attention to and awareness of present events and experiences, without evaluation, judgment, and cognitive filters' (p. 119). Glomb *et al.* provide a useful analysis of mindfulness-based practices in the workplace for the interested reader, but for now, the briefest of overviews will be presented to introduce the concept and its role in enhancing resilience.

Mindfulness is thought to affect self-regulation by creating a separation between the self and emotional reactivity to events. Roger (2002) calls this 'detachment'; Glomb *et al.* refer to it as 'de-coupling'. It essentially enables people to create a distance between themselves and their experiences and the associated thoughts and emotions. In forensic practice, where there are ample events that can provoke a range of intense emotions, it is easy to see how an ability to simply observe those reactions, rather than become overwhelmed by them, can be extremely beneficial. As one delegate on a mindfulness training programme encapsulated it, it is the experience of seeing the reactivity (e.g., anger) rather than being the reactivity (i.e., angry).

Much of the mindfulness research has been undertaken in the clinical domain, that is, outside the work place, but nonetheless the evidence is compelling that mindfulness-based practices have an organizational place. For example, Broderick (2005) found that individuals who practice mindfulness engage in less rumination, resulting in better adaption to events that might otherwise be perceived as stressful. In terms of affect regulation, mindfulness has been linked with both effective management of negative affect and promotion of positive affect. Tice, Baumeister and Zhang (2004) argue that while challenging situations may deplete important self-regulatory resources, which Giluk (2010) likens to energy, positive mood states associated with mindfulness can 'restore and replenish' these resources (p. 55). The association between mindfulness, energy management and resilience is further supported by Davis's (2009) assertion that a key ingredient of resilience is the capacity to harness positive emotion.

In summary then, energy management, supervision and mindfulness have a natural synergy that can enhance resilience for forensic practitioners with the ultimate benefit of improving performance and client outcomes. The challenge is to develop these skills alongside the technical skills to do the job, although hopefully the very clear benefits will provide plenty of motivation.

Intervention Point 4: Negative Psychological Outcome

Sometimes, despite best efforts, practitioners can find they are impacted negatively by their work, not just in terms of acute reactions to challenging events, but more chronically, over prolonged periods of time. As previously described, symptoms indicative of trauma, including intrusive imagery, avoidance, cognitive disturbance, mood changes and disruption of core beliefs, have been identified and variously referred to as burnout (e.g., Maslach and Jackson 1986), vicarious trauma (e.g., Pearlman, 1996), secondary traumatic stress and compassion fatigue (Compassion Fatigue Self-Test, Figley, 1995).

It is important to recognize that the prevalence of symptoms has been moderately low (see above), although ironically most organizations have resources in place for when things go wrong. Employee assistance programmes, in-house or contracted counsellors and occupational health are all examples of services aimed to respond to distress among the workforce, and are effective to varying degrees. They should not be dismissed as sources of support. However, for some, the prospect of disclosing distress to someone with whom no relationship has been established might induce almost as much stress as it is supposed to alleviate. Further, such services might not always be available when needed, and additionally it is not unusual to finds those in the helping professions somewhat resistant to acknowledging support needs (perhaps due to concerns that it undermines competence?).

An evidence-based intervention that negates many of the issues raised above, and has had extraordinary success in a range of spheres, is written (or trauma) disclosure (Pennebaker, 2000). Improved resilience and enhanced self-perception (Pennebaker and Keough, 1999), improved immune function (Esterling *et al.*, 1994), long-term improvements in mood (Pennebaker, 1997) and salutary effects on health (King and Miner, 2000; Pennebaker, 2000) are all consequences of this technique, which requires the individual simply to write about his or her traumatic experience on a number of occasions over a specified period of time. It is a technique that allows for uninhibited emotional expression and is consequently an ideal method for overcoming the intensely energy-inefficient and distressing experience of ruminating without an expressive outlet. It is also thought to promote the development of perspective and detachment. Pennebaker (2004) refers to the social, emotional and cognitive benefits of the process, all of which address many of the challenges of working in a critical occupation. For more details about this intervention see Pennebaker (1997, 2004).

CONCLUSION

Working in forensic settings with forensic clients is a challenging job. Physically, emotionally, mentally and spiritually, the very individuals we seek to help, support, develop and change can drain us of our energy in a way that probably few others can. Indeed, Scott (1989) contends that therapeutic intervention with criminals 'is the most demanding task in the entire arena of mental health' (p. 225).

It can also be one of the most rewarding and satisfying occupations; if one end of the continuum is so extreme, it is only reasonable to expect the other to be so too.

One way of ensuring we keep ourselves at the positive end of that continuum is to take the duty of care to ourselves seriously; to acknowledge negative impact when it occurs and to attend to our well-being needs promptly and efficiently. Knowing oneself, making use of all available resources (especially those that develop our competence), remaining mindful and managing our energy will all help ensure that our oxygen masks remain firmly in place, enabling us in turn to maximize our performance in pursuit of becoming skilled and effective forensic practitioners.

RECOMMENDED FURTHER READING

Much of the authors work in the field of resilience in critical occupations has been informed by the research of Douglas Paton, John Violanti and colleagues. Two of their books stand out as particularly useful:

Paton, D., Violanti, J. M., Dunning, C. and Smith, L. M. (2004). *Managing Traumatic Stress Risk: A Proactive Approach* (Charles Thomas, USA).

Paton, D. and Violanti, J. M. (2006). *Who Gets PTSD: Issues of Posttraumatic Stress Vulnerability* (Charles Thomas, USA).

In terms of individual well-being Roger, D. (2002). *Managing Stress* (2nd edn) (Maidenhead, Berkshire: CIM publishing) introduces the concept of detached compassion and is drawn from an evidence-based intervention designed to enhance resilience.

For a self-help book, based on research and full of strategies to develop resilience, try Reivich, K. and Shatte, A. (2003). *The Resilience Factor* (Broadway Books, New York).

Loehr, J. and Schwartz, T. (2003). *On Form* introduces the concept of energy management, an excellent skill for enhancing performance and keeping one's oxygen mask in place.

REFERENCES

Alexander, D. A. and Wells, A. (1991). 'Reactions of Police Officers to Body Handling after a Major Disaster: A before and after Comparison', *British Journal of Psychiatry* 159, 517–55.

American Psychiatric Association (1994). *Diagnostic and Statistical Manual of Mental Disorders*, 4th edition. Washington DC; American Psychiatric Assocoiation.

Atkinson, P. A., Martin C. R. and Rankin, J. (2009). *Journal of Psychiatric and Mental Health Nursing* 16, 137–45.

Brief, A. P. and Nord, W. R. (1990). *Meanings of Occupational Work* (Lexington, MA: Lexington Books).

Broderick, P. C. (2005). 'Mindfulness and Coping with Dysphoric Mood: Contrasts with Rumination and Distraction', *Cognitive Therapy and Research*, 29, 501–10.

Burke, K. J. (2007). Adjusting to Life 'on the Beat': An Investigation of Adaptation to the Police Profession. Unpublished PhD Thesis, University of Tasmania.

Carroll, M. (2007). 'One More Time: What is Supervision?', *Psychotherapy in Australia,* 13(3), 34–40.

Carroll, M. (2009). 'From Mindless to Mindful Practice: On Learning Reflection in Supervision', *Psychotherapy in Australia* 15(4), 40–51.

Carroll, M. (2010). 'Levels of Reflection: On Learning Reflection', *Psychotherapy in Australia* 16(2), 28–35.

Clarke, J. (2004). The Psychosocial Impact on Facilitators of Working Therapeutically with Sex Offenders: An Experimental Study. Unpublished PhD thesis, University of York, UK.

Clarke, J. M. (2008). 'Promoting Professional Resilience', in M. Calder (ed.) *Contemporary Risk Assessment in Safeguarding Children* (Dorset: Russell House Publishing), 164–80.

Clarke, J. M. (2011). 'Working with Sex Offenders: Best Practice in Enhancing Practitioner Resilience', *Journal of Sexual Aggression*, 18(3), 1–21.

Clarke, J. and Roger, D. (2002). 'Working Therapeutically with Sex Offenders: The Potential Impact on the Psychological Well-Being of Treatment Providers', L. Falshaw (ed.) *Issues in Forensic Psychology No. 3: The Impact of Offending* (Leicester, British Psychological Society).

Clarke, J. and Roger, D. (2007). 'The Construction and Validation of a Scale to Assess Psychological Risk and Well-Being in Sex Offender Treatment Providers', *Legal and Criminological Psychology*, 12, 83–100.

Creamer, M., Burgess, P. and Pattison, P. (1990). 'Cognitive Processing in Post-Trauma Reactions: Some Preliminary Findings', *Psychological Medicine* 20, 597–604.

Davis, M. C. (2009). 'Building Emotional Resilience to Promote Health', *American Journal of Lifestyle Medicine* 3, 60–3.

Department of Health (2007). http://www.dh.gov.uk. Primary, Secondary and Tertiary Prevention.

Dunning, C. (2003). Sense of coherence in managing trauma workers. In D. Paton, J. M. Violanti and L. M. Smith (Eds) *Promoting capabilities to manage posttraumatic stress: Perspectives on resilience*, Springfield, IL: Charles C. Thomas.

Edmunds, S. (1997) *Impact: Working with Sexual Abusers* (Vermont: Safer Society Press).

Eisenberger, R., Stinglahamber, F., Vandenberghe, C., Sucharski, I. L., and Rhoades, L. (2002). 'Perceived Supervisor Support: Contributions to Perceived Organisational Support and Employee Retention', *Journal of Applied Psychology* 87, 565–73.

Ellerby, L. (1998). *Providing Clinical Services to Sex Offenders: Burnout, Compassion, Fatigue and Moderating Variables* (Canada: University of Manitoba).

Esterling, B. A., Antoni, M. H., Fletcher, M. A., Margulies, S. and Schneider-man (1994). 'Emotional Disclosure through Writing or Speaking Modulates Latent Epstein-Barr Virus Antibody Titers', *Journal of Consulting and Clinical Psychology* 62, 130–40, 537.

Farrenkopf, T. (1992). 'What Happens to Facilitators Who Work with Sex Offenders', *Journal of Offender Rehabilitation* 16, 217–23.

Figley, C. R. (1995). *Compassion Fatigue: Coping with Secondary Traumatic Stress Disorder in Those Who Treat the Traumatised* (Levittown, PA: Bruner/Mazel).

Fox, A. (2010). Investigating the Factors that Contribute to Staff Well-Being and Professional Resilience at a Dangerous and Severe Personality Disorder Unit. Unpublished MSc Thesis, University of York.

Friedman, M. and Higson-Smith, C. (2003). 'Building Psychological Resilience: Learning from the South African Police Service', in D. Paton, J. M. Violanti, and L. M. Smith (eds) *Promoting Capabilities to Manage Posttraumatic Stress: Perspectives on Resilience* (Springfield, IL: Charles C. Thomas), 103–15.

Gillespie B., Chaboyer W. and Wallis M. (2007). 'Development of a Theoretically Derived Model of Resilience through Concept Analysis', *Contemporary Nurse* 25, 124–35.

Gilmer, B. and Markus, R. (2003). 'Personal Professional Development in Clinical Psychology Training: Surveying Reflective Practice', *Clinical Psychology*, 27, 20–3.

Giluk, T. L. (2010). Mindfulness-Based Stress Reduction: Facilitating Work Outcomes through Experienced Affect and High-Quality Relationships, Doctoral dissertation. Retrieved from Iowa Research Online: http://ir.uiowa.edu/etd/674. Accessed 26/4/12.

Gist, R. and Woodall, J. (2000). 'There are No Simple Solutions to Complex Problems', In D. Paton, J. M. Violanti and C. Dunning (eds) *Posttraumatic Stress Intervention: Challenges, Issues and Perspectives* (Springfield, Illinois: Charles C Thomas Publisher, Ltd).

Glomb, T. M., Duffy, M. K. Bono, J. E. and Yang, T. (2011). 'Mindfulness at Work', *Research in Personnel and Human Resources Management*, 30, 115–57.

Grove, W. M. and Meehl, P. E. (1996). 'Comparative Efficiency of Informal (Subjective, Impressionistic) and Formal (Mechanical, Algorithmic) Prediction Procedures: The Clinical-Statistical Controversy', *Psychology, Public Policy, and Law* 2, 293–323.

Haggerty, R., Sherrod, L., Garmezy, N. *et al.* (1994). *Stress, Risk and Resilience in Children and Adolescents* (Cambridge, Cambridge University Press).

Hanson, R. K. and Bussiere, M. T. (1998). 'Predicting Relapse: A Meta-Analysis of Sexual Offender Recidivism Studies', *Journal of Consulting and Clinical Psychology* 66, 348–62.

Hart, P. M., Wearing, A. J. and Headey, B. (1994). 'Perceived Quality of Life, Personality, and Work Experiences: Construct Validation of the Police Daily Hassles and Uplifts Scales', *Criminal Justice and Behavior*, 21(3): 283–311.

Hart, P. M., Wearing, A. J. and Headey, B. (1995). 'Police Stress and Well-Being: Integrating Personality, Coping and Daily Work Experiences', *Journal of Occupational and Organisational Psychology* 68, 133–56.

Hart, P. M. and Cooper, C. L. (2001). 'Occupational Stress: Toward a More Integrated Framework', in N. Anderson, D. S. Ones, H. K. Sinangil and C. Viswesvaren (eds) *International Handbook of Work and Organizational Psychology, Vol. 2: Organizational Psychology* (London: Sage Publications), 27–48.

Jacelon C. (1997). 'The Trait and Process of Resilience', *Journal of Advanced Nursing* 25, 123–9.

Jackson, K. E., Holzman, C., Barnard, T. and Paradis, C. (1997). 'Working with Sex Offenders: The Impact on Practitioners', in B. S. Edmunds (ed.) *Impact: Working with Sexual Abusers* (Vermont: Safer Society Press), 61–73.

Johnston, P. and Paton, D. (2003). 'Environmental Resilience: Psychological Empowerment in High Risk Profession', in D. Paton, J. M. Violanti and L. M. Smith (eds) *Promoting Capabilities to Manage Posttraumatic Stress: Perspectives on Resilience* (Springfield, Ill: Charles C Thomas), 136–48.

Kadambi, M. (2000). Working with Sex Offenders: Burnouts and Benefits, Paper presented at the Canadian Psychological Association Convention, June, in Ottawa.

Kadambi, M. and Truscott, D. (2006). 'Concept Mapping Professionals' Perceptions of Reward and Motive in Providing Sex Offender Treatment', *Journal of Offender Rehabilitation,* 42(4), 37–58.

Kilminster, S. M. and Jolly, B. C. (2000). 'Effective Supervision in Clinical Practice Settings: A Literature Review', *Medical Education* 34, 827–40.

King, L. A. and Miner, K. N. (2000). 'Writing about the Perceived Benefits of Traumatic Events: Implications for Physical Health', *Personality and Social Psychology Bulletin* 26(2), 220–30.

Kobasa, S. C. (1979). 'Stressful Life Events, Personality and Health: An Inquiry into Hardiness', *Journal of Personality and Social Psychology* 42, 168–77.

Loehr, J. and Schwartz, T. (2003). *On Form* (London, Nicholas Brearley Publishing).

Maddi, S. R. (2001). *Personality Theories: A Comparative Analysis,* 6th edn (Prospect Heights, IL: Waveland).

Manyena (2006). 'The Concept of Resilience Revisited', *Disasters* 30(4), 433–50.

Maslach, C. and Jackson, S. E. (1986). *The Maslach Burnout Inventory Manual,* 2nd edn (Palo Alto, CA: Consulting Psychologists Press).

McFarlane, A. C. (1987). 'Life Events and Psychiatric Disorder: The Role of Natural Disaster', *British Journal of Psychiatry,* 151, 362–67.

Moran, C. C. and Mossam, M. (1997). 'The Evaluation of Humour in Emergency Work', *The Australasian Journal of Disaster and Trauma Studies* 3, 26–8.

Murphy, S. A. (1991). 'Human Response to Catastrophe', *Annual Review of Nursing* 9, 57–76.

Myers, R. (1995). A Study to Investigate the Experiences of Staff Conducting National SOTP at HM Prison Wakefield, and to Compare the Psychological

Health, Emotion Control and Coping Strategies of These Staff to Non SOTP Group Work Facilitators. Unpublished MSc thesis: Middlesex University.

North, C. S., Tivis, L., McMillen, C., Pfefferbaum, B., Cox, J., Spitznagal, E. L. *et al.* (2002). 'Coping, Functioning, and Adjustment of Rescue Workers after the Oklahoma City Bombing', *Journal of Traumatic Stress* 15, 171–5.

Park, C. L., Cohen, L. and Murch, R. (1996). 'Assessment and Prediction of Stress Related Growth', *Journal of Personality* 64, 71–105.

Paton, D. (1994). 'Disaster Relief Work: An Assessment of Training Effectiveness', *Journal of Traumatic Stress*, 7, 275–88.

Paton, D. (1997). *Dealing with Traumatic Incidents in the Work place*, 3rd edn (Queensland, Australia: Gull Publishing).

Paton, D. (2006). 'Critical Incident Stress Risk in Police Officers: Managing Resilience and Vulnerability', *Traumatolgy* 12, 198–206.

Paton, D. and du Preez, H. (1993). *Job Demands Survey: Authority for the Intellectually Handicapped* (Perth, Western Australia).

Paton, D., Cacioppe, R. and Smith, L. M. (1992). *Critical Incident Stress in the West Australian Fire Brigade* (Perth, Western Australia).

Paton, D. and Violanti, J. M. (1996). *Traumatic Stress in Critical Occupations: Recognition, Consequences and Treatment* (Springfield, IL: Charles C. Thomas).

Paton, D., Violanti, J. M. and Dunning, C. (2000). *Posttraumatic stress intervention: Challenges, issues and perspectives.* Springfield, IL: Charles C. Thomas.

Paton, D., Violanti, J. M. and Smith L. M. (2003). *Promoting Capabilities to Manage Posttraumatic Stress: Perspectives on Resilience* (Springfield, IL: Charles C. Thomas).

Paton, D., Violanti, J. M., Johnston, P., Burke, K. J., Clarke, J. M. and Keenan, D. (2008). 'Stress Shield: A Model of Police Resiliency', *International Journal of Emergency Mental Health* 10(2), 95–107.

Pearlman, L. A. (1996). 'Psychometric Review of TSI Belief Scale, Revision L', in B. H. Stamm (ed.) *Measurement of Stress, Trauma and Adaptation* (Lutherville, MD: Sidran), 419–30.

Pearlman, L. A. and Saakvitne, K. W. (1995). *Trauma and the Therapist: Countertransference and Vicarious Traumatization in Psychotherapy with Incest Survivors* (New York: Norton).

Pennebaker, J. W. (1997). 'Writing about Emotional Experiences as a Therapeutic Process', *Psychological Science* 8, 162–6.

Pennebaker, J. W. (2000). 'The Effects of Traumatic Disclosure on Physical and Mental Health: The Values of Writing and Talking about Upsetting Events', in J. M. Violanti, D. Paton and C. Dunning (eds) *Posttraumatic Stress Interventions: Challenges Issues and Perspectives* (Springfield, Ill: Charles C Thomas), 97–114.

Pennebaker, J. W. (2004). 'Theories, Therapies, and Taxpayers: On the Complexities of the Expressive Writing Paradigm', *Clinical Psychology: Science and Practice* 11, 138–42.

Pennebaker, J. W. and Keough, K. A. (1999). 'Revealing, Organizing and Reorganizing the Self in Response to Stress and Emotion', in R. J. Contrada and R.

D. Ashmore (eds) *Self, Social Identity and Physical Health* (New York: Oxford University Press), 101–21.

Rich, K. D. (1997). 'Vicarious Traumatisation: A Preliminary Study', in S. Edmunds (ed.) *Impact: Working with Sexual Abusers* (Vermont: Safer Society Press).

Roger, D. (2002). *Managing Stress*, 2nd edn (Berkshire: CIM Publishing).

Roger, D. and Hudson, C. (1995). 'The Role of Emotion Control and Emotional Rumination in Stress Management Training', *International Journal of Stress Management* 2(3), 119–32.

Roger, D., Guarino, L. and Olason, D. (2000). Emotional 'Style' and Health: A New Three Factor Model. Paper presented at the 14th European Health Psychology Conference, Leiden, August.

Roger, D. and Najarian, B. (1998). 'The Relationship between Emotional Rumination and Cortisol Under Stress', *Personality and Individual Differences* 24, 531–8.

Rutter, M. (2007). 'Resilience, Competence, and Coping', *Child Abuse and Neglect* 31, 205–9.

Scott, E. (1989). 'Is There a Criminal Mind?', *International Journal of Offender Therapy and Comparative Criminology* 33, 215–26.

Stamm, B. H. E. (1995). *Secondary Traumatic Stress: Self-Care Issues for Clinicians Researchers and Educators* (Lutherville, MD: Sidran Press).

Tedeschi, R. G. and Calhoun, L. G. (2003). 'Routes to Posttraumatic Growth through Cognitive Processing', in D. Paton, J. M. Violanti and L. M. Smith (eds) *Promoting Capabilities to Manage Posttraumatic Stress: Perspectives on Resilience* (Springfield, IL: Charles C. Thomas), 12–26.

Tice, D. M., Baumeister, R. F. and Zhang, L. (2004). 'The Role of Emotion in Self-Regulation: Differing Roles of Positive and Negative Emotion', in P. Philippot and R. S. Feldman (eds), *The Regulation of Emotion* (Mahwah, NJ: Lawrence Erlbaum), 213–26.

Thornton, D. (2001). Issues of Risk Assessment. Personal Communication.

Turner C. (1992). The Experience of Staff Conducting the Core Programme. Unpublished MSc Thesis. University of London.

Index